SIGNS & SYMBOLS

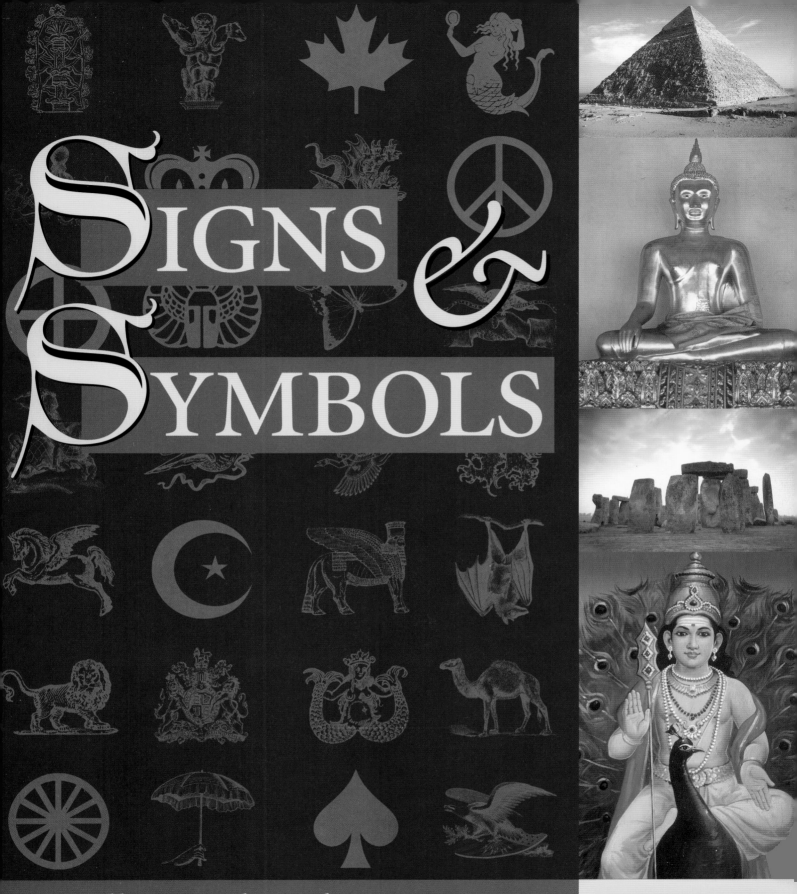

SIGNS & SYMBOLS

An Illustrated Guide to Their Meaning and Origins

CLARE GIBSON

BARNES
&NOBLE
BOOKS
NEW YORK

Above: This cave painting at Lascaux, in the Dordogne region of France, depicts a bull. Animals and natural phenomena are common subjects in prehistoric and ancient art.

Page 1: A heraldic crest, photographed in Edinburgh, Scotland, featuring the lion rampant, a Christian symbol widely used in medieval coats of arms.

For Marianne
and John Gibson and
Mike Haworth-Maden

This edition published by Barnes and Noble, Inc., by arrangement with Saraband Inc.

Copyright © 1996 Saraband Inc.

Design © Ziga Design

Library of Congress Cataloging in Publication Data available.

ISBN: 0-7607-0217-9

Printed in China

10 9 8 7 6 5 4 3

EDITORS
Martin Hill, Sara Hunt, Gail Janensch, Robin Langley Sommer, Julia Banks Rubel.

ART DIRECTOR/GRAPHIC DESIGNER
Charles J. Ziga

GRAPHIC ARTIST
Chris Berlingo

PRODUCTION COORDINATOR
Emily Elizabeth Head

INDEX COMPILER
Claire Gordon

NOTE ON CROSS-REFERENCES
Over the centuries and throughout the world, signs and symbols have evolved with increasingly complex, interwoven meanings, and many of the symbols illustrated in this book could be considered equally significant to more than one of the thematic headings used. Linked concepts can be pursued through the cross-referencing system: Throughout the text, **bold** type indicates that a symbol (or group of symbols) is illustrated and explored more fully elsewhere in the book. The main text entry for each featured symbol is highlighted in the index in **bold**. Index entries in regular type refer to references under another featured symbol.

Table of Contents

Introduction

Symbolism is an ancient and universal language that is a catalyst, triggering a complicated series of perceptions and beliefs, imparting information and arousing emotions through often little more than a brief glance. It is a truly international form of communication that transcends the barriers of language, history, nationality, cultures and religions. But why is this form of shorthand so powerful? Why does it evoke such profound instinctive responses? What, indeed, is a symbol or a sign?

What Are Signs and Symbols?

Generally speaking, a sign is denotive, in that it represents an object or direction, while a symbol is connotive, in that it arouses emotional responses. Dictionary definitions are of necessity brief and superficial: the word "sign" (which is derived from the Latin *signum*, a mark) will usually be defined as something that conveys specific information, while "symbol" (from the Latin *symbolum*) may be inter-

preted as something that represents something else; the two words are often interchangeable. The origin of the word "symbol" is particularly interesting. It derives from the ancient Greek custom of breaking a clay slate into pieces and giving a piece to each member of a group before their dispersal; when they reconvened, the pieces would be reassembled—*sumballein*, "to throw together"—like a jigsaw, and the individuals' group identity would thus be confirmed. The shells of the Eleusinian mysteries performed a similar function. So it was that the Greek word *sumbolon*, "a mark of recognition," came into being, from which the Latin *symbolum* evolved. But because they are bound by the limitations of language, the bald definitions of the lexicographers cannot encapsulate the full significance of signs and symbols, express the multitude of meanings that they represent, describe how they communicate their messages or explain why they speak to us so profoundly. They are so potent that, in words attributed to Confucius, "Signs and symbols rule the world, not words or laws."

Opposite: *This center-panel detail of Hieronymous Bosch's allegorical triptych* The Garden of Earthly Delights *(c. 1492) depicts humans dwarfed by gigantic birds and flowers. His art is packed with symbolic images of such extraordinary fantasy that Bosch has often been called the precursor of Surrealism.*

Above, left: *The red cross is a connotive symbol that was adopted by the Red Cross organization. Its red color symbolizes blood, and the cross, suffering and charity. It has become an internationally recognized symbol for medical aid.*

Below, left: *This generic sign indicates a restaurant. It is denotive because its components—knife, fork and plate—represent tools used for eating.*

Right: The crane has profound symbolic significance in the Orient, where it is believed to be a messenger of the gods and represents vigilance, longevity and happiness. This eighteenth-century depiction is by Lang Shih-Ning. Cranes were also important in the classical world. Nature symbols pervade the art of all cultures.

Symbolism and Early Man

Perhaps the earliest evidence of man's use of symbolism can be seen in the Paleolithic and Neolithic cave paintings and engravings of nearly thirty thousand years ago, such as those at Lascaux in France or on the African and Australian continents. In these pictographic depictions, early man not only portrayed hunters and beasts, but also drew geometric symbols, including circles, spirals and lines—forms that retain symbolic meaning to this day. Primitive as they are by modern standards, cave paintings demonstrate man's enduring need both to reflect his natural surroundings and to try to make sense of a seemingly chaotic world and determine his place within it. In the millennia before the development of modern science, man puzzled over natural phenomena which he was at a loss to explain: the rising and setting of the Sun, the phases of the Moon, the sudden appearance of thunder and lightning. In seeking to find explanations, and because he looked for these explanations in what was known and familiar, early man credited mythological supernatural beings with their cause: for example, the Sun was regarded as a manifestation of supreme male power in opposition to the female entity of the Moon, while thunder and lightning were evidence of celestial anger. The animals that lived alongside man were similarly believed to be endowed with supernatural power, as were trees, plants and geo-graphical features such as mountains and oceans. Such symbolic attributions inevitably raised cosmic questions regarding creation, the relationship between heaven and earth and man's position in the greater scheme of things, which could surely not be negligible. Drawing from humanity's familiar terms of reference, the universe gradually came to be identified with symbols such as the egg, which, in cosmic terms, emerged from the primeval waters to hatch out into heaven and earth, or the Tree of Life—an *axis mundi*, or world axis—which had its roots in the underworld, whose branches flourished on earth and whose pinnacle soared into the heavens, so uniting the three worlds.

Religion and Mythology

Such early symbolic cosmic concepts subsequently evolved into more formal religions, bringing with them different world views and new symbolic languages. The ancient Egyptians, for example, conceived a complex pantheon of deities that governed every aspect of life and death, and they represented these deities by means of a range of visual images, including hieroglyphics. Dating from at least 3100 BC, hieroglyphics, which were based on a complex representational language of phonograms (symbols that signify sound) and ideograms (symbols that depict concepts), were undoubtedly the most sophisticated of all the early symbolic systems, but this period also saw the emergence of symbols that still have relevance today, such as the Jewish pentagram and the swastika of the Indus civilization. The ancient Greeks, too, worshipped a variety of gods, whose collective symbolism was so powerful that they were adopted by the Romans, albeit with Latinized names, thus demonstrating the enduring resonance of particularly effective symbols. Similar practices can be seen in the assimilation of pagan symbols by Christianity or in the crossfertilization of the Hindu and Buddhist religions. Each of these religions additionally developed a wide range of symbols with which to represent specific aspects of their beliefs. Examples include the crucifix; Hinduism's elephant-headed deity, Ganesha; and the Buddha image. In man's search to explain the inexplicable, fantastic creatures—like the sphinx, the Greek Minotaur, the Hindu nagas or the Chinese and Western phoenixes, unicorns and dragons—also took

Left: Osiris, god of the underworld, is here surrounded by ancient Egyptian symbols, including the sacred eye, a hawk and a multitude of hieroglyphics. Osiris judged the dead, and here a recently deceased man kneels before him in supplication.

Below: Oak trees and mistletoe were sacred to the Druids. After the winter solstice, mistletoe was cut from oak trees (to release the oaks' strength) and caught in a white cloth to avoid its touching the earth.

their place in world mythology, their extraordinary hybrid forms symbolizing their respective characters and powers.

Macrocosm, Microcosm and Symbolic Systems

Religion and mythology were not the only ways in which humanity tried to find solutions to difficult questions such as man's existence and the relationship between macrocosm and microcosm: the cosmic man of medieval tradition, for example, was believed to be a microcosm that reflected and contained within his body all the elements of the macrocosm. Astrologers looked to the planets and constellations in their quest for cosmic understanding, in the process developing complicated symbolic systems; indeed, the horoscopes that date from ancient times are still consulted today in an attempt to predict the future, as are many other centuries-old symbolic systems of divination such as the Chinese pa kua, Tarot or numerology. Esoteric systems such as alchemy, the Jewish Kabbala, Rosicrucianism and Freemasonry each developed complex systems of belief which, adherents thought, could explain and influence life's mysteries. As well as simplifying complicated abstracts by arcane codification, the meanings of the respective symbols of such societies were known only to initiates in order to preserve their mystical secrecy and, by extension, their magical powers.

Above: This medieval tapestry from Cluny, France, depicts a virtuous lady to whom homage is being paid. Her purity is indicated by the presence of the unicorn, a fantastic creature that denotes chastity and goodness because it was believed that only a virgin could capture it.

The Symbolism of Opposition

Within the framework of his multitude of beliefs, man has furthermore made a primary distinction between good and bad. In non-religious cultures, this concept of moral opposition can be identified by positive symbols such as the color white, masculinity, the sun, sky, and heavens, or by negative symbols such as the color black, femininity, the moon, water, and the underworld. In religious analogy, Christianity for example, the power of goodness is symbolized by God and Christ, and evil by Satan. In mythology, the eternal battle between exalted and lowly forces is characterized by the conflict between the solar Garuda bird and the chthonic naga serpents in Hinduism or, in Western tradition, between the eagle and dragon. Many cultures have, however, recognized that true perfection is only achieved when the opposing forces present within the universe are reconciled and united: the Taoist yin-yang symbol and the alchemical figure of the Androgyne both represent this ideal, which is echoed in psychology.

Jung and the Archetypes

Remarkable similarities between fundamental concepts can therefore be seen within this apparently superficial disparity of religions and mystic belief, even where no historical religious or cultural associations exist. It was the pioneering work of the analytical psychologist Carl Gustav Jung (1875–1961) that made sense of these coincidences by identifying humanity's collective unconscious and the universal archetypes that are contained within it. According to Jung, the human psyche, or personality, consists of three main parts: the conscious mind (the ego); the personal unconscious, which stores our individual experiences, dreams, phobias and fantasies; and the collective unconscious, which stores the archetypes—universal blueprints of human experience which are inherited and shared by us all. In addition, there is a preconscious level, which contains recent memories.

The collective unconscious communicates with the conscious mind by means of the archetypes, which, in Jung's words, express

Jung was alerted to the presence of universal archetypes by both his study of alchemy and the spontaneous drawings of his patients, many of which demonstrated striking similarities to certain ancient mythic or religious symbols of which his patients could not have had prior knowledge. Indeed, Jung himself experienced this unconscious force when he felt himself inexplicably compelled to create abstract, geometrical designs based on a circle that was often divided into four parts. Jung interpreted these circular representations as archetypal symbols of the structure of the idealized, integrated self, but it was only later that he learned that such images had already existed for many centuries in the form of mandalas—Tantric cosmic symbols. Jung identified further archetypal images, such as the tree, which he described as a "symbol of the self in cross-section…depicted in the process of growth," whose roots represent the unconscious, whose trunk is the conscious and whose apex signifies a striving for individuation. In this context, the tree symbol was of particular importance in the work of artists such as Wassily Kandinsky, Paul Klee and Piet Mondrian. Jung's primary conclusion was that man unconsciously struggles to attain self-knowledge in order to achieve a personal psychological balance, and that this universal aim, which is evidenced by the archetypes, is expressed throughout history by all religions and systems of belief.

Left: Carl Gustav Jung identified the collective unconscious and the archetypal images that he believed are universal. According to his highly influential theory, the unconscious utilizes archetypes in its communication with the conscious mind.

humanity's "inborn disposition to produce parallel images" and which furthermore "represent the life and essence of a nonindividual psyche." Archetypes can be said to symbolize universal primordial experiences, including life and death, and psychic forces such as the emotions and moral values that are common to us all. They can find their expression in myths and fairy tales as examples of model human behavior, but they are also inherent in the collective unconscious as representations of the primitive and instinctual self. Among the most important of Jung's archetypes are the animus, representing the masculine side of the psyche; the anima, which symbolizes the feminine; the nurturing mother figure; the authoritative father figure; the trickster, the part of us that sabotages our own efforts; and the shadow—our primal, animal side. Sleep is the realm of the unconscious, and it communicates with the conscious mind by means of the archetypal symbols conveyed in dreams. On waking, the dream messages can then be interpreted and applied, so helping the conscious mind move closer to the harmonization of the conflicting complexes that are inherent in our minds, with the ultimate goal of achieving the individuation of the real self. As Jung explained, archetypes are therefore crucial instruments in the attainment of individuation, for they "act as transformers."

Left: Sigmund Freud first postulated the now widely accepted theory that dreaming is not simply an arbitrary phenomenon but the means of transmitting symbolic messages from the id to the ego. This theory was developed in his pioneering work The Interpretation of Dreams *(1900).*

Right and below: These symbols illustrate Charles Sanders Peirce's semiotic theory, in which there are three types of sign. The figure in the wheelchair is an "iconic" sign, as the image graphically depicts its subject. Leonardo's Mona Lisa *is an "indexical" sign, because the meaning behind the celebrated, enigmatic expression is entirely subjective. The sign for a nuclear hazard is "symbolic," in that, although its meaning is generally acknowledged, the image does not depict the subject it represents.*

Freud's Interpretation of Dreams

Jung had at one time worked closely with Sigmund Freud (1856–1939), the "father" of psychoanalysis, whose work, *The Interpretation of Dreams* (1900), first introduced the idea of dreaming as a form of communication between the unconscious (id) and conscious (ego and superego) minds. Unlike Jung, however, Freud believed that dream symbolism resulted from the repressed sexual desires of the individual, rather than from the archetypal vocabulary of Jung's collective unconscious, and the resulting conflict resulted in a parting of the ways. While Freud's theories are now sometimes regarded as taking too narrow a view, those of Jung have been widely accepted and, indeed, have been the primary influence on the modern psychological interpretation of symbolism.

Pioneers of Semiotics: Peirce and de Saussure

Semiotics (derived from the Greek *semeiotikos*, the study of signs), or semiology, is not the exclusive preserve of psychologists and psychoanalysts, but has also had great impact on a number of academic disciplines, including linguistics, anthropology, logic and mathematics. For example, the American philosopher Charles Sanders Peirce (1839–1914), often called the founding father of semiotics, based his research on language. Peirce came to believe that there are three types of signs: "iconic" signs, which clearly symbolize the objects that they depict; "indexical" signs, which represent concepts that can be regarded subjectively by each individual viewer; and "symbolic" signs, with meanings determined by conventional use, that

do not in any way resemble the objects to which they refer. It was Peirce who first postulated that because we each have unique viewpoints and terms of reference acquired by personal experience, individuals may perceive and interpret the same sign differently. His contemporary, the Swiss linguist Ferdinand de Saussure (1857–1913), identified two parts to a sign: the signifier (*le signifiant*) or word, which is itself meaningless until it gives form to an abstract concept, which he termed the signified (*le signifié*), whereupon it becomes a symbol and of "value." Because of the variety of systematic relationships between words, this relationship is not, however, rigid, but arbitrary.

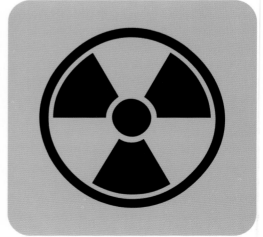

t The development of semiotics since the work of Peirce and de Saussure has resulted in different, and sometimes conflicting, schools of semiotic thought, but most generally recognize at least two basic components of a sign or symbol: the "representamen," which is the sign vehicle, and the "object," for which it stands.

Wittgenstein's Philosophy of Language

Ludwig Wittgenstein (1889–1951) also considered symbolism in the philosophy of language that he developed in his two major works on meaning, *Tractatus Logico-Philosophicus* (1922) and *Philosophical Investigations* (1953). In the former publication, Wittgenstein examines the statement of fact which, put in simplistic terms, can assume a pictorial character when conveying information. This relationship is, however, extremely abstract, for while statement and picture should have a shared form, this may be spatial or logical, and the latter form cannot be described accurately, if at all. At Cambridge University, Wittgenstein was a pupil of the British philosopher and mathematician Bertrand Russell (1872–1970)—himself the author of *An Enquiry into Meaning and Truth* (1940)—and a champion of the symbolic-logic theory developed by Gottlob Frege (1848–1925). Frege based his theory on the earlier attempts of George Boole (1815–64) to create a systematic notation for logic, and by using additional symbols—quantifiers— with which to represent mathematical ideas, Frege's symbolic logic succeeded in eliminating the ambiguities and uncertainties that had resulted from the use of imprecise language in mathematics.

Philosophical Investigations was Wittgenstein's first major published work written after he had reconsidered and largely rejected the premises underpinning his earlier writings. Like all his later works, it was published posthumously, leaving interpretations of his highly abstract writing (much of which was in the form of aphorisms without supporting explanation) open for debate, but its influence on subsequent work in the fields of linguistics, semiotics and the philosophy of mind was considerable. In *Philosophical Investigations*, he addressed the relationship between language development, meaning and the complexity of human thought. Contrary to his

Left: Sweethearts' names enclosed in a heart shape and pierced by an arrow form a popular symbol of love, and carving a heart on a growing tree symbolized love's endurance. This tradition has declined because of increasing awareness of the threat it poses to trees.

Most Western philosophers believed that love is an inherently "private" experience (as are all emotions and sensations) and the word "love" cannot have the same meaning for any two individuals. Wittgenstein's later philosophy allowed for shared, commonly understood meanings of words that describe inner experience.

earlier views that language is analogous to a kind of calculus or mathematical system, with simple, fixed elements (words correlated with private "pictures" in the minds of the speaker, listener or reader), he outlined a more sophisticated relationship between language, meaning and communicators. Although meanings of individual words shift, sentences and phrases can be understood because language is communicated in a context. A person claiming to be in pain is only understood (or believed) if he or she exhibits other symptoms of pain than simply saying the appropriate words. In the absence of such other signs, it is assumed that the person is either lying or has not mastered the rules of language sufficiently to understand the meaning of what he or she has said.

Wittgenstein likens language to a game, like chess, with publicly acknowledged rules allowing meaning that is genuinely understood and agreed upon in communication. Further, he suggests that many communication problems arise from misunderstandings caused by language itself creating a kind of false conundrum. For example, the language developed to describe the mind in Cartesian terms, as a separate realm residing in, but separate from the body, causes the belief that one person's experience of being in pain cannot be understood by another because the pain is inherently "private" and unique to the mental realm of that person, instead of something that can be shared in the "public" or demonstrable world. However, the meaning of a statement such as "I am in pain" is readily understood in context. To deny the possibility of meaningful communication about mental states or emotions on the grounds of their inherent privacy is thus a mistake caused by a concept of purely linguistic origin. By disconnecting words from picturelike, fixed or simple meanings and concentrating on contextual, game-like language use, Wittgenstein altered the terms of our understanding of language, signs and symbols.

The Semiotic Debate and Structuralism

Debates on symbolism and semiotic theories did not apply solely to linguistics, but to all forms of communication, thus later influencing modern sociology and also the Structuralist movement, among whose leading proponents were the anthropologist Claude Lévi-Strauss (b. 1908) and the literary Structuralist Roland Barthes (1915–80). In an interesting parallel to Jung's theories, Lévi-Strauss's major work, *Mythologiques* (1964–72), concluded that the similarity of structure seen in all human mythologies indicates a shared method, meaning and message, reflecting the common structure of the human brain and analogous human methods of attempting to impose order upon the universe. Barthes, too, used deconstructionalist techniques with which to identify language as a coded symbolic system whose individual signs (words) are interdependent. Meaning, he deduced, therefore depends on the structure of the "values" that are constituted by language as a whole.

The debate on symbolism and language continues to maintain its momentum, with Victor Turner, for example, arguing that symbols cannot be accorded a single interpretation; they are inherently ambiguous because they can mean different things according to their context and because they are perceived and interpreted in a variety of ways by individuals. Dan Sperber concurs with this latter thesis, additionally suggesting that symbols are symbolic precisely because their effect cannot be readily explained.

The Symbolist Movement

The impact of symbolic thought has not been confined to the domain of philosophers and theorists—art, too, has found it a rich palette from which to work. While religious and Renaissance art was especially addicted to the use of symbolic allegory, by the nineteenth century, Naturalism and Realism predominated, provoking a reaction in the form of the European Symbolist movement that prevailed from the mid–1890s until World War I, and which found its expression in art, literature and drama. Noted Symbolist writers included the novelist J. K. Huysmans and the poets Rimbaud and Mallarmé, as well as the dramatist Maeterlinck. Leading "literary" Symbolist artists included Gustave Moreau, Puvis de Chavannes and Odilon Redillon, and also the "pictorial" Symbolist Paul Gauguin. Following a loosely held doctrine that plastic art should be ideative, symbolist, synthetic, subjective and decorative, Symbolism freed art from the rigid constraints of Realism, thus preparing the way for later movements such as Expressionism, Abstraction and Surrealism, all of which relied heavily on symbolic images.

Right: Paul Gauguin emigrated from France to Tahiti in 1891. He drew endless inspiration from his new environment. His simplified, decorative and brightly colored figures stood in direct and revolutionary opposition to the conventions of Naturalism, thus identifying him as a "pictorial" Symbolist artist.

Surrealism

As well as inheriting Symbolist beliefs, the Surrealists were furthermore inspired by Freud's theories of free association, the unconscious and dream analysis. They enthusiastically used artistic forms as a way in which to represent and liberate the workings of the irrational, subconscious mind. Surrealist artists such as Max Ernst, René Magritte and, most notoriously, Salvador Dalí challenged Realist artistic conventions by consciously depicting the fantastic images of the unconscious mind. Ernst, for example, created extraordinary landscapes inhabited by bizarre animal and organic forms; Magritte intentionally mislabeled his paintings; while Dalí built up a unique new language of symbolic imagery, containing melting watches, crutches and spindle-legged creatures. Although not a Surrealist, Marc Chagall, too, used symbolic references to his Russian Hasidic past in his paintings, drawing on dreamlike images such as flying brides and floating animals with which to reflect both his personal experiences and his unconscious mind. Indeed, throughout the twentieth century, artists of all schools have continued to challenge conventional perceptions by the imaginative use of symbolism.

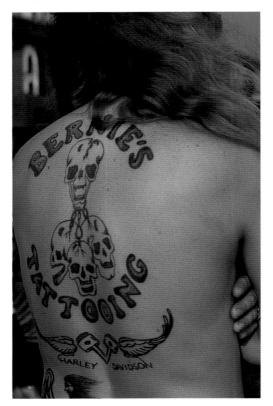

Left: By shaving their heads (representing purification) and donning the robes of their religious community, these Thai monks have made a symbolic statement of suppressing their individuality and embracing a collective identity.

Symbols of Identity

Symbolism has therefore had an enormous influence on the arts, but we need not visit an art gallery, a library or a theater in order to expose ourselves to symbolism in action, for it pervades our everyday lives. Since ancient times, symbolism has been used to denote identity and confirm adherence to social groups. People may be symbolized by a dominant trait of personality or attribute, such as wisdom, innocence or patriotism; while in psychological terms, as well as in reality, different personas may be assumed by the wearing of masks in order to conceal the true self and to take on some of the characteristics of the being that the mask symbolizes. Membership of a trade or profession may additionally define identity, and generic occupational symbols may thus be applied to those who practice within them: a chef, for example, may be denoted by a chef's hat, a barber by a barber's pole, or a king by his crown. Individual members of tribal cultures pronounce their collective identity through specific and insular symbolic marks such as body painting, piercing and decoration or tribal costume. This tendency holds true as much for the modern cult groups of Western youth (punks, for example), or for the supporters of sporting teams, as for tribal communities such as the African,

Left: Tattooing is an ancient practice—indeed, an art form—indicating tribal identity. Over the last century it has increased in popularity among youth groups. The cultural significance of this more recent practice can also be as an indicator of group identity (particularly military or gang membership). More generally, it is a symbol of rebellion against authority.

Right: It is not just the bagpipes that make this man's nationality instantly identifiable, for his tartan kilt is perhaps Scotland's best-known symbol. By the seventeenth century the kilt, whose pleated tartan fabric identifies the wearer's clan, had become so important as a symbol of kinship and nationhood that the English banned it after their victory at the Battle of Culloden in 1746. The restriction was lifted in 1782.

Below, right: A gift from France to the United States, the Statue of Liberty is the most emotive symbol of American nationhood. As the name suggests, the statue symbolizes the principle of liberty enshrined in the Constitution. The imposing figure was a powerful symbol of hope to the immigrants—the "huddled masses"—who arrived in New York from Europe during the nineteenth and twentieth centuries.

Opposite, above: Political symbols are powerful instruments in the manipulation of the masses. The image of former Chinese chairman Mao Tse-tung was made into a political icon, serving as a reminder of his power and presence and creating a "cult of personality."

Opposite, below: The looped, red AIDS empathy ribbon, worn here by Elizabeth Taylor and Clint Black, is an example of the power of symbols to evoke an instant emotional response.

Aboriginal or Native American, whose traditions have endured through the centuries. Medieval heraldic art also developed a unique, elaborate symbolic system with which to identify individuals or civic entities and to place them within the wider context of their dynasty or country.

Totemism and Symbols of Nationality

Totemism is another important way in which communities proclaim their collective identity, ties of kinship and belief: in tribal analogy, this concept may be seen in the respect that is accorded specific animals or supernatural beings—such as the Native American Thunderbird—as the totems, or protective entities, of a tribe. The stacked totemic figures that make up totem poles thus concentrate a tribe's history and beliefs in one powerful symbolic emblem. Countries themselves can be represented by totemic symbols in the form of national emblems—for instance, the Canadian maple leaf, the English rose, or the cock of France. Perhaps the best-known national symbols, however, are official national flags, whose combination of carefully chosen components symbolizes the unity of its people.

Symbols As Instruments of Political Propaganda

Political parties have long recognized and exploited the unifying and motivational power of symbols. In *Mein Kampf*, Hitler described the search for a suitable symbol with which to represent the Nazi party: "Not only was it to be a symbol for our struggle, but also had to be very effective on posters…those who have had experience with the masses realize just how important such a seemingly trivial thing is. A working and effective sign can be the deciding factor in hundreds of separate instances as to whether an interest is woken." The Nazis settled on the swastika, and, in a chilling example of the successful misappropriation of a symbol's subliminal power in order to manipulate the populace, transformed the meaning of this ancient symbol by skillful use of propaganda into one of racism, terror and annihilation—in the process tainting the symbol itself. Recognizing the latent power of the symbol (which, after all, initially signifies nothing until it is endowed with a specific meaning), the Third Reich promoted and strengthened its ideologies and position through a deliberate and systematic use of symbols, among which were the lightning-flash runes of the S.S., which recalled the mystical traditions of Germanic paganism; the yellow Star of David that Jews were forced to wear in order to identify their race; or the red and pink triangles that marked concentration-camp inmates as communists or homosexuals. Other dictatorships, like that of Stalin in the U.S.S.R., have also misused symbolism in the battle for the hearts and minds of the people and have saturated them with symbolic images such as, in the case of the Soviet Union, the ideographic hammer and sickle or the iconic portraits of political leaders.

Symbols of Commerce and Empathy

In a less sinister way, corporate logos also rely on the symbol's ability to arouse subliminal responses and are therefore carefully chosen to appeal to the unconscious mind. Psychologists are often consulted during the design process in order to propose symbols that will project a positive corporate image and thus persuade the consumer to endorse the product. As Barthes observed, advertisers, too, manipulate the unconscious, presenting their products in such a way that the consumer is encouraged to believe that a particular product will mystically transform their image and lifestyle. Advertisements and business logos are probably among the most prevalent of contemporary symbolic forms, but in recent times other generic types have also emerged, such as looped ribbons worn upon the lapel to signify support for certain social groups or those suffering from diseases: a red ribbon, for instance, promotes AIDS awareness and sympathy for its victims, a white ribbon represents breast cancer, while a pink ribbon expresses antipathy for homophobia.

Colors and Shapes

Such color codification demonstrates the ancient symbolic power that colors still exercise over us: white is generally agreed to be the color of purity and goodness, and black—its antithesis—of evil; in between is gray, the color of ambiguity or the unexceptional middle way; red is the color of fire or danger; purple, that of royalty; yellow, the color of both happiness and the sun; blue, the hue of the sea and sky that represents serenity; while green is the color of nature and growth. Like colors, shapes have also been used since humanity's earliest days to represent abstract concepts: gestalts such as the square, symbolizing the

Above and right: The generic man and woman images (based on gender-typed clothing conventions) and the no-smoking and airport signs are internationally recognized iconic images in everyday use. Traffic lights are based on a universally accepted colour coded system.

Below, right: Musical notation is a complex written symbolic system in which the pitch, tempo and relative duration of a combination of musical sounds are graphically represented. Modern Western musical notation, developed from an early system of neumes (dots and squiggles), is based on an eight-note scale (octave) and uses such symbols as a five-lined stave, clefs, bars, sharps, flats, quavers and semiquavers.

Far right: This double helix (spiral) is the biological symbol for DNA (deoxyribonucleic acid), the main constituent of chromosomes.

earth and solidity; the circle, perfection and the self; while the triangle is a triple entity representing the union and concentration of three separate forces into a powerful whole.

Symbolism In Everyday Life

Each of us makes use of symbols every day. When shopping, we pay for our purchases with money, which conveniently symbolizes the value of the goods that we have bought; a nation's economic strength can, moreover, be judged by its currency's foreign-exchange performance. Road signs are further examples of symbols that we routinely encounter; the signs are so designed that they can be seen and their messages absorbed while traveling in a moving vehicle, thus instantly and effectively imparting essential information that

not only regulates traffic flow, but also helps to save lives. Meteorology, too, employs a unique system of symbols with which to represent weather phenomena, and televized weather forecasts have familiarized us with many of these. In the media, people themselves are frequently described as being symbols: those who have survived tragedy are symbols of hope and endurance; criminals can be denounced as symbols of evil; while figures of exemplary selflessness, like Mother Teresa, are termed symbols of inspiration.

Symbols of Language and Science

As we have seen, language itself is a system of symbols with which we communicate ideas and information to others, both verbally and in writing; by applying single symbols to words or phrases, systems of shorthand such as Pitman, Teeline or Speedwriting have taken linguistic symbolism one step further, so speeding up the process of written notation in situations in which the formation of conventional words

would be too slow and unwieldy. In another context, how would one capture and preserve the elusive and transient sounds of the language of music if it were not for the system of musical notation that allows the transcription of tones and the duration of notes? Science relies especially strongly on symbolism as a means of

communication, and the study and expression of scientific disciplines such as mathematics, electronics, biology, chemistry, physics and pharmacy each use highly developed symbolic systems whose individual components can respectively denote extraordinarily abstruse and complex concepts by means of a simple sign. And in this technological age, we are being increasingly exposed to computers, whose basic operation is itself based on symbolic systems: those of binary notation, a number system in "base two," in which numbers are expressed by sequences of the digits 0 and 1; and the binary code, in which each set of numbers or letters is represented as a unique group of "bits." Computer software has introduced an entirely new set of symbols into the computer user's vocabulary, including menus, icons, trash cans, hourglasses, arrows and cursors.

Conclusion

Although every symbol is a microcosm, it may also be seen as an expression of the macrocosm, for each incorporates, reflects and connects the dynamic structure of both the cosmos and the human mind. When taken to its ultimate extreme, anything can be regarded as a symbol: any image, person, object or word—or even something as intangible as a smell—can represent something else. Furthermore, although symbols contain within their forms a rich legacy of millennia of humanity's experience and perception, their use, depiction and interpretation do not remain static, for new associations and, indeed, fresh images, are constantly being added to the fluid, dynamic entity that can be regarded as our collective symbolic vocabulary.

The following chapters examine a large selection of symbols that have been loosely categorized under the following headings: sacred symbols, symbols of identity, symbols of magic and the occult and symbolic systems, as well as nature symbols, the symbolism of fantastic creatures, and those of the emotions and inner mind. This selection cannot pretend to be a comprehensive catalog or definitive interpretation of the multitude of symbols that recur in our legends, history and art or arouse our responses. It should, however, represent the images most significant in a wide variety of cultures and provide a fascinating journey of discovery through which the effects of symbolism on our conscious and unconscious minds can be better understood, and which can then be further developed on a personal basis. The reader will discover that, in the words of Jung, symbols are a "perpetual challenge to our thoughts and feelings."

Above, left: *Semaphore (from the Greek for "sign-bearing") was developed in 1890 from an eighteenth-century English naval code. Based on the positions of the hands of the clock, each letter and numeral has its own position, which the signaler indicates by means of red-and-yellow flags held in each hand. Illustrated here are the positions for the distress message "SOS."*

Above: *The International Flag code performs the equivalent function to traffic signals in a nautical context. Pictured here are: A—Diver down; B—Dangerous cargo; C—"Yes"; and D—Keep clear. Morse code employs specific combinations of dots (rapid sounds) and dashes (longer sounds) to identify letters of the alphabet, with spaces (pauses) between each letter. Here, "SOS" is spelled out.*

Center, left: *Information— whether audio or visual—is encoded on a compact disc as a series of metallic pits and read by an optical laser. The data manipulated by electronic devices, however complex, can be reduced to a simple binary code.*

· 19 ·

Sacred Symbols

The rich variety of the world's religions is testimony to man's basic and enduring need to find an explanation for his existence and to discover his place in the cosmic scheme. Such religious and philosophical quests demand faith and the suspension of disbelief in what cannot be seen. They involve complex concepts that have become more elaborate and intricate through time. Thus, although not themselves objects of worship, sacred symbols are far more than mere graphic representations of the subjects of religious veneration. They are imbued with many layers of profound significance, which, when concentrated in one sign, serve to invoke both the tenets of faith and the history of belief. They may be regarded as powerful instruments of devotion, which, by crystallizing elements of the worshipper's religion, help to focus and develop faith. All of them can be regarded as meditational symbols, but some images, such as the Oriental lotus or the written syllable *Om*, are particularly effective in this respect.

Many of the most abstruse concepts are expressed by the simplest symbols: the Buddhist wheel for example, which signifies the round of existence or the Buddhist Law; the crucifix—the most important of all Christian symbols—which reminds of Christ's sacrifice; or the cosmic yin-yang sign of Taoism. Some symbols represent the power of sacred texts: the Jewish Tablets of the Decalogue and the Sefer Torah, the Buddhist prayer wheel and Islamic calligraphy. Symbols of the supreme deity are given different forms according to the particular religion: Native American tribes may represent it as the Thunderbird, while Judaism declines personification. Judaism and Christianity have used the Tetragrammaton or triangle of the Holy Trinity. The gods of Ancient Egypt and Hinduism, the Greco-Roman pantheon and the Buddha are all depicted in bodily—if sometimes hybrid—form. Creatures from the natural world can also signify a sacred concept: in Australian Aboriginal and Native American belief, animals like the kangaroo and the buffalo are totems imbued with supernatural power. The bull has symbolic resonance in Hinduism, while in Christianity, the dove and lamb represent Christ. The fish is a creature used to represent both Buddha and Christ.

There are often striking similarities among religious symbols, indicating both the cross-fertilization of early religious thought, and common cosmic interpretations. This can be seen in the Roman adoption and renaming of the Greek pantheon, for example, and in the evolution of early sun gods' aureoles into the haloes of Christianity. Haloes are also features of Hinduist imagery, which, like Christianity, professes a trinity. And Hinduism shares many sacred symbols, including footprints and canopies, with Buddhism. Nor are sacred symbols restricted to two-dimensional representation: architecture also conveys religious belief, as seen in the Buddhist stupa, the Shinto Buddhist torii, or such Druidic constructions as Stonehenge, all of which are far more than mere places of worship.

While this chapter cannot fully encompass the world's multitude of sacred symbols, it aims to give a broad introduction to some of the most enduring.

Opposite: This is an unusual image of Buddha in that it depicts him with three heads. Trinities are common in many religions, including Christianity (the Holy Trinity) and Hinduism (the Trimurti). The triple-faced Buddha image can represent the Triple Jewel that consists of Buddha himself, the Dharma (the Buddhist Law) and the Sangha (the Enlightened Community). It can also symbolize the past, present and future, or the Three Bodies of Buddha: Essence, Bliss and the Created Body. In common with Judaism and Christianity, and unlike religions such as Hinduism, early depictions of Buddha were not human in form .

Buddhism

Buddha *Below*

Initially, representations of Buddha were not given human form. The now familiar, serene figure of Shakyamuni became an icon of Buddhism in the second century AD. These depictions date from the Kushan period and the Gandhara or Mathura schools. Buddha is usually portrayed deep in meditation and his physical characteristics assume some of the thirty-two ways of identifying Buddhahood. Thus he is often shown dressed in simple monastic robes, with a **halo**, with lengthened or enlarged ears, with an urna (a mark on his forehead representing a third eye of spiritual vision) and with the ushnisha, a cranial protuberance (signifying knowledge).

Wheel *Above, right*

The wheel is a powerful ancient symbol for the cycle of life and has significance in most religions. When shown with twelve segments, as here, it symbolizes the months of the year, or the twelve Adityas. The twelve spokes of the wheel represent the twelve links (*nidana* in Sanskrit, *tendrel* in Tibetan) in the circle of interdependent existence, the whole

representing a natural law whose transcendence is called enlightenment. The wheel also denotes the **sun** with rays radiating out from the center and is the sign of sun gods in many cultures. With its implication of movement, it can also be a sign of the cosmos and of time and fate. It has particular resonance in the Buddhist religion as both the Wheel of Life and the **Wheel of Law** (usually eight-spoked, signifying spiritual power and enlightenment). It can also serve as an aniconic depiction of **Buddha**. Along with the **lotus**, it makes up one of the chakras—the spiritual and psychic centers of energy.

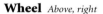

Hand of Buddha *Below*

In images of **Buddha**, the portrayal of his hands carries great significance. The various gestures that can be made are collectively termed the mudra (these symbolic gestures can also be seen in Indian dance and in Hindu and Buddhist rituals). While the hand of Buddha generally signifies protection, the mudra symbolize the power of enlightened spirituality. Although there are over five hundred mudra positions, Buddha is usually portrayed making one of five: raising his right hand to show fearlessness; making

the shape of a **wheel** to signify his law; joining his hands upward in meditation; pointing a hand downward to call the earth as witness (the *bhumi sparsha* mudra, shown here); or with an upraised palm offering gifts.

Dharma Chakra *Opposite, top*

The **eight**-spoked dharma chakra is the Wheel of Law of Buddha (chakra meaning "wheel," and dharma "the law" in Sanskrit). **Buddha** is sometimes referred to as "He who turns the Wheel of the Word and the Law," and when he first preached at Sarnath he set the dharma chakra in motion. While the **circle** symbolizes the completeness of dharma, each spoke represents the Noble Eightfold

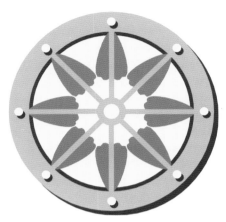

Path (the path consisting of the right faith, values, speech, conduct, livelihood, endeavor, awareness and meditation), to lead the believer to enlightenment and Nirvana. Through its endless turning, the dharma chakra exposes ignorance and illusion, and its spokes converge on the center, which is sometimes equated with Buddha. Buddha can be portrayed making the dharma chakra mudra with his hands, and the symbol is sometimes depicted on the **footprint** of Buddha, when it signifies the universal ruler. The first turning of the wheel of dharma is believed to have taken place in the deer park of Sarnath, modern-day Varanasi (Benares). The Wheel of Law, Truth and Life is one of the Eight Symbols of Good Augury to Chinese Buddhists.

Conch Shell *Below, right*
According to Buddhist tradition, the conch shell, when sounded, symbolizes the voice of **Buddha** preaching the law and thus **wisdom**, the power of oration and sound. In addition, it is a sign of victory over samsara (a state of suffering existence loosely equated with reincarnation). A white conch signifies power on **earth**. In Chinese Buddhism, the conch shell is one of the Eight Symbols of Good Augury and can signify a prosperous journey, as the shell is associated with the beneficial effects of **water**. The conch shell also plays an important role in Hindu symbolism, where it is sacred to Vishnu and articulates his call to his followers to awaken from their ignorance. In Islam it signifies the ear that hears the divine word.

Parasol *Below*
The parasol, sun-shade or umbrella is a symbol of elevation, dignity and honor in Buddhism, as well as in India, China and Japan. Important personages, such as kings and princes, were traditionally protected from the hot Asian **sun** by parasols, which became marks of temporal distinction and sovereignty and were associated with religious figures such as **Buddha** and the bodhisattvas. Thus a parasol is held over Buddha by Indra, and in the hands of Mo-li Hung—the celestial king of the south in Buddhism—it symbolizes earthquakes and

darkness. The parasol's mystical significance as a link between heaven and earth is further compounded by its shape: its canopy is reminiscent of the sun, of the radial effect of the sun's rays and of the vault of the heavens, while its shaft acts as an *axis mundi*. Most para-

sols used in religious ceremonies have many layers (echoed in the **stupa**'s tower), signifying the hierarchy of heaven and the stages of the path toward Nirvana. As well as being a symbol of sovereignty, the parasol also represents protection because of its function. The golden *Chattah* is one of the Eight Symbols of Good Augury in Chinese Buddhism, and in Hinduism the parasol is held by Vishnu in his appearance as a dwarf and by Yashoda, the mother of Krishna.

Fish *Below*
In a striking parallel with Jesus in Christianity, **Buddha** is the Fisher of Men, and the symbolism of the fish is therefore closely linked with him. As one of the Seven Appearances, the fish is sometimes depicted on **footprints** of Buddha, when it represents freedom from the restraints of desire and attachment. It can also signify the followers of Buddha.

Guardian Spirits *Above*

The guard shown here protecting the royal palace of Bangkok, Thailand, wears an elaborate costume and fearful **mask** with which to frighten away evil intruders. By investing himself with a nonhuman face, he calls upon the supernatural powers of the guardian spirit symbolized by the mask. Guardian spirits play an important role in the traditions of Buddhism (in which they are usually gods, demons or bodhisattvas) and Japanese Shintoism (as well as in many other cultures, including Native American) and have the positive attributes of protection, spiritual power and the bringing of good fortune. In particular, they are believed to protect sacred places.

Lotus *Above, center right*

As well as having profound symbolism in Ancient Egypt and Hinduism, the lotus flower is sacred to Buddhas, who are often portrayed seated on a lotus or issuing as a flame from the lotus center. A variety of waterlily, the lotus rises in the morning from muddy waters to flower and is therefore a symbol of purity, resurrection and perfect beauty in Asia. The lotus symbolizes the creation of life from the slime of the primordial waters. With the **wheel**, the open lotus flower constitutes a **chakra**, the spiritual Wheel of Existence. With **eight** petals, the flower signifies cardinal directions and cosmic harmony and is used in **mandalas** as a meditational symbol; with a thousand petals, it denotes spiritual revelation. The closed lotus bud symbolizes potential. The union of bliss and emptiness that is the goal of tantric practice is termed *mani padme* ("Jewel in the Lotus")—the lotus with **Buddha** as its heart. The lotus is also imbued with sexual symbolism, the jewel and lotus representing the phallus and yoni respectively. In addition, the lotus is an attribute of the Buddhas Amitabha, Kwan Yin and Maitreya Buddha, and of Tara—Mother of Buddhas. In Chinese Buddhism, the lotus is one of the Eight Symbols of Good Augury. It is now the emblem of India and Egypt.

Stupa *Below*

The stupa is a widely seen monument in India marking the resting places of the ashes of emperors and religious figures such as the Buddha Shakyamuni, and later also Buddhist monks and sacred relics. Derived from a simple burial mound and cairnlike in shape, the stupa has a distinctive domed roof that is sometimes many-layered (a form from which the **nine**-story pagoda of eastern Asia derived). The Tibetan chörten (as shown here) is identical to the stupa in style. Built on a **square** base (to represent the **earth**), the stupa is a cosmic symbol: four **doors** on each side represent the cardinal directions, its circular levels (representing **water**) signify the path of knowledge leading through the planes of existence, and its dome (anda) symbolizes **fire**. Balanced on a dish (signifying **air**) on the dome's apex is a spike, variously symbolizing Buddha, the Bodhi tree under which Buddha achieved enlightenment and the *axis mundi,* which reaches for the ethereal. The rings (chattra) encircling the spike represent elements of the higher world. Thus spiritual energy flows upward through the stupa from its earthly base to heaven. As well as representing the stages of life, knowledge, initiation and elevation, the stupa is the architectural embodiment of the Buddhist law, dharma, and, like the **mandala**, whose combination of shapes it shares, it is designed as an aid to meditation.

Taoism/Confucianism

Yin-Yang Circle *Below*

The yin-yang (ta-ki, or tai-chi) **circle** is the primary symbol of Taoist religious and philosophical belief, based on the mystical teachings of Lao Tse. It is also important in Confucianism, especially in the theories of the Han Confucian, Tung Chung Shu. Tao ("the way") teaches that everything in the **universe** is made of, and controlled by, two conflicting forces: the yin, the negative and passive power (depicted in black, which represents femininity); and the yang, the positive and active power (depicted in white, which signifies masculinity). Yin represents the soul, wetness, cold, night, the **moon**, darkness, the Earth and sustenance, and is associated with the broken line. The yang denotes the spirit, light, heat, dryness, day, the **sun**, heaven, creation and dominance, and is associated with the unbroken line. The yin always comes before the yang, as it represents primeval darkness before creation. The influence of yin and yang can be seen in the changing of the **seasons**—and, indeed, in the whole of the natural order. Harmony can only be achieved when the two are perfectly and complementarily balanced. The yin-yang circle symbolizes this concept. Its equal areas of yin and yang are divided by a sigmoid line (denoting dynamism) and are contained within a circle of revolution and unity. A small circle of the opposite color is contained in each, signifying the seed of the other, and therefore their interdependence.

Prayer Wheel *Above*

The Buddhist prayer **wheel** is mainly seen in Tibet and takes the form of a cylindrical drum, to which a handle is attached. Prayers or mantras (usually including the mystical lines *Om Mani-padme hum*, referring to the Jewel in the Lotus) are repeatedly printed on a scroll of paper wound around the cylinder and secured by a metal cover that is also inscribed with a mantra. When the wheel is spun in a clockwise direction, the rotational effect is believed to stimulate the offering of the prayers to heaven to ensure their effectiveness throughout the world. A variation on the prayer wheel is the prayer barrel, which is placed at the entrance of Lamaist temples. The prayer wheel is a symbol of the power of the sacred texts and of the creative force generated by the wheel.

Canopy *Below*

To Chinese Buddhists, the canopy is one of the Eight Symbols of Good Augury. Like the **parasol**, it was traditionally held over the heads of dignitaries to shield them from the elements. It is a symbol

of both importance and protection (a white canopy represents the protection of the dharma) and shelters buddhas such as Maitreya. Depending on its shape, it can be equated with the sky and **sun** if it is circular or with the **earth** if it is **square**—in Hinduism these respectively signify the temporal power of royalty and the spiritual authority of priests.

Shinto Torii *Left*

Shintoism, which evolved in the sixth century, is Japan's national religion. The torii, or wooden **gateway** leading to the Shinto shrine (Jinja) where the gods reside, is believed only to date from the sixteenth century. The torii is traditionally made of **three** pieces and symbolizes the right entrance to the sacred way—the way of the gods.

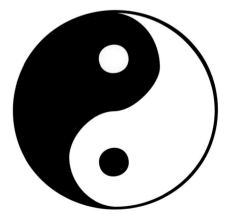

Hinduism

The Hindu Trinity *Right*

In classical Indian belief, **Shiva**, Vishnu and Brahma—the three mightiest gods of India—together form the Hindu trinity, the *Trimurti* (which means "having three forms" in Sanskrit). Vishnu the Preserver maintains the harmony of the universe and is the agent of light; Shiva the Destroyer, by contrast, represents the powers of darkness and annihilation; while Brahma, the Creator (who is sometimes depicted with four faces), provides the balance that links the opposing forces of Vishnu and Shiva. This triad, respectively representing the cosmic forces of creation, preservation and destruction, is said to make up the supreme, formless being (*Brahm*) that rules the cosmos. Many Indian cults, however, do not worship Brahma and consider either Vishnu or Shiva the supreme being (indeed, his devotees call Shiva himself the Trimurti, as this complex god also personifies the supreme being's triple aspects).

Shiva *Below*

Shiva (or Siva) is one of the **three** most powerful gods of the Hindu pantheon. In the *Rig Veda* he is identified as the lesser deity, Rudra, who later evolved into the omnipotent Shiva. As one of the Trimurti, Shiva is named only as the Destroyer, yet

he is a deity of contrasting and often contradictory characteristics. While he is the supreme god of masculine virility (symbolized by a phallic lingam, whose counterpart is the female yoni), he is also an ascetic yogi; he is additionally an agent of both good and evil. As Nataraja he is lord of the universal dance of creation and destruction, who dances on the vanquished demon of chaos or dwarf of ignorance. He is portrayed with **four** hands, and they can carry a consuming flame, the rattle of creation or a drum with which to beat out the rhythm of life. In iconic depictions Shiva is represented riding the white **bull**, Nandi. One of his wives is the terrible Kali and, like her, he can carry a rope or serpent with which to kill trans-

gressors and sometimes wears a necklace of human **skulls**. He may also carry the skull of the murdered Brahma in his hand or wear it in his hair. A crescent **moon** ornaments his head, representing his power over life and death; the ashes of corpses flow through his veins. He wears a **tiger**-skin loincloth and carries a weapon such as a **trident** (symbolizing the past, present and future), **bow**, ax or **torch**. From his head springs the Ganges River (whose personification, Ganga, is another wife). In the middle of his forehead is a third eye; as well as destroying with fire those who look upon it, this grants him transcendent wisdom. The third eye variously symbolizes the **sun**, **moon**, **fire** and day and night.

Ganesha *Above*

In the Hindu pantheon, the **elephant**-headed Ganesha, son of **Shiva** and Pavarti, is the god of sagacity, good luck, prudence and invincibility because he can remove all obstacles. He only has one tusk, the other having been broken off in battle. The elephant head is that of Airavata, mount of Indra (signifying wisdom). Ganesha is shown with **four** arms (one of which holds the ax of Shiva) with which he protects and confers gifts on humanity. He rides a rat, also a symbol of **wisdom**. Ganesha is the lord of the Ganas, the lesser deities. The patron of learning (in popular tradition he was the author of the ancient epic poem, the *Mahabharata*) and merchants, Ganesha's image is often placed above commercial buildings or painted on the title pages of books. He is saluted before a journey and before embarking on an important task.

Om *Above, center right*

The Sanskrit calligraphy of this symbol spells out the mystical monosyllable *Om*, (or *Aum*), which is regarded in Hinduism, Buddhism and Jainism as a sacred sound with divine potency. The *Upanishads*, the ancient writings of Hindu philosophy, describe *Om* as the fundamental sound of the universe that brought about creation and sustains the cosmos. The

sounds made when A, U, and M are pronounced represent the Trimuti, the **three** gods, Brahma, Vishnu and **Shiva**, who control life. They also signify the three states of man: dreaming, sleeping and waking; the three times of day and the three human capacities of desiring, knowing and acting. The everlasting sound is used as a mantra in meditational yoga, as an invocation, or at the beginning and end of the chanting of prayers to denote self and spirituality. Outside Hinduism, it is used today in occult contexts, where it denotes both goodness and spirituality.

Yoga *Below*

Yoga is an ancient system of Hindu religious philosophy requiring a rigorous preparation of the body for the achievement of spiritual goals. By exercising a variety of physical or meditational techniques, the yogi may cast off his earthly concerns and achieve a liberating, blissful state of higher consciousness (moksha). There are four primary spiritual approaches of yoga: ritual (karma-yoga), devotional (bhakti-yoga), intellectual (jnana-yoga), and meditational (dyana-yoga). Other forms of yoga include kundalini-yoga, which awakens vital energy, and mantra-yoga, in which sounds are repeated.

Sacred Footprints *Above*

In Hinduism, as in Buddhism, footprints represent the divine presence of a deity, usually Vishnu the Preserver (originally a Vedic sun god). The footprints of Vishnu indicate his omnipresence. Hindu and Buddhist beliefs are often intertwined, and Vaishnava Hindus believe that Vishnu's ninth incarnation, or *atavar*, is Buddha. In Buddhism, footprints are frequently decorated with symbols of the Seven Appearances: a **fish**, **swastika**, diamond mace, **conch shell**, flower vase, **Wheel of Law** and crown of **Brahma**. If the devotee follows in Buddha's footsteps, he may attain enlightenment.

Bull *Above*

As in other cultures, the bull in Hinduism symbolizes strength, power and fertility. As a fertility symbol, it is a form of Indra, the Vedic god of the sky. The powerful bull, Nandin, is a vehicle of **Shiva** the Destroyer (associated with the Vedic god Rudra); Agni, "the mighty bull" and god of **fire**; and the all-embracing Aditi, mother of the gods. Its symbolism is linked with that of the sacred **cow** (which also represents fertility) and, when depicted with a cow (symbolic of the **earth**), the bull represents heaven.

Jainism

Jain Temple *Below*

Jainism is a highly ascetic Indian religion, formed as a reaction against certain Hindu practices. It shares many of the principles of Buddhism. Self-discipline, detachment and meditation are the main tenets of Jainist philosophy, which is dominated by a strict policy of *ahimsa*—the avoidance of causing harm to any living creature (itself derived from the Jainist belief in the eternal cycle of reincarnation ending only when the soul attains perfection and is liberated). There are many magnificent Jain shrines and temples in India, whose style echoes those of Buddhism and Hinduism and whose majesty and elaborate decoration (as shown here) contrast sharply with the austere lifestyles of the Jainist monks. Such temples were often erected in tribute to any of the twenty-four *tirthan-kara*—the teacher-founders of Jainism—but, rather than paying homage to any god or individual, they symbolize the principles of Jainism.

Sikhism

Turban *Above*

The turban is a symbol of Sikh identity, worn as a mark of commitment to the faith and representing spiritual authority and courage. According to the Khālsā, Sikhs are required to wear **five** articles of faith, the "five Ks." These are *keś*, or uncut hair, which signifies spiritual strength; *kanghā*, a comb worn in the hair symbolizing discipline because of its grooming function; *kirpān*, a ceremonial **sword** with which to fight injustice; *karā*, a steel bangle worn on the right hand to represent the wearer's union with divinity (and as a reminder to use the right hand for good deeds); and *kachh*, a pair of shorts representing sexual restraint as well as readiness to fight for the Sikh faith (because the stitched, rather than unstitched, garment is more appropriate for fighting). Although the turban, or *keśkī* is not stipulated as one of the five Ks, it has come to symbolize Sikh identity because it is worn to protect the *keś* and *kangā*. The Sikh code of discipline based on the teachings of Guru Gobind Singh (the *Rahit Maryada*) recommends the wearing of a turban. Political and religious affiliation within Sikh communities can be expressed by the color of the turban's cloth: adherents of the Punjabi, Haryana and Himchal Pradesh Akali Dal party wear blue turbans; those in the movement for an independent Sikh state of Khalistan wear orange turbans; while white turbans are worn by Namdharis, followers of the reformist Baba Balak Singh (1799–1861). Some sects, such as that of Bhai Randhir Singh (1878–1971), regard the turban as itself one of the five Ks, integral with the *keś*, and require women as well as men to wear it as a sign of their faith.

Khanda *Below*

The emblem of Sikhism, known as the khanda, is depicted in black on the triangular yellow Nishan Sahib, the flag of respect. The emblem incorporates a khanda, or double-edged **sword** (which represents the Sikh concept of the martial saint), encircled by the chakkar, or steel quoit (a symbol of the unity of god and humanity). On either side are two kirpāns, symbolizing spiritual and temporal power. This symbol is also the emblem of the Khālsā, the Sikh community created to purify the Sikh tradition by Guru Gobind Singh in Anandpur, India, in 1699.

Ancient Egyptian Religion

Eye of Horus *Above*

The Eye of Horus, or the All-Seeing Utchat, had many complex meanings in Ancient Egypt. Horus was the falcon god, Lord of the Skies; his right eye was the "Eye of Re," (the **sun** god), and his left the "Eye of Horus," symbolic of the **moon**. When depicted as an eye and eyebrow it denoted strength and power. This sacred-eye symbol was regarded as powerful protection against evil and retains its resonance today.

Sacred Cat *Below*

In Ancient Egypt cats were sacred to the goddess of love, Bast (or Bastet), who was often portrayed as a woman with the head of a cat. The male cat was regarded as the incarnation of the **sun** god, while the female cat was the personification of

the solar eye, probably because cats enjoy basking in the heat. Also associated with the **moon**—the dilation of its pupils was considered symbolic of the waxing and waning of the moon—it was sacred to the gods **Isis**, Bast and Set.

Ankh *Below*

The ankh is the most recognizable symbol of Ancient Egypt. Its original meaning is unknown; one theory is that it combines the male and female symbols of **Osiris** (the T-cross) and **Isis** (the oval) and signifies the union of heaven and earth. It came to symbolize life and immortality, the universe, power and

life-giving air and **water**. Its keylike shape also encouraged the belief that it could unlock the gates of death. Presented by gods to the pharoah, it is generally portrayed in Egyptian art in the hands of a deity. Coptic Christians adopted it as a symbol of life after death. Extensively used in magic, today the ankh symbolizes peace and truth.

Scarab *Top right*

The scarab (or dung) beetle was one of the most powerful symbols of Ancient Egypt. Erroneously believed to be exclusively male, it laid its eggs in balls of dung, and thus came to symbolize regeneration. It represented the god of the morning **sun**, Khephri (or Khepera), for by rolling its ball of dung, it signified the sun being rolled across the sky, thus also symbolizing resurrection. As well as being worn, scarab amulets were often placed

in tombs, signifying the renewal of life. As here, it was sometimes shown with falcon's wings, symbolizing transcendence and protection.

Ba *Below*

The Ancient Egyptians believed that the ba, symbolized by a human-headed **hawk**, was the human soul: man's spiritual aspect, whose psychic energy survived death. After mortal death, the soul would take flight to the realm of **Osiris** (where its happiness was assured), but would later return to the body—either in the next world, or after reincarnation on earth. The symbol was extensively used in Egyptian tomb decoration.

Sphinx *Overleaf*

Generally depicted in the shape of a **lion** with the head of a pharoah, the Egyptian sphinx symbolizes the unification of natural and spiritual power and hence came to represent benevolent regal power and protection. In addition, it was associated with **Horus** in the Horizon, the son of the sun god Ra (or Re). As well as this type of sphinx (the androsphinx), the pharoah's head was sometimes interchanged with that of a falcon (the hieracosphinx), so embodying solar power, or a **ram** (the criosphinx), signifying silence.

The celebrated limestone Giza sphinx is 66 feet high and 240 feet long, and was created about 2620 BC on the orders of the pharoah Khafre, whose face it bears. The Egyptian sphinx should not be confused with the riddle-asking sphinx of Greek mythology, who was a hybrid creature with a woman's head.

Isis *Below*

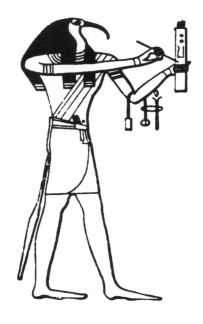

Isis was the principal goddess of Ancient Egypt, the faithful wife and sister of **Osiris**, and devoted mother of **Horus**; she was a protective deity exemplifying both the ideal woman and the divine mother. She is usually portrayed as a queen, wearing a cow-horn headdress (for the **cow** was sacred to her) symbolic of the **moon**, within which is set the solar disk. Possessed of great magical powers, Isis is sometimes portrayed as a kite, the form she assumed to search for Osiris's scattered body parts. She is also sometimes shown with lotuses, signifying rebirth, and a jackal, representing Anubis, god of embalming. Isis was worshipped as a goddess of nature by the Romans.

Osiris *Above, right*

The democratic god Osiris was the epitome of perfection to his worshippers and was the subject of extensive symbolism. Initially a god of life and fertility, he was particularly associated with **corn**, the flooding of the Nile (in which the evil Set had him drowned) and the **moon**. One of his attributes is the djed pillar, which was originally used in fertility rites and came to represent the god's backbone and thus stability because of its ridged structure. It was believed that Osiris was once a human ruler, and that, by living on as lord of the underworld, he represented the renewal of life. He is always personified as a mummy (which sometimes sprouts corn), carrying the insignia of royalty—the white **crown**, scepter and flail, and is sometimes accompanied by **Isis**, as here. A further symbol of Osiris is the tau (or T) cross, signifying life.

Thoth *Below*

The god of wisdom, learning and the **moon**, Thoth was believed by the ancient Egyptians to have given them both their language and **hieroglyphic** script. Thoth was symbolized in a number of ways: with an ibis's head, whose long, curved beak was believed to represent the crescent moon as well as the search for **wisdom**; by the lunar crescent; and with the head of a baboon, whose form he took at Hermopolis (the baboon in turn became associated with scribes, of whom Thoth was patron). Because of his limitless wisdom, and because he helped **Osiris** with the judgment of souls in the underworld, Thoth was believed to have occult powers, and his name is still invoked by those in search of arcane and esoteric knowledge.

Vulture and Cobra *Below*

This depiction of Queen Nefertari shows her elaborate vulture headdress—a protective symbol, for, as a scavenger of corpses, in the land of the dead the vulture represented purification. Isis sometimes took the form of a vulture, and so it came to embody motherhood and the female principle and became the emblem of both the goddess Nekhbet and Upper Egypt. Hathor, goddess of love, was sometimes depicted with a vulture's head, and the bird was the sacred animal of

Mat (or Mut), goddess of maternity. The cobra, or *uraeus*, is an important feature of this headdress; to the Egyptians it personified wisdom, rulership and protection, for it was believed to rise up from the sun and destroy its enemies with its fiery breath. An emblem of Lower Egypt, the cobra was associated with rebirth and solar power and is frequently shown crowned with the solar disk.

Obelisk *Left*

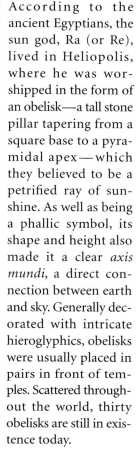

According to the ancient Egyptians, the sun god, Ra (or Re), lived in Heliopolis, where he was worshipped in the form of an obelisk—a tall stone pillar tapering from a square base to a pyramidal apex—which they believed to be a petrified ray of sunshine. As well as being a phallic symbol, its shape and height also made it a clear *axis mundi*, a direct connection between earth and sky. Generally decorated with intricate hieroglyphics, obelisks were usually placed in pairs in front of temples. Scattered throughout the world, thirty obelisks are still in existence today.

Pyramid *Above, right*

Perhaps the most recognized symbol of Ancient Egypt and now the symbol of the modern-day country, on the most basic level the pyramid represents the awesome power of the kings of the Old and Middle Kingdoms. Massive funerary monuments of the pharoahs, the pyramids were built according to strict principles. Sadly, many of the reasons governing their complicated construction are no longer known, but it is believed that they symbolized the mound of creation and were erected in alignment with the sun and stars, thus creating a ramp between earth and the

heavens over which the dead pharoah could cross to the afterlife. Pyramids are not exclusive to Egypt: human sacrifices to the gods were performed at Aztec pyramidal shrines (such as Templo Mayor). The Mayans worshipped their deities from temples on stepped pyramids, as did the Mesopotamians at their ziggurats. All such pyramids are believed to have represented the cosmic mountain. In esoteric thought, the pyramid can be considered not only a representation of the world axis, but also a symbol of enlightenment: its apex is spiritual attainment, which can only be reached from the lowly base by means of a toiling ascent of its steeply sloping planes.

Winged Sun Disk *Below*

To the ancient Egyptians, Ra (or Re) was the creator of the world, ancestor of the pharoahs and god of the sun (symbolized by the solar disk) and skies (symbolized by a pair of wings). The winged sun disk thus signifies the life-giving power of the sun, and the spiritual attributes of the heavens. Closely associated with this representation of Ra was the Aten (or Aton)—the sun disk whose rays culminate in hands—which was subsequently worshipped in Ancient Egypt. The sun disk is sometimes represented surrounded in the coils of the *uraeus*, the protective flame-spewing cobra.

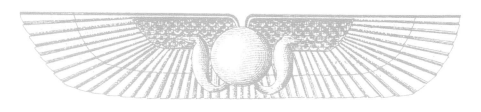

Greek/Roman Mythology

related symbols of the Norse god, Wotan (or Odin), and the Babylonian deity, Adad, god of thunderstorms.

Janus *Below*
This Roman coin shows Janus, the guardian of heaven and, thus, of **gates** and **doors** in general. Janus is always shown with two heads looking in opposite directions (to see those who enter and leave). He has thus come to signify ambiguity and being two-faced. The Romans opened his temple in war, but closed it in times of peace, and so his name can be associated with war. Janus can also signify journeys and new beginnings, and he lives on today in the name of January—a month which contemplates the past year as well as looking forward to the future.

Neptune's Trident *Above, right*
The trident of the Roman god **Neptune** (Poseidon in Ancient Greece) is a three-pronged **spear** whose prongs are sometimes barbed with arrowheads. Neptune was the god of the sea and the trident is

Jupiter's Staff *Above*
This graphic symbol represents the staff of the Roman supreme deity, Jupiter (**Zeus** in Greece). It is composed of a double **trident** (the sign of Neptune/Poseidon), and thus symbolizes not only power over the waters, but also **thunder**, **lightning** and storms, since a triple prong signifies a lightning flash. Furthermore, if this sign is turned on its side, it becomes the zodiacal symbol of **Pisces**, of which Jupiter and Neptune are the ruling planets. It is strikingly similar to the

a clear symbol of his authority and power: in the human world, it was an instrument forcefully used to spear **fish**, and in the mighty hand of Neptune it created life-giving springs of **water**, destructive floods or devastating storms at sea, depending on his will. The trident shares the characteristics of the signs for water (which Neptune rules) and **fire** (like the related symbols of lightning and the thunderbolt, a symbol of divine omnipotence). Its prongs have also been equated with the **sun**'s rays and the teeth of sea monsters. In astronomy, the trident is the symbol of the planet Neptune and can be depicted with a crossbar over the handle. The trident has become a general symbol of sovereignty over the sea and appears as such in Minoan art. It is, in addition, an attribute of Britannia, the female personification of Britain.

Caduceus *Opposite*
The caduceus (or *Kerykeion*—"herald's wand" in Greek) was given to Hermes, the herald of the Greek gods—**Mercury** in Roman myth. This winged staff had the power to transform strife into harmony—in mythology, placing it between two fighting **snakes** caused them to entwine themselves around the staff and face each other in peace. This universal symbol is also depicted in the hands of ancient Egyptian, Phoenician and Indian deities. Along with the rod of Aesculapius, the caduceus has come to symbolize homeopathic medicine and the medical profession in general. Its prime meaning, however, is that of dualism and balance and the union of opposing forces. It is also the astronomical symbol of Mercury.

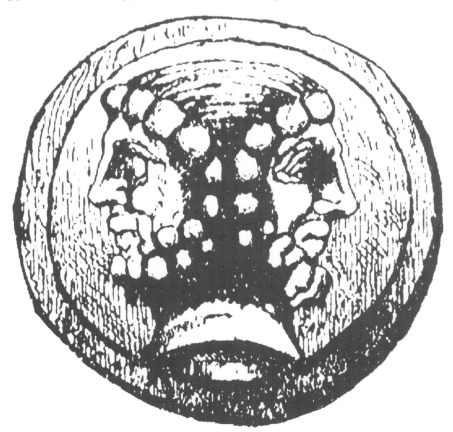

Zeus *Above*

Zeus (**Jupiter**) was the greatest god in the Greco-Roman pantheon. As well as dominating the lesser Olympian gods, he also governed the sky and humanity. He is primarily symbolized by the solar emblems of the thunderbolt or **eagle**, but his authority is further underlined when he is portrayed with a **crown**, scepter or throne. His image, along with images emblematic of Zeus—the chariot, thunderbolt, eagle, **bull**, **oak** leaves and **laurel wreaths**—symbolize supreme power, even omnipotence.

Athena *Above, center right*

The Greek goddess Athena (Pallas Athene), daughter of **Zeus** and Metis (Thought), was the goddess of **wisdom**, the arts, trade and patron goddess of Athens. As the Roman goddess Minerva, she sprang fully formed from Jupiter's temple. She is represented wearing a hel-met, bearing a **spear** and the aegis—the shield of Zeus with the Gorgon's head in its center, signifying protection (it can also be represented as a cloak fringed with **serpents**). Together, spear and shield symbolize the *epheboi* (adulthood) and also chastity. As part of the aegis, the serpent represents knowledge.

Owl of Athena *Below*

Athena (Minerva) was the goddess of **wisdom**, learning and the arts. Owls were prolific in Athens, the city of which Athena was patron, and this, along with its wise appearance and ability to see in the dark (in symbolic terms, thus penetrating ignorance), led it to become an important symbol of wisdom. It was also the attribute of Ceres (Demeter), goddess of the harvest, and with a prophetic quality: its hoot was believed to warn of impending death and its appearance preceded the death of Dido, Queen of Carthage, and several Roman emperors.

Judaism

Tetragrammaton *Below*

The tetragrammaton comprises the four letters, Y, H, W, H, which spell the true name of God in Hebrew. This is so sacred that it is never spoken aloud and is referred to as "the name" (*ha shem,* or the word *Adonai,* "my Lord") because it is forbidden to take God's name in vain. Although the letters signify the name Yahweh, Christians mistranslated them, thinking that they spelled Jehovah. According to tradition, God revealed the tetragrammaton to Moses. It was engraved on both the rod of Aaron and the magic ring of Solomon. In Kabbalism, the symbol was believed to signify life and to possess magical and healing powers. Its correct pronunciation has now been forgotten. Today the tetragrammaton is written on amulets and on the shivviti plaques displayed in the synagogue and in Jewish homes, as a reminder of God's omnipresence.

Tablets of the Decalogue *Overleaf*

The Tablets of the Decalogue, or the Law, are two stones said to be engraved with the Decalogue (the Ten Commandments) by the finger of God. The first contained the text from Exodus and the second that from Deuteronomy. Moses received the tablets on Mount Sinai as a symbol of God's covenant with the Israelites and, because of the divine text, found them light to carry. On his descent from Mount Sinai, he discovered the Israelites worshipping the Golden Calf; this idolatrous behavior caused the text to disappear, and Moses dropped and smashed the now heavy stones. Returning to the summit of Mount Sinai, he engraved replacement tablets himself. The text could be read from both sides, and the divine words hovered miraculously above the stone tablets. The new versions (symbolizing the Old Covenant) and the fragments of the old tablets were placed in the Ark of the Covenant, as a reminder that scholars should remain figures of respect.

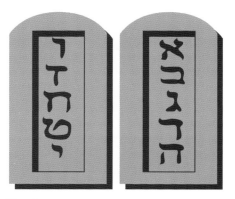

Torah *Below*

The sefer torah, or torah scroll, contains the word of God as given to man through Moses and is one of the most sacred symbols of Judaism. Its message, contained in the Pentateuch and handwritten in Hebrew, is given in the form of mystical symbolic stories, whose inner meaning will only be revealed at the coming of the messiah. The scroll is kept in the synagogue's holy Ark, where it is covered with a mantle, a silver breastplate and a **crown** surmounted with bells.

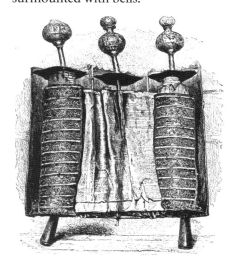

Menorah *Below*

The golden, **seven**-branched candelabrum—the Menorah—is among the most ancient of Jewish symbols. It dates back to the days of the Jewish Exodus, when it burned in the tabernacle of the Sinai Desert. According to tradition, it created itself from gold that Moses cast into **fire**. Miraculously, fueled by olive oil, one flame always burned, while the remainder were extinguished. It was subsequently placed in the Second Temple in Jerusalem until Titus destroyed the city in AD 70. Symbolizing divine wisdom, the seven branches of the candlestick are believed to have derived from the Babylonian tree of lights and represent the seven days of Creation as well as the **sun**, **moon** and **planets**; the seven heavens; and the seven stars of Ursa Major. In 1949, the Menorah became an official emblem of the State of Israel, and is featured on the president's flag.

Star of David *Above, right*

The Star of David, or Magen David (Shield of David) is one of the most recognized signs of Judaism and is today a symbol of the State of Israel, appearing on its national flag since 1948. It derives its association with David from the tradition that he carried a hexagrammic shield against Goliath. The symbol is made up of two interlocked triangles which form a **six**-pointed star, or hexagram. The white of the upper triangle and the black of the lower symbolizes the union of opposites. Also known as the Seal of Solomon, the Kabbalists believed that the emblem had protective power and magical properties. In magic and

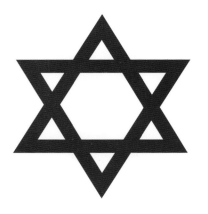

alchemy, it symbolizes the unity of the elements—the upward triangle signifying **fire**, the downward **water**—and also masculinity, femininity and the soul. When the six points are combined with a mystical seventh, the seventh, invisible point signifies transformation. The Star of David can also be called the Creator's Star, with each point representing the days of the week and the central hexagram symbolizing the Sabbath.

Harp of David *Below*

The harp is a symbol of David, vanquisher of Goliath and king of Israel. David's musical prowess found favor with King Saul as a salve for his depression. It is said that when David became king, at midnight the wind played upon a harp which hung above his bed, thus summoning him to study the **torah**. In symbolic terms, the harp is interchangeable with the lyre and signifies harmony with the **universe** and the ascent to higher things. This depiction of a lyre-type harp is adorned with the six-pointed Magen David (**Star of David**, Shield of David or Seal of Solomon), a symbol of the Jewish faith and of the state of Israel.

Shofar *Below*

In Jewish tradition, the blowing of the shofar, the Hebrew ritual horn (usually made of a hollow ram's horn, a reminder that a **ram** was sacrificed instead of Isaac), can signify the approach of an enemy. Today it is usually heard as part of the Jewish New Year, or Rosh Hashanah, when it is a summons to penitence. There are three main sounds blown on the shofar, but one hundred are sounded during Rosh Hashanah, divided into two parts to confuse Satan. The shofar can also be blown in the morning during Elul (the month preceding Rosh Hashanah) or to signal the end of the Yom Kippur fast. It is also used in exorcism and excommunication rituals. It is believed that on the Day of Judgment, Elijah will blow a shofar to summon both the living and the dead.

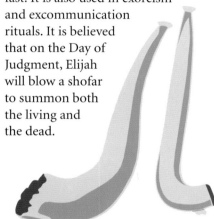

Palm Tree *Right*

The palm tree is important in the iconography of Judaism, where, according to the Kabbalah, it symbolizes the righteous man (*tzaddik*) and was an emblem of Judea after the Exodus. Along with the myrtle, citrus fruit and willow, the palm branch, the *lulav*, is one of the four agricultural species paraded on the Sukkot to celebrate God's bounty. Each represents a type of Jew, and the palm signifies one who studies the **torah**, but does not obey the commandments. In addition, the palm branch symbolizes the spine which bends before God and is a symbol of God himself. In Christianity, the palm signifies righteousness, resurrection, Christ's entry into Jerusalem and pilgrimage to the Holy Land. In Babylonia, Egypt, Ancient Greece and Rome, it signified victory.

The Sacrifice of Isaac *Above*

Sacrifice, a common feature of many religions, was crucial to the ritual of the early Judaic faith. In general terms, the act of sacrifice expresses a desire for union with a deity by means of placation and submission. The death of the victim (be it animal or human) is intended to invoke the next stage of the cycle of creation—life. Sacrifice was an important ritual of biblical Judaism: priests offered up ritually clean animals at least once a day. The near-sacrifice of Abraham's cherished only son, Isaac (illustrated here by Caravaggio), is known as the akedah (a Hebrew word meaning "binding") and is a poignant symbol of the testing of faith. God required Isaac's sacrifice on Mount Moriah as a proof of Abraham's obedience; at the last moment, however, Abraham's hand was stayed by the archangel Michael as a sign of God's compassion, and a **ram** was substituted in Isaac's place. Sacrificial practices were abandoned after the destruction of the Third Temple in 70 BCE. During the persecutions endured by Jews in medieval times, Isaac was adopted as a symbol of martyrdom. Today, the akedah is read at Rosh Hashanah (the Jewish New Year festival), when a ram's horn (**shofar**) is also blown in commemoration of God's **mercy**. At pesach (Passover), the deliverance of the first-born children of the Israelites (whose doorposts were smeared with the blood of the Paschal **lamb** to identify them to God) is celebrated.

Note: Judaism and Christianity share much of their symbolism. Some Judeo-Christian symbols—the Eye of God, dove and olive branch, altar and bishop's miter—appear in the following pages.

Christianity

Eye of God *Above*
This symbol is a combination of Judeo-Christian symbols. The eye is that of God, the all-seeing father, from which radiates divine light (often shown within a **triangle**, it represents God at the center of the **Trinity**). The three links of the chain also represent the Trinity and symbolize the golden link that binds the faithful to God. The tent represents the house of God—the Tabernacle, the temple of the nomadic Jews—whose flaps are opened to reveal the inner truth to believers.

Halo *Above*
This detail of an Italian painting of the Annunciation depicts the Archangel Gabriel announcing to the **Virgin Mary** the news of her impending motherhood. A **dove**, symbolizing the Holy Spirit, hovers above him and he holds a **lily**, representing purity. The halo (aureole, or nimbus) above his head signifies divine radiance but can additionally symbolize sainthood, sovereignty, wisdom and vital

energy. The halo is usually portrayed as a golden disk above, or rayed corona around, the head, but God is sometimes represented with a triangular or diamond-shaped halo, Christ with a cruciform halo and living people, such as the pope, with a square-shaped or hexagonal halo. The halo was originally an ancient **sun** symbol (signifying solar power in religions such as the Mithraic) and can also be equated both with a crown of glory and a personal aura. It is not unique to Christianity but adopted from earlier cults. Originally signifying majesty and power, the Greco-Roman god **Zeus** (Jupiter) has a blue nimbus and **Buddha** a red halo. The Hindu God **Shiva**'s fire-fringed halo signifies the cosmos. Roman emperors were portrayed with haloes and in Christian Byzantium, even Satan was depicted with a halo of power.

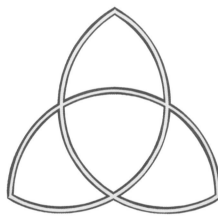

Triqueta *Above*
Geometrical shapes, such as **three** interlocked **circles**, **triangles** or an equilateral triangle, are often used in Christian iconography to express the Trinity—the three-in-one—of God the Father, the Son and the Holy Spirit. Consisting of three connected arcs, the triqueta signifies eternity, while its central, triangle-like shape represents the Trinity. Along with the trefoil and Y-shaped fork, the triqueta denotes the intangibility of the Trinity. It appears on **Celtic crosses** and was a popular motif in Gothic art. The Trinity is also symbolized by a trio of **fish** or **hares**, the pentalpha and the Arms of the Trinity, or *scutum fidei*.

Angel *Below*
Angels are divine messengers and existed as such in the beliefs of the ancient Sumerians, Babylonians, Egyptians, Greeks and Romans. They are also present in Hinduism and Islam. In Christian tradition, angels are spiritual beings created by God who act as intermediaries between God and man (or heaven and Earth). There are nine orders of angels—seraphim, cherubim, thrones, dominions, virtues, powers, principalities, archangels and angels—arranged in a triple hierarchy. Archangels represent aspects of God and protect against demons. The attributes of other angels such as Michael (a **sword**), Raphael (a pilgrim's staff), Uriel (a **book**) and Gabriel (a **lily**) symbolize divine judgment, protection, wisdom and mercy. Mortals may also have guardian angels to protect them and guide them through life. Angels are generally depicted with a halo and wings; as men, women or *putti* (cupids*)*; and may carry scrolls or musical instruments.

The Holy Family *Above*
This Italian depiction of the Holy Family includes a sleeping Christ child, the shadowy figure of Joseph and a winged angel. The Madonna's special significance is symbolized by her halo, veil of chastity and protective cloak (see **Halo, Virgin Mary, Nativity** and **Angel**).

Dove and Olive Branch *Below*
In the Judaic and Christian cultures, the dove holding an olive branch symbolizes peace. After the biblical flood, Noah sent out a **raven** and a dove from the ark to search for dry land. Only the dove returned, grasping in its beak an olive branch from the Mount of Olives, thus signifying God's forgiveness of man and the deliverance of humanity. In Christian iconography, the dove also symbolizes the Holy Spirit, with seven doves signifying the seven gifts of the Holy Spirit. The dove and olive branch has now become a general, nonreligious symbol.

The Nativity *Above, right*
Botticelli's painting *The Mystic Nativity* (c. 1500) is replete with symbolism. The **Virgin Mary**, wearing her blue cloak of purity, bends over the Christ child in adoration while an **ox** (which, according to Isaiah, knows his owner and warms Christ with his breath) and **ass** (which knows his master's crib) look on. To Christ's left can be seen Joseph and the **Magi**. Heavenly and fallen **angels** clasp each other in reconciliation, while a trio of angels reads from the Holy Book on the roof of the manger. Above is a circle, or choir, of dancing angels who dangle three **crowns**, signifying both the **Holy Trinity** and the cycle of birth, life and death. **Olive** branches abound, representing God's covenant with man, peace and the **Tree of Life**.

Mandorla *Below*
Related to the **halo** is the almond-shaped mandorla, or aureole, which, in Christian iconography, surrounds a holy figure or theophany. Also known as the *vesica piscis*, it is associated with the **fish** shape that once represented Christianity but also symbolizes the **cloud** upon which Christ ascended to heaven.

The Virgin Mary *Above*

The Virgin Mary appears frequently in Christian depictions of key events such as the Annunciation, the **Nativity**, the **Crucifixion** and the Assumption and is usually accompanied by a number of symbols of her purity—including a **lily** and a **veil** of chastity. A **halo** and the presence of **angels** signify her holiness as the mother of Jesus. She is often associated with the crescent **moon**, cypress and **olive** trees, the **Tree of Life** (with Jesus the fruit) and the white **rose** (for she is the rose of paradise). She wears a blue cloak, signifying faith, compassion and the baptismal waters. She can also be portrayed as the queen of heaven, with a **crown** of stars and other royal attributes; as the Lady of Mercy (*Misericord*), sheltering the faithful under her blue cloak (signifying protection); or as the Lady of Sorrows (*Dolorosa*), with her breast pierced by seven **swords**. Duccio's *Madonna and Child* (seen here) combines much of the iconography of Byzantine art with medieval innovations: while the Madonna is a static icon, the Christ child and surrounding angels are given more a lively representation.

The Crucifixion *Right*

Guidi's harrowing portrayal of the Crucifixion shows the Virgin Mary prostrate with grief at the foot of the cross, flanked by praying figures. See **Crucifix, Crown of Thorns,** and **Virgin Mary.**

The Magi *Right*

In Christian tradition, the Magi (Latin for wise men) are also known as the Three Wise Men or Three Kings. According to the Gospel of St. Matthew, God told the Magi by means of a **star** that a great king would be born in Judea, so they traveled from the East to attend his birth. Guided by the star, they continued to Bethlehem, where they found Jesus and adored him, presenting him with costly gifts of gold (signifying royalty), frankincense (divinity) and myrrh (suffering and death). In early tradition, it was believed that the Magi represented both the three ages of man and the three continents of Europe,

Africa and Asia. In addition, they were said to represent Christ's divinity, majesty and sacrifice. It was not until the eleventh century that they were named as Caspar (or Gaspar), Melchior and Balthasar, respectively king of light, "the white one" and king of treasures.

Crucifix *Below*

The crucifix, or Latin cross with an image of Christ nailed to it, is the most profound and enduring symbol in Christianity, depicting in graphic detail the supreme sacrifice that Jesus made for man's salvation. Christ is portrayed in his death agony, bearing a **crown of thorns** and five wounds. Fixed above is often a scroll displaying the letters I.N.R.I. (the abbreviation in Latin for "Jesus of Nazareth, King of the Jews"). Paleochristian iconography avoided the depiction of the Crucifixion, and the image was first used after the Council of Constantinople in AD 692. The type of crucifix shown here dates from the eleventh century.

Crown of Thorns *Below*

Often used in images of the crucified Christ, the crown of thorns is one of the instruments of Christ's passion and can sometimes be depicted as a holly wreath (whose red berries signify Christ's blood). Thorns are a universal symbol of adversity and, in Christianity, the crown of thorns symbolizes both the derision when Christ was "crowned" King of the Jews (in parody of the Roman emperor) and his suffering on the cross. The thorn can also signify sin. A **skull** surmounted with a crown of thorns is a Christian symbol of eternal damnation.

Shepherd's Cross *Above*

One of the many variants of the Christian cross is the shepherd's cross, whose vertical apex is shaped like a shepherd's crook. This symbol indicates both the Christian faith and Jesus' role as the Good Shepherd, who guides man safely through life and saves lost souls. Jesus is frequently depicted with a **lamb** draped over his shoulders. As well as being a sign of the apostles, the shepherd's crook (or crozier) is part of the regalia of bishops, signifying their pastoral authority over their flock. In ancient Egypt, **Osiris** was often portrayed carrying a crook.

Celtic Cross *Above*

The Celtic (also Iona, or Ring) cross was prevalent in Ireland even before the eighth century. It is typically depicted as a cross (signifying Christian faith) with arms enclosed by a **circle** (solar power and eternity), together symbolizing the unity of heaven and earth. Although it is now primarily identified with Christianity, the Celtic cross dates from pagan times, when it was a symbol of fertility and life—the cross signifying male potency and the circle female power.

Cross Fitchy *Below*

In heraldry, a cross which terminates in a point is termed a cross fitchy. This cross is frequently used in heraldry and signifies the unshakeable Christian faith of the bearer. The combination of cross and **sword** is a clear symbol of the determination to fight the infidel, if necessary, to defend the values and tenets of Christianity.

Heraldic Lion *Below*

The lion (shown here rampant) is one of the most popular images in heraldry. It signifies bravery, strength and ferocity. Christian art represented the king of the beasts as a benevolent creature; indeed, the Bible described Christ as the Lion of Judah and the winged lion became the symbol of St. Mark. In heraldry, it symbolizes valor, royalty and protection and is part of the English royal coat of arms. The rampant lion shown here bears aloft a **crucifix**, denoting its role as the mighty protector of Christianity.

Lamb of God *Above*

The lamb symbolizes innocence, gentleness and purity. In ancient times, it was commonly used for **sacrifice** and in Christian symbolism it denotes the sacrificial **crucifixion** of Christ for the sins of the world. Depending on the manner of its depiction, the Agnus Dei can have many meanings. Here the Lamb of God is shown with a **halo**, holding a **cross** and pennant, thus signifying both the crucifixion and the resurrection.

Labarum *Above*

The labarum has a number of alternative names, including Constantine's Cross, the Monogram of Christ, the Chrismon, the Christogram and the Chi-Rho. The use of this symbol in Christian iconography dates from AD 312, when on the eve of the battle of Milvean Bridge, it is said that the Roman emperor Constantine I had a vision of a **cross** and the words *in hoc signo vinces* ("with this sign comes victory"). He obeyed the command to have the cross and motto placed on his army's shields and the enemy Maxentius was duly vanquished. This experience prompted

Constantine's conversion to Christianity. The labarum was one of the earliest symbols of Christianity and is a monogram composed of the Greek letters X (chi) and P (rho)—the first characters of the Greek spelling of the name Christ. However, it was also a potent pre-Christian symbol, signifying both a good omen (*chrestos*, in Greek) and the Chaldean sky god. As well as signifying the Christian faith, the symbol became Constantine's emblem and the imperial standard of the Roman empire from AD 324.

Fish *Below*

The fish is one of the earliest symbols used in association with Christ and has multiple significances. Christ called his apostles (Andrew, Peter, James and John) the "fishers of men" and fed the five thousand with just two fishes. The initial letters of the Greek words for Jesus Christ, Son of God, Savior (*Iesous Christos, Theou Huios, Soter*) are used as an acrostic to spell out the Greek word for fish, *ichthus*. As well as signifying unity with Christ, the fish symbolizes baptism by **water**, life and spiritual nourishment. The early Christian fathers called the faithful *pisculi* (fish). The fish was employed as an ideogram from the first century AD, when Christians suffered persecution; it can be found on graves in the Roman catacombs—an ancient, secret meeting place. It remains a widely used symbol among Christians today.

Candle *Right, top*

The burning candle has significance in many religions and cultures as a symbol of light, life and spirituality, but it has particular importance in Christianity, in which it symbolizes both the divine light

of Christ and faith itself. It is much used in the rituals of the Catholic liturgy. In funeral rites, candles represent the light of heaven. They are frequently lit by worshippers and placed before shrines, where they can signify either the souls of the departed or a request for illumination by prayer. When flanking the **cross** on the altar, the two candles represent the dual nature of Christ—both human and divine.

Altar *Above*

The altar is not exclusive to Christianity, but is significant in many religions, including Judaism and Hinduism, and in pagan cultures in which it was used for sacrifice. In Christianity the altar symbolizes **sacrifice**, death and resurrection: its tomblike shape is a reminder of mortality, while its position at the eastern end of a church, facing the **sun**, signifies rebirth. The wood and stone used to construct the altar symbolize the **cross** and the rock of Calvary, while the linen covering represents Christ's burial shroud. By raising the altar, ascension is signified, and the three steps leading to it symbolize the **Trinity**. As the place of the **Eucharist**—the host and consecrated wine—the altar can also recall the Last Supper.

Eucharist *Below*

In Christian ritual, the sacrament of the Eucharist is the most important act of worship. Consecrated bread (the host) and communion wine are associated with the body and blood of Christ. Many believe that when the Eucharist is distributed among the congregation, consubstantiation occurs and the faithful become filled with the essence of Jesus. The Eucharist is clearly symbolic of Christ's bodily sacrifice, and the vessels in which the bread and wine are contained are treated with reverence and placed at the center of the altar. The chalice containing the communion wine can be associated with the Holy Grail, from which Christ urged the disciples to drink at the Last Supper and in which Joseph of Arimathea caught the spilled blood of Christ.

The Funeral *Below*

In Christianity, as in many religions, death may be the end of mortal life, but the soul of the deceased faithful will live on in heaven. At a Christian funeral, therefore, the body is laid in a casket or coffin, indicating a return to the womb and subsequent rebirth. The **crucifix** and cross banner draped over the casket symbolize salvation through belief, while the flames of the attendant **candles** signify truth and eternal life.

Bishop's Miter *Above*

Along with the episcopal **ring** and crozier, the consecrated position of a bishop is signified by the miter, which symbolizes authority. The miter is a direct link with Christianity's early origins in the Middle East because it is believed to date from the **fish**-head headdress worn by the Babylonian priests of Ea-Oannes and also from the regalia of the Jewish high priest. This example is elaborately decorated and includes a stylized trefoil, symbolic of the **Trinity**.

Rosary *Above*

Also an attribute of Buddhism, Hinduism and Islam, the rosary in Christianity is mainly used by Roman Catholics and less commonly by Protestants. Initially the rosary, or rosarium, meant the repetition of devotional prayers, but it came to represent the string of beads used as a memory aid. The rosary symbolizes the **Virgin Mary**—the Mystical **Rose**—and consists of 50 or 150 small beads, divided by a large bead into five or fifteen "decades," each of which signifies the various glorious, sorrowful and joyful events of the Virgin's life. An *Ave Maria* (Hail Mary prayer) should be said for each small bead, while the larger beads represent a *Gloria* and the *Pater Noster* (Our Father prayer). Attached as a trailer are usually two large and three small beads and a **crucifix**.

Stained-glass Window *Above*

Because windows let in light, the windows of churches symbolize the penetration of the divine light that illuminates the faithful. The jewel-like colors of stained-glass windows are both a way of paying tribute to God and a reflection of the vivid imagery and color of biblical tales. The stained-glass window pictured here is the work of the nineteenth-century medieval revivalist William Morris and, in accordance with his beliefs, faithfully echoes the principles of the ecclesiastical windows of the Middle Ages. Its overall shape is that of the Gothic arch, a form that is reminiscent of the triangle, thus associating it with the Holy **Trinity**; the apex, with its looped cross, is reserved as a homage to God; while the two smaller windows represent **swords** of truth. The holy figures portrayed in the window also follow tradition by providing a narrative of the Christian story, and the whole window is replete with rich Christian imagery.

Islam

Star and Crescent *Below*

The star and crescent is the premier symbol of Islam and signifies concentration, openness and victory, as well as sovereignty and divinity. According to tradition, in 339 BC a brilliant waxing **moon** saved Byzantium (now Istanbul) from attack by Philip of Macedon. To mark their gratitude, the citizens adopted the crescent of **Diana** as the city's emblem. When the city became the Christian Constantinople in 330 BC, its crescent assumed the significance of an attribute of the Virgin Mary. In 1299, before conquering what is now Turkey, Sultan Osman had a vision of a crescent moon stretching over the world; it thus became a symbol of the Ottoman dynasty, and, when Constantinople fell to Mohammed II in 1453, the crescent came to represent both Islam and the Turkish empire. The star was added under Sultan Selim III in 1793 (its **five** points being established in 1844). The star and crescent is now a universal Islamic symbol and is displayed on the national flags of Turkey, Algeria, Malaysia, Mauritania, Pakistan, Tunisia, North Cyprus and the League of Arab States. It is also the emblem of the Islamic counterpart of the Red Cross, the Red Crescent Society.

Calligraphy *Above, center right*

Figurative representations are not encouraged in Islam, as they are considered tantamount to idolatry. This accounts for the abundance of decorative patterns and Arabic calligraphy employed in the beautification of mosques. Along with architecture, calligraphy is regarded as an acceptable aesthetic form of the adulation of Allah and is highly valued. Many styles of calligraphy have evolved over the centuries—including *kufic, naskhi,* and *rukah*—and, in its most revered form, it is used in the transcription of passages from the Koran into books and onto plaques hung in mosques and in the homes of the faithful.

Mosque *Above, right*

The mosque (or *masjid*—"place of prostration") is the sacred building in which Muslims worship Allah. Originally just a rug-hung canopy, the mosque has evolved into a more permanent edifice, whose characteristic architectural features include an enclosing courtyard (in which fountains for the ablutions required by Islam are situated), domes and minarets—the towers from which the muezzin call the faithful to prayer. Mosques are oriented toward Mecca (whose direction is indicated by a mihrab, or niche, in the wall). Since Islam forbids the representation of living beings in art, mosques are decorated with graceful calligraphic texts from the Koran and the geometric or vegetal patterns of tiles, carpets or inlays. Worshippers gather before the imam and prostrate themselves in prayer five times a day. The Friday noon prayers are obligatory. Mosques are also used as places of education and congregation. The mosque symbolizes the transcendence of Allah: while its base represents the **earth**, its domes and minarets represent his celestial power.

Mausoleum *Below*

The mausoleum of Hunuman in Delhi, India is a beautiful example of Indo-Islamic architecture, featuring a simple, flat façade, a relatively low dome and a tall minaret at each end, an elegant Mughal fusion of traditional geometric Persian and Indian architecture. The mausoleum's architectural style is derived from that of the Persian **mosque**, and it shares its courtyard and vaulted windows. The **square** foundation of the tomb housing the body of Hunuman represents the **earth**, while the central dome is a symbol of the heavens to which his soul has ascended. As well as housing the body of the deceased, mausoleums such as this and the **Taj Mahal** are intended to recreate an earthly version of the celestial paradise to which the occupant has ascended. The tomb is therefore an impressive tribute to the importance of Hunuman in life, and a symbol of his stature.

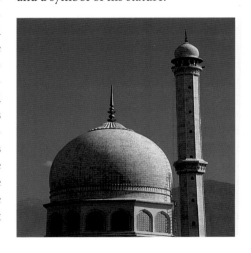

Native American Religions

Buffalo Skull *Below*

To many Native American cultures, particularly those of the Plains and Southwest, the buffalo, or bison, epitomizes supernatural power as well as strength and bravery. Native American faith is closely associated with the natural world: many of the creatures that inhabit America are attributed special powers. Before their virtual extinction, buffalo herds roamed the plains, providing good hunting; they therefore played an important role in both the material and spiritual life of the Native Americans. The Cheyenne practised the Buffalo Head Dance, while a buffalo skull placed on a dwelling acts as a powerful protective symbol, or guardian spirit, against the forces of evil.

Thunderbird *Above, center right*

Thunderbirds (or skyamsen) are the most potent deities in northwestern Native American belief. They are supreme beings that create, control and destroy nature. Usually depicted as huge **eagles** with human faces, they live in the sky, feed on killer **whales** and wage eternal battle against the underwater panthers and giant horned **snakes**. In some traditions there are four Thunderbirds, representing each quarter of the cosmos; the chief Thunderbird is Golden Eagle (*Keneun*). Although generally benevolent to man as bringers of **rain** and thus creation, they also possess terrible powers of death and destruction, manifested in natural disasters. They must therefore

be appeased, and many ritual ceremonies and dances (such as the Plains Sun Dance and the Iroquois and Shawnee War Dance) are dedicated to them.

Feathered Headdress *Below*

Native American cultures consider feathers symbolic of both the **sun** and the Great Spirit. Birds are regarded by some Native American tribes as being messengers between man and **Thunderbird**, and are therefore especially respected. Their feathers (particularly those of prairie **eagles**) thus assume great importance in Native American ritual and are worn by chiefs in magnificent ceremonial headdresses reminiscent of the rays of the sun. The headdresses also recall the absolute power of the Thunderbird and demonstrate the spiritual authority of the wearer.

Calumet *Below*

In Native American tradition the calumet is the peace pipe smoked in rituals of worship, pacification and conciliation. It is believed that smoking is a means of prayer and communion. Calumets are usually intricately carved with natural symbols and decorated with feathers. The elements and spirits can be addressed while the calumet is smoked, while, in the tangible world, peace treaties can be forged and cemented. It is possible that the pipe of peace derived from the shaman's suckling pipe (used to remove toxins from the body and to create a state of ecstasy by inhalation), but many tribes believe that their calumet derives from a sacred archetype and represents a being whose strength is transferred to the smoker. Thus in South Dakota there is a

"calf" pipe, and the Arapaho cherish a flat pipe representing the supreme being. The White Buffalo Woman's pipe of the Oglala Sioux symbolizes a microcosm of the **universe**, its clay bowl representing the globe and substance of the **earth**, its wooden stem plant life, its carved decorations animals and birds and the grains of tobacco all living things. In terms of the **human body**, the bowl can represent the heart, the stem the spine and the pipe's channel the life force—the smoke is the spirit. Moreover, while the pipe itself acts as a medium for man's spiritual communion with the Great Spirit, the rising smoke produced by the calumet is believed to connect man with the supreme being and powers of nature.

Dreamcatcher *Below*

The Native American dreamcatcher is believed to have the power to protect vulnerable sleepers from any evil spirits that may wish to cause them harm. Its circular exterior provides the framework for an intricate fibrous web (very similar in design to that of the **spider**), whose construction is believed to be able to snare any spirits that wander into its mesh, trapping them so inextricably that they are unable to escape in order to pursue their malicious intentions. As important symbols of protection against destructive supernatural manifestations, dreamcatchers can either be worn as amulets or hung by beds. Yet the dreamcatcher also has a different purpose in those tribes that place great importance on the lessons contained in dreams. Some Native American communities believe that personal dream guides help humans find their way in life by controlling their dreams. Dreamcatching is an initiation ritual in certain tribes, in which the initiate mediates in the center of a magic **circle** and tries to "catch" the messages that the spirits are sending him through the **air**; the dreamcatcher itself embodies this concept.

Kachina Doll *Above*

Kachinas are the ancestral spirits or representatives of the gods of the Pueblo (Hopi and Zuni) peoples of the American Southwest, and their carved, masked kachina dolls are personifications of these spirits. It is believed that the kachinas once lived among man, but now only return from the otherworld for part of the year (when they are represented by **mask**-wearing tribal members), in order to intercede between humans and gods. These periods are celebrated with sacred annual rituals and celebrations. At the end of their period on earth, kachinas, in their guise as human dancers, present their doll images to the children of the tribe as a reminder of their existence until their return the following year or to women as fertility talismans. Kachina dolls are usually carved from cottonwood roots or pine and each doll is carefully fashioned according to the distinctive characteristics and garb of its particular kachina (of which there are many). As symbolic representations of the kachinas, kachina dolls are important totemic images.

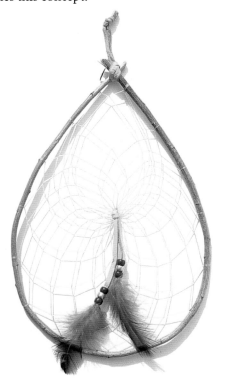

Navajo Sand Painting *Below*

According to the Navajo tribe of America's Southwest, the **universe** is divided according to pairs of opposites. Chaos inevitably ensues from this duality, and several Navajo ceremonies and rituals are designed to restore cosmic harmony. Rituals, or "sings," are directed by a chanter, in whom the tribe's collective history and spirit is invested, who recites the oral traditions of the tribe. It is he who is responsible for the correct procedure in the creation of sand paintings, or dry paintings—symbolic pictures that are unique to the tribe. These are "painted" by allowing a delicate stream of powdered sandstone of various colors to flow from hand to ground. The paintings depict scenes from the tribe's creation myths, in which likenesses of the Yeis—holy people—that govern various aspects of the world are portrayed. The Yeis, who drew the first sand paintings in the sky, are believed to be attracted to their sand images and to enter the paintings, bringing their supernatural powers, which, although they are invoked to benefit the tribe and restore reorganization to the universe, can also be dangerous if misdirected. Sand paintings are therefore sacramental and symbolic of both ancestors and supernatural powers. They are also believed to have healing powers. A sick tribal member sits on the sand painting during the healing ritual, and the source of the illness is transferred to the painting; after the completion of the ritual the sand, along with the disease, is destroyed.

Paganism

Thor's Hammer *Right*

In Norse mythology, Thor (whose name means "**thunder**") was the god of thunder, winds, storms and fertility and was the most powerful of all the deities. The god of law and order, Thor dispensed punishment by hurling his double-headed hammer, Mjöllnir, with fatal and unerring aim. Mjöllnir symbolized the lightning or thunderbolt and, like a boomerang, always returned to him. As well as causing death, it could also revive the dead. The **swastika** is sometimes known as Thor's Hammer, as is the T (or tau) **cross**; these, as well as ornamental hammers, were revered as sacred symbols and were widely used as protective amulets and decorations with which to ward off fire and evil and invite fertility.

Funeral Ship *Above*

In many pagan traditions of northwestern Europe, a ritual funeral boat was used to launch the dead on their journey to the other world (as told in the Anglo-Saxon poem *Beowulf*). In Scandinavia the ship was a funereal symbol as early as the Bronze Age, but ship funerals do not appear to have been practised until the seventh century. A ship funeral involved laying the body of the deceased in a boat, surrounding the corpse with treasured possessions and animal sacrifices and covering the boat with a burial mound. Sometimes the ship and its contents were cremated, as in the case of Viking chieftains; the **fire** represented cleansing, and the smoke symbolized the ascension of the spirit to the life-giving **sun**. The use of ships as graves probably results from the association between ships and the Vanir, Scandinavian fertility gods who were equated with dead ancestors. Beautifully crafted model ships of precious metals were regarded as prized oblations in Scandinavia. This illustration by Arthur Rackham depicts King Arthur and Queen Guinevere sending off the funeral ship of Elaine of Astolat.

Foliage *Above*

To the pagan peoples, particularly the Celts, everything in the natural world possessed its own magical meaning. **Trees** held a special significance, signifying life and the mystical connection of the Earth with both the heavens and the under, or other, world. The **oak**, beech, hazel, ash, rowan and yew each had individual symbolism. Artistic representations frequently include **spiral** shapes and knots, often in the intertwining of vegetation, as here, signifying an association with the sky and the **sun**.

Stonehenge *Below*

Stonehenge, located near Salisbury, England, is the best-known Stone Age megalith of menhirs (standing stones) arranged in the shape of a **circle**. Its exact meaning remains uncertain, but it is believed that it was erected in alignment with the **stars**, the solstices and the paths of the **moon** and was a place of pagan worship. As seen here, modern-day Druids have reclaimed it as a sacred place and assemble there in celebration of such significant dates as the **summer** solstice.

Aboriginal Beliefs

Kangaroo *Above*

Along with the **emu**, the kangaroo is a symbol of Australia. Unique to that country, it appears as a supporter of Australia's coat of arms. However, the kangaroo has a far deeper significance to many Aboriginal cultures, dating back to ancient times. It was believed that supernatural ancestors (*wondjina* in western Australia) created the land at the time of the Dreaming (*altjiranga*), and filled it with creatures and plants. In central Australia, each person is the incarnation of a totemic ancestor, from whom he receives his totem—if a kangaroo, he must ensure the constant supply of kangaroo meat. Hence the kangaroo, as well as being an important source of food, has magical associations. Many rock paintings in Australia were once believed to have been created by such supernatural ancestors.

Ayers Rock *Above*

The distinctive form and color of the monolithic Ayers Rock (named after a premier of Southern Australia) in the Northern Territory of central Australia is a sacred place for Australian Aborigines. With a circumference of nine kilometers and a height of 1100 feet, its red sandstone surface changes color spectacularly according to the position of the **sun**. The Aborigines call the rock *Uluru* ("great pebble"), and believe that it is home to mythical creatures such as **snake** people, sleepy **lizard**-women, dingos, hare-wallabies, marsupial moles and willy-wagtails. Their stories are illustrated by means of the rock paintings that cover the face and sacred caves of Ayers Rock; created in the distinctive desert-art style, the animal-like figures are accompanied by mystical, abstract geometric patterns, whose symbols underline the enduring significance of the ancient legends.

Cave Paintings *Below*

The cave paintings in Kakhadu National Park, Australia, symbolize the totemic ancestors of the Aboriginal people. Pictured here are female spirits giving

birth to the first human beings at the time of the Dreaming (*altjiranga*), when all living things were created and when the landscape and order of existence was imposed upon the world. Rock art of this type is prevalent in northern Australia, particularly in the Northern Territory; Arnhem Land, for example, was believed to have been populated by the Djanggau sisters. Sacred emblems (such as solar signs) are also embodiied in the ancient rock art of Native American tribes.

Totem Pole *Below*
This New Zealand Maori totem pole depicts the animal spirits sacred to the tribe, in ascending hierarchical sequence, to invoke their protective powers. Animal skins, as worn by this shaman, are worn for the same purpose. In common with other totemic systems, particularly the totem poles of northwestern Native American tribes and Oceania, Aboriginal totem poles can also represent the social history and legend of a tribe or family group and are placed in front of dwelling places to denote ancestral identity.

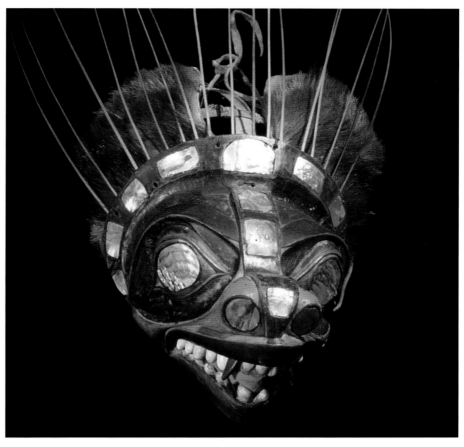

Shamanism

Mask *Above*
The shaman's mask is intended to frighten off evil spirits, but it can also magically confer the characteristics of the animal or spirit whose features the mask bears. The shaman's robes are also often fashioned of animal skins and decorated in a similar fashion to the mask. During an ecstatic trance, the shaman "becomes" the bird or animal spirit (which his mask and clothing invoke) and may even speak in their voices. He can thus draw on their benevolent supernatural powers for the benefit of the community.

Rattle *Right*
The shaman's rattle (usually fashioned from a gourd) is regarded as a powerful instrument crucial to the attainment of the ecstatic state. The rattle is used in conjunction with a drum; when shaken rhythmically, its hypnotic beat, reminiscent of a heartbeat, induces a trancelike condition that frees the shaman's mind from the shackles of earthly matters and allows him direct communion with the spirits. This bestows on him magical powers (such as the power of healing) and grants him a vision of the future. The rattle is sometimes used to ward off evil (and is therefore sometimes worn as a protective amulet) or to invite good fortune.

Symbols of Identity

The search for identity is inherent in the human condition: in order to know oneself fully, one must first be familiar with one's kin, one's tribe, and one's nation. The collective history and beliefs of social groups inform the personalities of their members and define their identities. This chapter explores both personal symbols and those of various types of communities within whose framework the beliefs and attitudes of the individual are shaped.

Because identity consists of many, often contradictory, components, it is impossible to represent its entire complexity by means of a single symbol. However, one can extract and symbolize some of the individual facets that make up the whole. Thus a dominant attribute of a person's character can be singled out as a means of definition. Joan of Arc, for example, believed so strongly in France that she became a symbol of martyrdom and patriotism. The characters of children, like the babes in the wood, are as yet untainted, so they represent innocence. A knowledgeable individual can be symbolized by the owl of wisdom, or an ignorant one by a dunce's cap. Idealized traits, such as the cardinal virtues, have themselves become symbols, as in the blindfolded figure of Justice bearing a pair of scales and the sword of truth.

People are also given identity by their occupations, and most of us are familiar with such occupational symbols as the barber's pole, the pirates' flag, or the royal crown, which evolved from being objects of practical use into generic signs. Heraldry is a very specific symbolic system in itself. It can be used both to represent an individual and to indicate his position in the family history: the pope, for example, is signified by the keys of Rome and the papal crown, while the British royal arms signify sovereignty and the monarch's place in the royal dynasty.

Following on from symbols of individuality are tribal symbols, which proclaim the particular customs, history, and beliefs of kinship. Thus totem poles are both an emblem of faith and a record of tribal history. Body decoration, too, serves to emphasize a communal identity. In many cultural rituals—when invoking a supernatural power, for example— it is important to assume another identity, which is frequently symbolized by the wearing of masks. Other closed communities, whose members are bound by ties of purpose rather than of kinship, also have powerful symbols: each of the weapons and accouterments of the military, for example, has a very specific symbolism that serves to unify and to motivate.

The symbols of political bodies also play an inspirational role, but their powerful effect has sometimes been sadly misused, as can be seen in the devastating results of Hitler's misappropriation of the ancient swastika. Perhaps the best-known symbols of collective identity today, however, are national flags and emblems, which proclaim the patriotism and unity of the citizens of the lands that they represent.

This chapter presents an overview of all these types of symbols whereby feelings of identity are shaped.

Opposite: In many cultures, the donning of a mask is symbolic of the wearer relinquishing his ego and suppressing his identity, allowing a spirit or god to enter his body. In ceremonial rituals, the mask itself represents the god or spirit invoked. Often with exaggerated or terrifying features, masks are also intended to arouse fear, emphasizing the supernatural power of the incarnation. This Indonesian mask is of painted papier mâché and represents a demon.

Tribal Symbols and Body Adornment

Totem Pole *Left*
The Native American totem pole has a variety of significances: as an *axis mundi*, it links Earth to the heavens; its stacked and carved totemic visages act as guardian spirits to protect the tribe; and the careful selection and position of the individual images also tell the story of the tribe's history. The majority of the creatures depicted on totem poles are animals or birds (and sometimes plants), illustrating the importance of the natural world in Native American cultures. The totems are placed in ascending order of importance: a Thunderbird often sits on the apex of the totem pole, underlining its position as the supreme being or chief deity. The totem pole is a unique and individual tribal emblem, asserting a tribe's beliefs, history and kinship in graphic visual form.

Body Piercing *Above*
Distinctive forms of body ornamentation have been adopted in many cultures to assert tribal identity, and this practice has continued (albeit in modified forms) to this day. As well as painting their members' faces and bodies with special marks, wearing ritual **masks**, jewelry and costumes and performing initiation rites such as circumcision, many cultures practise body piercing. This involves a certain amount of pain—a necessary and important part of some initiation ceremonies—but ultimately allows the wearer to assert kinship by means of an identifying decoration in the ears or nose; in some traditions it also acts as a protective or religious amulet. This Wisham woman of the Pacific Northwest wears a bone in her nose from an animal hunted and killed by her tribe. It signifies her tribal membership and her acceptance of tribal customs and history, and was traditionally believed to ward off evil spirits.

Face Painting *Above*
This tribesman from Papua New Guinea in the Southwestern Pacific has painted his face and decorated his body with patterns and objects of ancient traditional significance. Like the **mask**, face painting has its origins in the rituals of prehistoric man, and the practice survives in many tribal cultures today, including in Africa and in Native American tribes. The primary purpose of face painting is to transmit the embodiment of the painted image to the character of the wearer: markings can variously represent a god or demon, assert the tribe's identity or be specific to a particular ritual. Today facial decoration is usually only applied during ceremonial rites or for war. Melanesian tribes, such as those of Papua New Guinea, have exclusively male rituals, including those of initiation or purification. Tribal ancestors (*tumbuna*) are particularly important in Melanesian belief, and can be invoked in dances and rites such as the singsing, for which the participants decorate their bodies carefully.

Tribal Mask *Above*
Many African tribal masks incorporate animal features. They are most often worn during healing rituals, during which the healer invokes the power of the animal spirit, or transfers the disease (or evil spirits thought to cause the disease) to an animal which is then sacrificed to purify the patient. Animal masks are also used by several Native American tribes in a variety of ceremonial rituals. The function of these masks is to superimpose another identity on the wearer, suppressing his own, rather than to assert kinship.

Tragedy/Comedy Masks *Below*
The Greek mask originated in the Dionysian festivities of Ancient Greece. The most famous are the opposed masks that denote tragedy and comedy, whose faces are respectively fixed in expressions of mirth or doom. These masks together symbolize the essential components of existence and were intended to rouse the audience's awareness of fate and man's ultimate destiny in the drama of life. The masks were the attributes of the muses of tragedy and comedy, Melpomene and Thalia, and Cupid was often portrayed as wearing the mask of tragedy in Roman funerary art. Today they symbolize the theatrical and dramatic arts.

National Flags

Stars and Stripes *Above*

The flag of the United States, the Stars and Stripes, dates from 1777, marking America's independence from Britain. Originally the flag had thirteen white **stars** (one for each colony) on a blue field and thirteen red-and-white stripes, symbolizing—according to George Washington—the stars of heaven, the red of the mother country and the white of independence. Over the centuries, new stars were added as further states joined the Union, and today there are fifty. The Stars and Stripes are shown here borne by the personification of the cardinal virtue of bravery, Fortitude (*Fortitudo* in Latin). Fortitude is frequently accompanied by the attributes of war—a **club**, **sword** and **shield**—and sometimes a **lion**. When she carries a flag, she represents victory through bravery; she is often depicted as a national symbol and represents the defense of all that the nation holds dear.

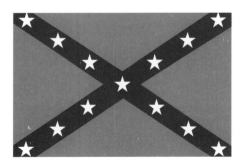

Confederate Flag *Above*

In 1861, during the prelude to the American Civil War, the seven Confederate states adopted their own flag, known as the "Stars and Bars." It consisted of a white bar sandwiched between two red stripes, in whose left-hand corner was a **circle** of seven white **stars** (representing the breakaway states) on a blue field. Later, however, the Confederacy comprised eleven states, making this original emblem inappropriate. It was replaced with the "Southern Cross," or "Flag of the South": a blue **cross** of St. Andrew dotted with white stars, placed on a red field. This became the Confederacy's battle flag after it was flown at the battle of Manassas in 1861 and until the Confederacy's demise in 1865. Today the Southern Cross forms part of Mississippi's state flag.

Union Jack *Above*

Popularly known as the "Union Jack," the Union Flag of the United Kingdom symbolizes the union of England, Scotland and Ireland as pronounced by the Act of Union of 1801. The flag is composed of the white saltire **cross** and blue field of St. Andrew (patron saint of Scotland), upon which is superimposed or "fimbriated" the red saltire cross of St. Patrick (patron saint of Ireland); the red cross of St. George (patron saint of England) surmounts both and is fimbriated in white. The earliest version of the flag dates from 1606, three years after the unification of the kingdoms of England and Scotland under James I of England (who was also James VI of Scotland); this flag was originally flown exclusively on royal ships. The Union Flag later appeared in the canton of the Red Ensign and is now part of the flags of many Commonwealth countries, including Australia, New Zealand and Fiji, as well as colonies and former colonies such as Hong Kong, Bermuda, the Cayman Islands, the British Virgin Islands and the Falkland Islands.

Japan *Above*

The land of the rising **sun** (*Nihon-Koku*), Japan flies a flag incorporating this emblem, reflecting the belief that the Japanese emperor is a descendant of the sun. One of the world's simplest flags, it was adopted in 1870 and represents a spherical, blood-red sun disk (possibly styled after a chrysanthemum) on a white field. During World War II, sixteen rays were added to the sun, and this variation was used as Japan's imperial battle flag; naval flags had eight rays.

South Korea *Above*

The flag of South Korea is known as the *pakwa* or *taeguk*, and bears in its center the distinctive Eastern **yin-yang** symbol that represents the perfect union of opposites. The top half of the yin-yang sign is colored red, the lower half blue, and it stands on a white field. Radiating diagonally from this central feature are four black kwae, or trigrams taken from the Chinese *I Ching—The Book of Changes*. Pointing symbolically toward the four corners of the Earth, the kwae represent the four winds, **seasons**, cardinal points and the **sun**, **moon**, **Earth** and heaven. The flag was first adopted in 1883 but fell into disuse during South Korea's occupation, first by the Japanese, then by the Allies. It was readopted by the Republic of Korea in 1948.

National Emblems

American Eagle *Above*
The bald-headed eagle is indigenous to the United States and, as the national bird of America, signifies the strength of the nation. When portrayed holding an **olive branch** in its right talon, it symbolizes peaceful intentions. The bundle of thirteen arrows represents the thirteen original states of the Union and also signifies America's readiness for war when defense against aggression becomes necessary. The eagle appears on the Great Seal, a symbol of the federal government's authority designed in 1782, and also on many State flags, including those of Illinois, Iowa, North Dakota, the Virgin Islands and American Samoa.

Liberty Bell *Above*
The Liberty Bell is one of America's most potent civic symbols—a reminder both of the fledgling nation's struggle for independence and of the citizen's right to liberty. The vast iron bell, weighing 2080 pounds (943 kg), and with a circumference of 12 feet (3.7 m), was commissioned from Thomas Lester's London foundry in 1752 for the state house of the [then British] province of Pennsylvania. It was cracked by its clapper soon after its arrival and had to be recast locally. Fittingly, but coincidentally, it bears the motto "Proclaim liberty throughout the land unto all the inhabitants." The bell was sounded on July 8, 1776, when the Declaration of Independence was first averred in the state hall. When the British threatened Philadelphia, it was hidden in Allentown for nearly a year. Eventually cracked beyond repair, it was last rung in 1846 and was displayed in Independence Hall from 1852. Today it can be seen in Philadelphia's Liberty Bell Hall. As well as being a symbol of the War of Independence, the Liberty Bell was also associated with the nineteenth-century antislavery movement.

Mount Rushmore *Below*
A unique tribute to four of the greatest American presidents, today the Mount Rushmore National Memorial in the Black Hills, South Dakota, is a powerful symbol of the national identity of the United States. The idea for such a memorial was conceived in 1923 by Doane Robinson, director of the South Dakota Historical Society. Dynamiting at the 5725-foot-high (1745 m) mountain began in 1927, under the direction of the sculptor Gutzon Borglum. It took fourteen years to carve the massive portraits of George Washington, Thomas Jefferson, Theodore Roosevelt and Abraham Lincoln into the hard granite rock. Borglum died a few months before its completion in 1941, but the monument was finished under his son, Lincoln. Each face is approximately 60 feet (18 m) high.

Maple Leaf *Above*
The maple leaf is the emblem of Canada. It replaced the Red Ensign of Britain on the country's flag in 1965. Represented as a red leaf with eleven points, the maple is of particular importance to Canada because of its prevalence in that country and its vital role in the economy (the sap from the maple tree produces maple sugar and syrup, and the hard wood is used in furniture-making and flooring). In China and Japan the maple leaf is both the emblem of lovers and of **fall**.

Tudor Rose *Below*

The Tudor **rose** represents a unified England. Between 1455 and 1485, England was torn apart by the Wars of the Roses, a struggle caused by the dynastic ambitions of the houses of Lancaster and York (whose devices were the red and white rose respectively), both of which wished to place their claimant on the English throne. When the Lancastrian Henry Tudor finally came to the throne in 1485 as Henry VII (the first Tudor king), the red and white roses were combined to form a single red-and-white rose—the Tudor rose.

Thistle *Below, right*

The prickly thistle, with its accompanying motto, *Nemo me impune lacessit* ("No one provokes me with impunity"), is the national emblem of Scotland. It is a symbol of defiance and of a willingness to defend Scotland. According to legend, in the eighth century the Scots were alerted to an imminent Danish attack when one of the barefooted Norsemen trod on a thistle and yelped with pain; as a result, the invaders were successfully routed. The thistle was officially adopted as the Scottish emblem during the reign of James III of Scotland (1451-88) and later also appeared in the British **royal arms**. The British Order of the Thistle is an important order of chivalry. In Christian analogy, however, the thistle is equated with both the **crown of thorns** and the fall of man, thus representing sorrow and sin. Scotland is also symbolized by the sporran and kilt (the kilt's tartan pattern further identifies membership of a clan) and by the bagpipes.

Beefeaters *Above*

Beefeaters symbolize England's proud historical tradition. More properly called the Yeomen of the Guard, their popular name is derived from the French *boufitiers*—guardians of the king's buffet. Constituted in 1485 by Henry VII to serve as the sovereign's bodyguard, the corps is England's oldest military formation. Today its members are most often seen on state occasions and on duty as warders at the Tower of London. The yeomen are drawn from the ranks of retired soldiers, and their idiosyncratic military hierarchy ranges from their captain (usually a peer), to a lieutenant and ensign, through the "clerk of the cheque," and "exons," down to messengers, sergeants major, yeoman bedgoers and bedhangers, and privates. Their colorful formal uniforms date

from the fifteenth century and consist of red tunics faced with purple stripes and gold lace, red knee-breeches and stockings, a ruff and plumed hat. On less formal occasions they dispense with the ruff and substitute a derby (bowler) hat.

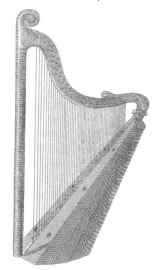

Harp *Above*

Along with the **shamrock**, the harp is an important emblem of Ireland, reflecting its Celtic heritage. It is an attribute of the good god and father of all, Dagda—one of the Irish Tuatha Dé Dannan—who caused the changing of the **seasons** by playing his harp. In Scandinavian mythology, as well as Celtic, the harp was regarded as a mystical **bridge** between heaven and **Earth**. The symbol also indicates the outstanding musical heritage of Ireland.

Cock *Right*

The cock's history as the emblem of France dates from its adoption by the warlike Goths as their battle emblem, in tribute to its fighting spirit. The medieval bestiaries called the cock "Gallus"—perhaps a derivation of the name Gaul. During the French Revolution, the depiction of the cock on the French flag was revived. In the revolutionary context, the cock assumes the attributes of vigilance and supremacy. Today the French cock signifies pride and positive aggression.

Shamrock *Above*

The association of the shamrock with Ireland dates back to the fifth century, when St. Patrick (whose emblem it is) used the three-leaved shamrock to illustrate the concept of the **Holy Trinity** to Christian converts. Its name is derived from both the Arabic word *shamrakh*, which represented the Persian Triads, and the Irish *seamrog*—"little clover." The shamrock (or green clothing and adornments) is worn on March 17, St. Patrick's Day, in Irish communities.

Bullfighter *Above*

Although bullfights are staged in all the countries once colonized by Spain, its popularity at home has made it a symbol of the mother country itself. The origins of bullfighting are uncertain, but the first enclosed bullfight is documented as occurring in 1090. At first the *toreros* (bullfighters) were mounted on **horses**, but from 1725 they began to bait the unfor-

tunate **bulls** on foot, aided with capes (*capas*) and **lances**. The first permanent bull-ring was erected in Madrid in 1743, and today there are at least four hundred such arenas in Spain. Each hosts the torture and killing of six bulls every Sunday between April and November. There is a strict hierarchy of bullfighters, from *toreros*, *matadors* and *espadas*, down to *banderillos* and *picadors*, and many become fêted heroes. Along with other bloodsports, bullfighting has become controversial due to increasing awareness of animal rights, and the bullfighter, for some, also symbolizes gratuitous cruelty and lack of respect for animals.

Great Wall *Below*

The Great Wall of China has come to symbolize that country. It was built in the third century BC as a defensive wall against the incursions of the Mongols, and stretches over 1500 miles (about 2400 km), following the contours of the land

Leo Belgicus *Above*

The lion is a historical emblem of Belgium and features in the country's national arms. The date of this map precedes Belgium's independence in 1830, but the featured lion is a symbol of Belgian pride and autonomy. The cartographer has ingeniously combined the geography of the Belgian region with its national emblem, resulting in the "Leo Belgicus"—a symbol of national defiance. The fearsomely rampant lion is depicted with its back turned on England, roaring ferociously at its neighboring countries, who are identified by their heraldic shields (as are the various provinces of Belgium). Portrayed in the borders of the map are notable Belgian personalities.

from mountainous Western Gansu to the Gulf of Liaodong. A massive engineering feat, the fortification's stone walls are, on average, approximately twenty feet (six meters) high and wide. Although substantially rebuilt during the fifteenth century, and despite social and military upheavals over the centuries, it has survived to this day, signifying the indomitable spirit of the Chinese people.

Parthenon *Below*

The ruined Parthenon in Athens, which is acknowledged as one of the finest examples of Doric architecture, is perhaps Greece's most recognized national symbol. The Persians destroyed the original temple on the sacred rock of Athens around 480 BC. Pericles commissioned the architects Iktinos and Kallikrates to

construct a new temple on the Acropolis (the "High City"), to be dedicated to **Athena**, the goddess of Athens. Work began in 447 BC, and the splendid marble temple was finally completed in 432 BC. Steps led up to the column-surrounded temple, at whose center was a rectangular room in which the 36-foot-high, ivory-and-gold figure of Pallas Athena, sculpted by the Phedias, was enshrined. Games and festivities were held at the Parthenon in honor of Athena each year. Since ancient Greek times, the Parthenon has come to symbolize Greece's outstanding cultural achievements.

Sydney Opera House *Above, right*

Along with the Harbour Bridge, the Opera House is the leading symbol of Sydney and, by extension, of Australia. Situated on Bennelong Point, this extraordinary concrete-and-steel edifice is a

unique landmark that resembles the billowing sails of a ship. In 1957 the government of New South Wales invited architects to tender their designs for the projected opera house; the winner was the Danish architect Jørn Utzon. Construction started in 1959. When it was finally opened by Queen Elizabeth II in 1973, it had cost A$102 million, a sum generated by state-run lotteries. The Opera House is an impressive 4.5-acre complex of opera, concert and drama theaters, bars and restaurants, and it boasts the world's largest mechanical organ. It is an unparalleled cultural symbol.

Taj Mahal *Below*

India's celebrated Taj Mahal is a dual symbol, representing India itself and the power of **love**. When Arjumand Banu Begum (*Mumtaz Mahal*—"Chosen of the Palace"), the favorite wife of the Mughul emperor Shah Jahan, died in childbirth in 1631, her inconsolable husband ordered this magnificent mausoleum to be erected on the River Yamuna on the outskirts of Agra, where it could be seen from his palace. Work started the same year, and the Taj Mahal was completed, with the efforts of twenty thousand workers during its construction, in 1648. A formal garden leads to a raised platform upon which stands the tomb, faced with white marble from Makrana, Rajastan. Amid a fantasy of arched recesses and screens decorated with semiprecious stones, a huge dome rises above the central chamber in which the bodies of Arjumand and Shah Jahan lie in marble sarcophagi.

Royalty and Heraldry

Crown *Above*

The crown, coronet or diadem is the premier symbol of royalty, nobility and success. Because it is worn on the most "noble" part of the body—the **head**, seat of the soul—it emphasizes the wearer's temporal and spiritual elevation and authority. Although mainly worn by sovereigns, crowns are also symbols of religious authority: the pope wears a triple crown. The deities and pharoahs of Ancient Egypt wore double crowns that were endowed with magical power. In Eastern religions, crowns signify spiritual elevation. In some religions, including Christianity, the crown signifies divine glory, and crowns were once placed on the heads of the recently deceased as a sign of their unification with God. Crowns generally incorporate the symbolism of the **circle**—infinity and perfection—and can imply solar power, light and enlightenment when decorated with rays. In most cultures in which a system of nobility prevails, different forms of crown are worn by peers according to their rank: thus the coronets of dukes, counts and barons are all distinguished by specific forms which become less splendid according to the decreasing hierarchical position of the noble wearer.

Fleur-de-lys *Above, center right*

The fleur-de-lys (or fleur-de-lis, which means "flower of the lily" in French) is a much-used floral heraldic symbol. It depicts a stylized **lily** or **lotus**, signifying perfection, light and life and traditionally represents the kings of France. In French

legend, Clovis, the Merovingian king of the Franks, converted to Christianity in AD 496, whereupon an **angel** gave him a golden lily as a symbol of his purification. Alternatively, it is sometimes said that Clovis adopted it as his emblem after waterlilies in the River Rhine alerted him to a safe spot at which to ford the river and cross to achieve victory in battle. In the twelfth century the fleur-de-lys became the symbol of French royalty. Louis VII used it on his shield and "*lys*" is also thought to be a contraction of "Louis." Between 1340 and 1801, English kings used the emblem on their coats of arms to signify their claims to the French

throne. Because it consists of a triple lily, the fleur-de-lys can also represent the **Trinity**, the **Virgin Mary**, the trinities of God, the creation and royalty and also mankind's **body**, mind and soul. Its resemblance to a **spear**head also links it with masculine martial power. The fleur-de-lys is the symbol of Florence, Italy, known as the "City of Lilies."

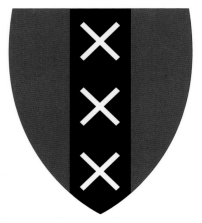

The Arms of Amsterdam *Above*

The arms of the Dutch city of Amsterdam, which date from the fifteenth century, are described in heraldic terminology as "gules on a pale consu sable three saltires argent"—three white saltire crosses on a black strip placed in the center of a red shield. The three crosses are believed to represent justice. They are derived form the arms of the counts of Amstel whose house of Persijn granted Amsterdam privileges in the thirteenth century when it was just a humble fishing village, or alternatively from the arms of the lordship of Breda (which also appear in those of the princes of Orange). Amsterdam's heraldic shield is sometimes shown supported by two black **lions** and is surmounted with the imperial **crown** with the motto: *Heldhaftig, Vastberaden, Barmherzig* ("Heroic, resolute, charitable").

British Royal Heraldic Arms *Left*

The royal armorial bearings of Queen Elizabeth II of England date from the reign of Queen Victoria. Quartered in the center, enclosed by the garter with its motto *Honi Soit Qui Mal y Pense*, are the arms of England (symbolized by **lions** passant guardant), Scotland (the lion rampant) and Ireland (the **harp**). The royally crowned lion and the **unicorn** act as supporters and stand above the monarch's motto: *Dieu et Mon Droit*. Balanced above is the royal helm and lion crest. The effect of this masterpiece of heraldry is one of majestic power and authority.

Papal Emblem *Above*

The heraldic emblem of the pope consists of the crossed **keys** of St. Peter (the first bishop of Rome and guardian of the gates of heaven), surmounted by the conical papal tiara and draped with the pallium, from which hangs a **cross**. The keys are a reminder of the legacy of St. Peter; the pallium was once worn exclusively by the pope; while the triple-crowned tiara denotes the **Holy Trinity**. All are symbolic of ecclesiastical authority.

German Eagle *Below*

The black **eagle** of German heraldry dates from its use as the emblem of the Holy Roman Empire, whose emperors regarded it as a symbol of the authority they claimed they had inherited from the Romans. Throughout the period of the dissolution of the Holy Roman Empire, the unification of the German nation in 1871, the abdication of the Kaiser, the Weimar Republic and the Third Reich, the eagle remained a German emblem.

Military

Gun *Right*

The gun, in whatever form—pistol, revolver, rifle or machine gun—is a classic phallic and phobic symbol, its rigid shape (like that of the **sword**, **spear** or **arrow**) signifying masculine potency, and its effect injury or death. It is a symbol of authority and domination and, when fired, its explosive flash and bang can also represent **thunder** and **lightning**. A gun that does not fire can signify impotence and, when associated with men, sexual impotence. As a wounding weapon, its significance can simply be that of the power of injury or death.

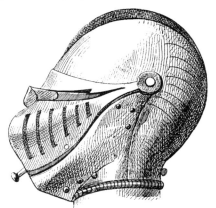

Helmet *Above*

The helmet, or helm, is a clear martial symbol of strength, protection and invulnerability. Depending on whether the visor is open or closed, it can represent spiritual or hidden thoughts. It is the attribute of the Greco-Roman gods **Mars** (or Aries, signifying war), **Pluto** (or Hades, darkness) and Minerva (or **Athena**, thought). In Greek legend Perseus's helmet (the helmet of Hades) bestowed invisibility when he slayed Medusa. The helmet is part of the heraldic crest and can be portrayed in many historical forms; different styles also signify the various ranks of nobility: royalty (gold, with seven or five bars in the visor), peers (silver or gold, with five visor bars), knights (steel, with an open visor) and esquires (steel, with a closed visor).

Knight and Lance *Below*

Both the mounted knight and his lance have symbolic significance. The knight represents the soul guiding the **body** (represented by the **horse**), and his quest can be equated to man's journey through life, with its attendant trials, tribulations and obstacles. The Green Knight of tradition signifies the apprentice or the powers of nature and death; the Red Knight represents bloody victory; the White Knight symbolizes purity and illumination; while the Black Knight is the embodiment of evil, sin and sacrifice. The knight can be regarded as the universal hero or the animus figure. The lance is a phallic masculine symbol associated with the **spear** (from which it evolved). It can also represent the solar rays, war and sacrifice. While the **sword** has celestial associations, the lance (as the lesser weapon) is associated with the **earth** and can assume the symbolism of the *axis mundi*. In medieval times, if a knight held the point of his lance forward, he declared war; if he held it behind him, he came in friendship. In Christianity, the lance, or spear, of Longius is an emblem of Christ's passion (from which it may draw its association with the legendary Holy Grail). The lance is an attribute of the cardinal virtue of bravery (*Fortitudo*).

Bow and Arrow *Below*

With its curved shape and martial use, the bow has both masculine and feminine symbolism: the tension of its string represents male prowess, vigor and vitality; its shape mirrors the crescent **moon**. The arrow, however, is a clearly masculine phallic symbol, signifying penetration, **lightning**, virility, speed, the **sun**'s rays, war and death. Because of its phallic connotations, in Roman times it was associated with lust, as were archers such as the centaur. Together, bow and arrow generally signify war, power and the ability to hit a target. In Buddhism the bow and arrow signify the mind and the five senses respectively; together they symbolize willpower and the sacred syllable *Om*. This significance is shared in Hinduism, but the arrow, when associated with Indra, represents the sun's rays and lightning, and when fired by Rudra, pain and healing **rain**. The bow is also an attribute of **Shiva**. In China, the bow and arrow form a fertility symbol and can represent the Tao. In Islam, the bow signifies Allah's power and the arrow his wrath; while in Christianity, the bow symbolizes temporal power and arrows **martyrdom**. In Japan, the meditation technique kyudo, involving the unintentional aiming of an arrow, represents the shedding of the ego. In the Greco-Roman pantheon, Artemis (**Diana**) carries a bow (signifying the crescent moon) and arrow (symbolizing light), and they are also the attributes of Apollo and Eros (Cupid)—the latter firing arrows of **love**. In shamanistic cultures, a feathered arrow represents a birdlike flight to heaven. The bow and arrow are carried by the zodiacal centaur, **Sagittarius**.

Shield *Above*

Since the times of earliest man, the shield has been used for defense and protection, and this is its prime symbolic meaning, although it can also signify both spirituality and chastity. In Ancient Greece, the shield of **Zeus**, the aegis, conferred divine protection. It was made by Hephaestus and covered with the skin of the goat Amalthea. Thunderstorms were produced when Zeus shook it, and **Athena** carried it emblazoned with the **Gorgon**'s head. Together with the **spear**, the shield is the emblem of Ares (**Mars**) and Athena (Minerva, who also wore the aegis as a cloak); with the spear it also symbolized epheboi, or adulthood. In the Middle Ages, **knights** wore their coats of arms upon their shields in order to identify themselves when their features were obscured by **helmets**; as a result, as the escutcheon, it is the fundamental component of heraldry and is the base upon which other emblems are placed.

Spear *Right*

As well as being a universal and ancient weapon of war, the spear shares much of the symbolism of the **lance**. It also represents the *axis mundi*, the magician's **wand** and—through its phallic shape—masculinity and fertility. In Ancient Greece, it was part of the epheboi (along with the **shield**), which symbolized adulthood, and was the attribute of **Athena** (Minerva), Ares (**Mars**) and Achilles (the rust from his spear produced the plant milfoil, which cured Telephus). In Hinduism, Indra carries a spear representing victory and wisdom. In Japan, spears represent the heavenly spear of creation borne by Izanagi, the first male god. Two crossed spears behind a shield are part of the flags of Lesotho and Kenya and signify defense.

Maltese Cross *Above*

The Maltese Cross (also called the cross of eight points) was the badge of the Knights Hospitaller (or Knights of St. John of Jerusalem), a prominent military order of the Crusades. In 1529 they set up their headquarters in Malta and became known as the Knights of Malta, thus providing the name for their emblem. The Maltese cross is white, displayed on a black background. Its eight points represent the beatitudes (blessings) and are formed from four barbed arrowheads. This form of cross also had resonance in Ancient Assyria, where its points symbolized the gods Ra, Anu, Belus and Hea.

Iron Cross *Above*

The Iron Cross, whose arms splay outward, is also known as the formy or paty cross. It is a heraldic symbol associated with Germany, as that country's highest military decoration. It was first awarded by Frederick William III of Prussia during the war with Napoleon in 1813 and was made of iron edged with silver. It was awarded in all subsequent military campaigns, including World War I. Adolf Hitler supplemented the Iron Cross with a **swastika**, but this was removed after World War II; unlike the swastika, the Iron Cross has not been excised from Germany's iconography.

Occupations

Seafaring *Left*

The anchor is the universal symbol of seafarers and has been adopted by many navies as their emblem. As the anchor stabilizes a ship and therefore protects sailors from death on storm-tossed seas, so in the Christian tradition, the anchor was a sign of religious steadfastness and of **hope** and salvation through faith. The anchor was a sign of the theological virtue of Hope (*Spes*), often symbolized by a woman (sometimes winged and accompanied by a globe, cornucopia, beehive or pear) with an anchor at her feet.

Chef's Hat *Right*

The chef's hat is now a universal symbol for cooks and gastronomy. It is a common sign in guidebooks used to denote restaurants and to categorize their standard of cooking. Because it covers the **head** and restrains the hair, the hat serves a hygienic purpose, but it is also a symbol of the chef's authority over his staff. A culinary apprentice must work his way up the hierarchy of the kitchen, progressing from a menial position through various intermediate levels before finally earning his chef's hat. As well as identifying the principal cook (the word "chef" is French for "chief"), the chef's hat is a sign of prowess that symbolizes his culinary experience and skills.

Piracy *Below*

The **skull** and crossbones is famous as the "Jolly Roger" flag of marauding pirates. It is an age-old symbol of death and therefore also a universal symbol of danger. While the skull denotes the impermanence of human life, the crossed thigh-bones signify the vital force of the loins. This terrifying symbol was also used by the Nazi S.S. and by many armies as a regimental military emblem. Today it is most commonly seen as a warning sign on poisonous substances.

Barber's Pole *Below*

A pole with red-and-white spiral stripes stands outside the barber's shop and symbolizes haircutting. The significance of the barber's pole has nothing to do with this service, however, but dates back to the days when barbers also performed certain medical functions. One of these was blood-letting—a procedure believed to cure many ailments. Patients were given a pole to grip in order to make the veins in their arms stand out, after which the barber lanced a vein and drew blood. Between appointments, the pole, around which a blood-stained bandage was tied, was left outside. The real version was eventually replaced by a custom-made, symbolic pole whose red stripes signify blood. The gilded knob seen at the end of some poles represents the barber's basin.

Virtues

Temperance *Above*

Along with her sisters, Justice, Prudence and Fortitude, Temperance is the female personification of one of the four cardinal virtues and warns against the dangers of excess. She can be depicted with a number of attributes, including a sheathed **sword** (signifying the control of temper), two urns (representing balance), an **hourglass**, a horse's bridle and bit (symbolizing restraint) and wine diluted by **water**. Temperance is, in addition, the fourteenth of the major-arcana cards of **Tarot**, represented by an androgynous figure pouring water from one vessel into another. Its meaning underlines the need to maintain harmony by achieving the perfect balance of emotions and actions. Because it stores water in its hump and uses it sparingly, the **camel** can also symbolize temperance, as can the **dove**.

The Three Graces *Above, center*

In ancient Greco-Roman mythology, the three Graces (*Gratiae* in Latin, or *Charites* in Greek) were the sisters Aglaea, Thalia and Euphrosyne, the daughters of **Zeus** (Jupiter) and Eurynome (herself the daughter of Okeanos). They were collectively celebrated for their loveliness and charm, but Aglaea (whose name means "radiance") was particularly praised for her beauty, Thalia ("revelry")

for her laughter and Euphrosyne ("mirth") for her grace. As well as embodying these virtues, the goddesses were believed to have the power to bestow them upon deserving humans. They attended many of the deities of the Greco-Roman pantheon but were especially associated with Aphrodite (**Venus**), whose attributes (such as the **apple**—seen here in Raphael's painting—**rose**, myrtle and **dice**) they were portrayed as carrying. Their symbolism is varied: Seneca said that they embody generosity and the giving, receiving and requiting of favors, while in Neo-Platonic interpretation they represent the three stages of **love** (beauty, desire and fulfillment). In Christian tradition they symbolize chastity, beauty and love. Because they are three in number, they also symbolize perfect unification (of two opposites by a third, transcendent member).

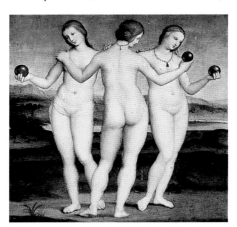

Justice *Right*

Justice (*Justicia* in Latin) is one of the quartet of cardinal virtues, which also include Fortitude (*Fortitudo*), Prudence (*Prudentia*) and Temperance (*Temperantia*). Justice (who is associated with the goddess Astraea) is portrayed as a woman wearing a blindfold (so that her eyes will not betray her into making false judgment), holding a **sword** with which to separate good from evil and a pair of scales (symbolizing balance and equality before the law). She is occasionally also depicted with an **olive branch**, cornucopia and law book. Justice is also one of the major arcana of the **Tarot** system.

Mercy *Above*

According to the Gospel of St. Matthew in the Christian New Testament, there are six acts of mercy, the performance of which is crucial in separating those who will go to heaven from those who will go to hell on the Day of Judgment. They are feeding the hungry, giving drink to the thirsty, housing the homeless, clothing the naked, nursing the sick and visiting or ransoming those in prison. A further act, burying the dead, was later added as a sign of respect for the **body** as "God's temple, where the Spirit of God dwells" (I Corinthians 3:16). Illustrated here is Caravaggio's depiction of the seven acts of mercy. In Gothic imagery, Charity was depicted carrying out all the acts of mercy but in later centuries was restricted to clothing the naked only.

Attributes

Owl of Wisdom *Above*

Today the owl is one of the most popular symbols of learning and is frequently portrayed (as here) perched upon a stack of books with a serious-looking expression. This symbolism can be attributed to its ancient significance as the bird sacred to the Greek goddess **Athena**, goddess of wisdom. In more recent times, its ringed eyes suggest the wearing of spectacles, and thus bookishness. In this association it is also a symbol of opticians, implying keen eyesight.

Innocence *Below*

The story of the babes in the wood dates from a sixteenth-century ballad (properly called *The Children in the Wood*). Having been left rich orphans by the death of their father, a young boy and girl are entrusted to the care of their greedy uncle, who decides to kill them in order to inherit their wealth. He therefore employs two men to take them into the woods and murder them; one is moved by the children's plight and kills the other, but he then abandons the helpless children, thus condemning them to death through exposure. Fittingly, God punishes both uncle and his employee with penury and death. The story is a morality tale—a warning that evil will not go unpunished—in which the babes are emotive symbols of innocence, goodness and defenselessness. In symbolic terms, children generally represent these virtuous qualities.

Thrift *Left*

Because children store their money in them, piggy banks have been accorded the symbolism of thrift. Just as **pigs** are slowly fattened for slaughter, so the piggy bank gradually accumulates pennies until it is full and a tidy sum has been saved, demonstrating to the child the benefits of thrift. As the modern equivalent of the purse, however, which was an attribute of the deadly sin of avarice (as, indeed, was the pig itself), the piggy bank can also represent **greed**; the unfortunate pig furthermore represented the deadly sins of sloth and lust. Other symbols of thrift include the **bee** and **ant**; all three creatures are commonly used in the corporate signs of savings institutions.

Martyrdom *Above*

Joan of Arc, also known as the Maid of Orléans, is a potent symbol of both patriotism and martyrdom. Born in 1412, she was merely a humble peasant girl until she experienced heavenly visions commanding her to save her country, then in the grip of the Hundred Years' War. After convincing the dauphin of her extraordinary mission, she went on to lead the French army that relieved Orléans, an action which enabled Charles VII to be crowned in 1429. She was captured by the enemy in 1430, sold to the English, then pronounced a **witch** and a heretic and burned at the stake in 1431. She was canonized by the Catholic church in 1920. Her youth, courage and conviction, as well as her tragic death, have caused her to become a symbol of France and, more generally, of fervent patriotism and noble martyrdom or self-sacrifice in the service of one's country.

Political Emblems

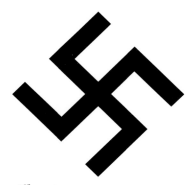

Swastika *Above*
Today the swastika is inextricably linked with twentieth-century Nazism, but it has ancient and overwhelmingly positive symbolism. Before its appropriation by Hitler in 1919 as the Hakenkreuz (hooked cross), it was a symbol of **good luck**. The name is derived from the Sanskrit word *svasti*, meaning "well-being." Also known as a fylfot (in medieval times it was used as a decoration to "fill the foot" of stained-glass windows), gammadion (because it is made up of four gamma characters) or the heraldic cross cramponné, it is an equilateral hooked cross spining around its center. When it spins clockwise, it symbolizes solar and male dynamism; when anticlockwise (called the swavastika), it represents the lunar and female. It can also signify the union of opposites, such as male and female, dynamic and static, beginning and end, **yin** and **yang**. The swastika dates from prehistoric times and is found all over the world, including Asia, Greece, Europe, Scandinavia and America. It was an ancient symbol of the Aryans, for whom it represented the **sun** (the arms signifying solar rays), and it was sometimes superimposed upon a solar disk. Hitler adopted it as a symbol of Aryan racial supremacy. Although its primary meaning is solar energy, it can also symbolize the pole and the **stars**, the four cardinal points, winds and **seasons** (as in Islam), the four quarters of the **moon**, the whirlwind, the wheel of life, the creative force and the squaring of the **circle** (and vice versa). In Greek tradition, it was an attribute of **Zeus** and Helios,

as well as Hera, Ceres and Artemis. The Celts, Scandinavians and Teutons regarded it as the battle ax or hammer of **Thor**, god of air, **thunder** and **lightning**. The swastika has particular significance in Buddhism: as the Round of Existence it is one of the Eight Symbols of Good Augury, and it is one of the signs of the Seven Appearances. To Shinto Buddhists, it is the heart of **Buddha**. In China, it was an early form of the fang sign, meaning the four parts of the world, and signified immortality and infinity. It is also an important symbol in Jainism (where the four arms signify the four levels of existence, consciousness and divinity) and Hinduism, where it is an attribute of Vishnu, Agni, Indra, **Shiva** and **Ganesha** (god of the crossroads). Early Christian tradition equated the swastika with the gammadion, symbolizing Christ as the cornerstone. In black magic, the anticlockwise-spinning swastika signifies the power of evil.

Hammer and Sickle *Above*
Until recently, the hammer and sickle represented communism, particularly in the Soviet Union. Derived from the Bolshevik emblem of a hammer crossed with a plow, the hammer and sickle represents the alliance between the proletariat (industrial workers) and the peasantry (agricultural workers). After the czar had been overthrown, in 1922 the gold hammer and sickle on a red field was adopted as the emblem and flag of the U.S.S.R., signifying the power of working people. President Gorbachev ordered it to be removed from the flag of Russia in 1991, when it was replaced by the Russian tricolor, which had been used in precommunist times.

Neo-Nazism *Above*
There are many variants of the **swastika** in use by neo-Nazi groups today, and this version takes the form of the triskele (triquetra or fylfot), the three-legged symbol of Ancient Greece which signified progress and competition, as well as the **sun**. It is the device of the *Afrikaaner Weerstandsbeweging*, (Afrikaner Resistance Movement—A.W.B.), a South African fascist organization dedicated to white supremacy, founded in 1973 by Eugene Terre Blanche.

United Nations *Below*
The flag of the United Nations, which was founded in 1945 and today has nearly 180 members, reflects the international unity and worldwide peace that the organization promotes. Placed on a field of "United Nations blue," it consists of a maplike representation of all the continents of the world as seen from the north pole in a globe that symbolizes unity. The globe is enclosed by two crossed **olive branches**, representing peace. In times of conflict it is carried into war zones by United Nations peacekeeping forces and observers, as a sign of their impartiality and desire to work for world peace.

Peace Symbol *Above*
The peace cross was designed by Gerald Holtom in 1958 for C.N.D. (the Campaign for Nuclear Disarmament). The symbolism he employed for the emblem was simple: within a **circle**—signifying unity—are the semaphore characters N (for nuclear) and D (disarmament). Despite its positive peaceful connotations, the peace cross also became associated with anarchy through its use by anarchists (among others) in the peace marches of the 1960s.

Black Power *Below*
The black clenched fist is the symbol of the Black Power social, economic and political movement that found its expression in the mid to late 1960s in the United States as a development of, and in reaction to, the civil rights movement. The achievements of the civil rights movement, which had come to prominence during the previous decade and was still active, were seen by many African Americans as inadequate, the pace of change too slow and the tactics insufficiently aggressive to attain real equality. Black

Power was also inspired by the separatist policies advocated by the Black Muslim movement (founded by Elijah Muhammed in 1930 and later led by Malcolm X), by Stokeley Carmichael's Student Nonviolent Coordinating Committee (set up in 1966) and by the more radical Black Panther organization, established in the same year. The Black Power fist graphically represents the strength of African American unity, determination to achieve the movement's goals—by force if necessary—and the separatism of the movement (through its black color). The fist sign has been adopted by political equality campaigning organizations worldwide.

Ku Klux Klan *Above*
Along with the burning **cross** and white hoods and robes, the initials K.K.K. are symbols of this white supremacist movement. The emblem shown above depicts a cross with a flame at the center, symbolizing destruction and purification. The Ku Klux Klan was founded by white Southerners in 1866 with the primary purpose of intimidating emancipated slaves, to prevent them from voting. This particular battle having been lost, the Klan reemerged in Georgia in 1915 and spread to other parts of America, including the Midwest and Oregon, during the 1920s. Its violent "persuasive" techniques included arson, lynchings and bombings, tactics assumed during the Klan's revival in the 1960s as a desperate response to the civil rights movement. Then, as now, Klansmen are mainly drawn from the ranks of disenchanted white men who blame other ethnic groups for all society's ills.

Donkey *Above*
The donkey is the emblem of the Democratic Party of the United States. Its use as such dates from 1828, when it was adopted by Andrew Jackson (U.S. President, 1829–1837) as a humorous allusion to his derogatory nickname "jackass." Its mascot role was further consolidated by Thomas Nast's cartoons, published in *Harper's Weekly* during the 1880s.

Elephant *Above*
Since 1874, when *Harper's Weekly* published a cartoon by Thomas Nast of an elephant trampling on inflation and chaos, the elephant has been the symbol of the Republican Party of the United States—the party whose traditional priorites include social and economic conservation and law and order. Nast used the elephant to symbolize Republican determination to uphold these priorities uncompromisingly.

*Note: see also **Donkey** and **Elephant** in Nature Symbols.*

Symbols of Magic and the Occult and Symbol Systems

Throughout his history, man has consistently refused to believe that the purpose of his existence is solely to be born, to live and then to die. For many, it is inconceivable that humanity has no greater role to play in the universe, and in earlier times such concepts as that of cosmic man were first propounded. This symbolic figure reflected in his body all the many components and qualities of the universe.

Another ancient theory, which still endures today, is that of zodiacal man, who is mystically related to the stars of the zodiac which both govern the parts of his body and influence his personality and actions. The twelve signs of the Western zodiac, which are themselves symbolized by sigils and pictorial representations, are each believed to govern not only their individual spheres of time and space but also those who are born under their signs; the creatures of the Chinese zodiac have a similar influence over those born in their respective years.

As well as trying to determine his place in the cosmic scheme, man has also tried to control his environment by attempting to invoke supernatural powers by means of occult practices. The rituals of Satanism, for example, are intended to enlist the support of Satan for evil purposes, while those of Wiccanism, which call up the benevolent Earth Mother, are less malevolent; both make extensive use of symbolism. Alchemy, although based on pseudoscientific princi-

ples and popularly believed to be concerned only with the transformation of base matter into gold, also sought a spiritual answer to the cosmic question. Its tracts are rich in symbolism, and the alchemical signs for basic ingredients such the elements can be seen as a blueprint which, if used in the correct combination, will lead to perfection, represented by the androgyne. Related to the esoteric theories of alchemy are the beliefs and rituals of such secret societies as Rosicrucianism and Freemasonry, both of which use a complicated symbolic language into which their members are initiated.

There are many other examples of symbolic systems that signify more than is apparent at first sight: each piece of a chess set or each individual playing card, for example, has a specific connotation, and together they have an altogether more cosmic significance. Tarot cards and the Chinese *pa kua* hexagrams are divinatory systems whose individual components symbolize separate personal concepts that in combination also mirror the universe. Other symbolic systems with which we are all familiar include those of shapes, numbers and alphabets like Egyptian hieroglyphics and the Greek and Roman letters. Used as tools for artistic, mathematical or written communication, they can also signify more profound concepts.

This chapter introduces a representative cross-section of each of these symbolic types, offering revealing insight into the world of esoteric symbolism.

Opposite: *Goya's nightmarish painting* Witches' Sabbath *illustrates a coven of witches gathered around Satan (who has taken the form of a goat), while bats swoop overhead. Although the women do not entirely reflect the traditional Western portrait of witches as black-garbed, wrinkled hags, they present sacrificial children to their evil master, leaving no doubt as to their allegiance.*

Witchcraft and Satanism

Witch *Above*

The archetypal symbol of the witch presents her as an aged hag wearing long, black robes and a pointed hat and flying on a broomstick. The original significance of the broomstick is uncertain, but it is possible that it is derived from pagan phallic symbols; it was a symbol of womanhood in the Middle Ages when it was usually made of hazel twigs. In this depiction, the witch is shown brandishing her broomstick and riding a goose. The Celts believed that the goose was a messenger to and from the spiritual world and that it signified the negative characteristics of conceit and stupidity.

Cloven-hoofed Satan *Above*

Satan is sometimes personified as the **serpent**, the **dragon** of the Apocalypse and the tempter of man. This abhorrent representation, in which the cloven-hoofed devil is entwined by a serpent (in mockery of the garter), exemplifies Satan's qualities of evil, destructiveness and craftiness.

Winged Satan *Right*

This depiction of the devil, based on Eliphas Levi's Sabbatic Goat, or Baphomet, is redolent with symbolism. Satan has the **head**, haunches and cloven feet of the **goat**, and the wings of an infernal **angel**. Centered in the abdomen is the **caduceus**; the hexagram (usually depicted as a pentagram) acts as his third eye. A triple **crown** of **fire** rises from his head, and his hand points to the symbol of the moon. The presence of both horns and breasts indicates the union of masculine and feminine power in evil.

Black Mass *Below*

Many satanic practices deliberately parody the most sacred symbols and rituals of Christianity. A sacrilegious inversion of the Christian mass, the black mass mocks God and venerates **Satan**. Here the "priest," symbolizing the devil, raises a goblet aloft above an **altar** while an acolyte member of the coven carries one of the altar **candles**. Satanic rituals vary in content but are popularly believed to culminate in sacrifice.

Succubus/Incubus *Opposite, top left*

The succubus is the monstrous demon that personifies nightmares, waking the sleeper to face evil incarnate and mocking his terror. The succubus, a female demon, was believed to prey on men, while the male incubus terrorizes women; both were said to visit their victims at night and have sexually threatening connotations. They symbolize nightmares and threats to **innocence**.

Familiar *Below*

Witches, servants of the devil, are said to have assistants to aid them with their infernal tasks. These creatures, known as familiars, are often horned and winged imps as shown here, but they can also take the form of seemingly ordinary animals. A woman accused of witchcraft would often find that her pet animal (often a **cat**) was alleged to be her familiar, a malicious imp in disguise.

Witch in Flight *Right*

The ancient crone flying on her broomstick to join her coven is a common symbol in Western tradition. She is invariably garbed in black and crowned with a cone-shaped hat and is usually accompanied by her **familiar**, here shown as a black **cat**. In medieval times, the witch was regarded as the servant of **Satan** and thus symbolized evil on earth; this image is still evoked on Hallowe'en.

Wand *Below*

Innocent young children cower before the wicked **witch** and her magic wand. The wand is a symbol of power and magical knowledge as well as a conductor of supernatural forces; it is an indispensable part of the magical ritual. Being touched by a magic wand has either a harmful or beneficial effect, depending on the will of the witch or magician.

Toad *Above, right*

The toad is associated with Satanism and witchcraft mainly because of its repulsive, warty appearance. While many cultures regarded the **frog** as a symbol of life, the toad (although it sometimes shared the

frog's positive symbolism of the **moon** and resurrection) has generally attracted the reverse significance. As a cold-blooded amphibian believed to spit poison when threatened, the toad avoids the **sun**, preferring damp and dark places; it was therefore often believed to be a creature of the devil, a **familiar** of witches and one of the forms into which these figures could transform themselves. The possessor of diabolical wisdom, it was thought that, like the **serpent**, the toad had a jewel—the Borax—embedded in its head, which could act as an antidote to poison. Furthermore, in Western tradition, this maligned creature also became associated with lust and covetousness.

Wiccanism and White Magic

Herbalist *Right*
Under the light of the **moon** and **stars**, the female herbalist practises her esoteric art in a lushly verdant wood. Plant life generally symbolizes the cycle of life (birth, death and resurrection) and is particularly linked with the Great Mother, the universal goddess of nature and fertility. When associated with the feminine moon cult, the spiritual aspect of **trees** and **plants** is more emphasized. Some cultures in Central Asia, Japan, Korea and Australia regarded trees as mythical ancestors frozen into a vegetable form; they believed that one could tap into their wis-

dom. Because of their traditional role as preparers of food, women developed an extensive knowledge of the properties of plants and the purposes for which they could be used. Certain plants and herbs were vital ingredients in magic potions and in early medicine. As well as being curatives, many, such as henbane, belladonna and hemlock, were hallucinogens, which expanded the consciousness—a magical experience to the medieval mind. In less enlightened times, villagers would approach their local "wise woman" for simple (but to them mysterious) help with their ailments. However, possession of such powers was a double-edged sword: if the cure was successful, the herbalist might gain a position of respect; if it failed, she would be branded a **witch** and persecuted.

Erda *Left*
Like the early pagans, adherents of Wiccanism revere nature in all its forms. Wiccanists believe in reincarnation and magic and ritually celebrate astronomical and agricultural phenomena. Their credo is rooted in both the God and the Goddess—male and female divine energies. These modern "white witches" hold a special reverence for the earth, personified as Erda—one of many goddess incarnations.

Black Cat *Above*

Although in modern times the black cat has come to signify good luck, traditionally it has been regarded as a symbol of the devil, whose favorite creature it is. Thus it can denote evil and death. It was believed that **witches** could transform themselves into black cats, and that possession of a black cat as a **familiar** was incontrovertible proof that its owner was a witch.

Diana *Below*

The Roman goddess Diana (also known as the Greek goddess Artemis) personified the **moon** and thus became representative of fertility—of both women and nature. Shown here as a beautiful young girl, she wears a torc of authority around her neck, is crowned with **mistletoe** (a Celtic feminine symbol of immortality and fertility) and carries a sickle, which combines the symbolism of the crescent moon and harvest. Many Wiccanists revere Diana as the lunar goddess. She was also the goddess of wild beasts and hunting and, as such, was symbolized by the **bear**.

Fairy Godmother *Below*

In the fairy tale, Cinderella was helped by her fairy godmother to achieve her dreams of **love** and marriage against all the odds. The concept of benevolent spirits (symbolized here by the fairy godmother) protecting humans against the forces of evil dates back to the ancient civilizations and parallels Christianity's guardian **angels**.

Mandrake *Right*

The forked mandrake root of the mandragora plant is curiously human-shaped and contains toxic hallucigens. In pagan belief, it was sacred and symbolic of the Great Mother. In Egyptian and Hebrew tradition, it symbolized fertility and was eaten as an aid to conception; it was also the symbol of the Hebrew tribe of Reuben. The emblem of Circe, the Greek sorceress, the mandrake was considered to have powers of magical enchantment and was used in magic potions. During the Middle Ages, the mandrake was believed to be a curative plant, and it was used in early medicine. It was popularly believed to grow beneath gallows from the sperm of hanged men and to scream when uprooted. Despite this, it was also associated with the positive attributes of happiness and wealth.

Magic Circle *Above*

This medieval woodcut shows the devil brought to his knees by a magician. Secure within his protective magic circle which the devil cannot penetrate (around which powerful symbols such as **crosses** and the signs of the **zodiac** are inscribed) and clutching his magic **wand**, the magician neutralizes the evil spirit with powerful words from his book of spells.

Astrology

Astrological Key *Right*
Astrology can be seen as a way of unlocking the spiritual meaning of the **universe** and thus finding a path to wisdom and knowledge. By studying the movement and cycles of the **stars** and **planets**, the **sun** and the **moon**, it is believed that man's mystic fate can be divined. The **zodiacal system** of twelve celestial symbols has been known since the second century AD. Seen here are the sigils of **Aries, Taurus, Gemini, Cancer, Leo, Virgo** and **Libra**.

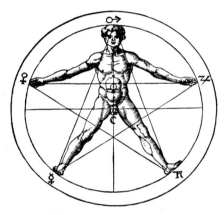

Cosmic Man *Above*
Ancient belief in the creation of the **universe** from a single being, as well as an understandable and widespread bias in ancient and medieval times, put man firmly at the center of the cosmos; it was thought that he represented the microcosm of the greater celestial macrocosm. Thus the universe's various qualities are mirrored in cosmic (or universal) man, whose body represents the element of earth, his body-heat, **fire**; blood, **water**; and breath, **air**. Furthermore, cosmic man's **head** symbolizes the heavens; his stomach, the sea; and his legs, the **earth**. In this medieval illustration the position of the **planets** is reflected in cosmic man: the astronomical symbol of the **sun** is placed in his stomach—the center—and that of the **moon** between his legs. In the wheel encircling him are (clockwise from top) the signs of **Mars, Jupiter, Saturn, Mercury** and **Venus** (the remaining three

planets had not yet been discovered). The **mandala**-like diagram is composed of the central figure of cosmic man, surrounded by the **circle** of completeness (also known as the zodiacal wheel), itself bisected by quadrants—signifying earth and the cardinal directions—imposed upon which is a **five**-pointed star (pentagram). All these geometrical forms symbolize perfection. Cosmic man's association with the pentagram derives from Pythagoras's theory that five is the perfect number of man as microcosm, and the medieval belief that the number five is special to man, for he has five senses, five digits on each extremity, and his height is composed of five equal parts, as is his width. The concept of cosmic man, related to that of zodiacal man, is crucial to astrology and is also important in areas of alchemy.

Zodiacal Man *Right*
In association with the cosmic-man principle and before the advent of modern medical diagnostic practices, it was believed that each part of the human body was controlled by a zodiacal sign. The celestial macrocosm was paralleled in the microcosm (man) and therefore believed to govern the body. This representation illustrates the perceived relationship and was consulted by medieval physicians in the diagnostic process called melothesia (which remains in use today).

According to this theory, because the relative positions of **stars** and **planets** influence man, they inevitably affect his physical and mental health. In more specific usage, ailments can be determined by consulting the patient's birth sign and horoscope. As shown in the diagram, the zodiacal signs each influence separate parts of the body: **Aries**, the head and face; **Taurus**, the throat and neck; **Gemini**, the shoulders, lungs and arms; **Cancer**, the chest and stomach; **Leo**, the heart, liver and lungs; **Virgo**, the stomach and intestines; **Libra**, the spine, kidneys and bone marrow; **Scorpio**, the kidneys and genitals; **Sagittarius**, the liver, hips and thighs; **Capricorn**, the knees, bones and teeth; **Aquarius**, the calves, ankles and blood; and **Pisces**, the feet and lymph glands.

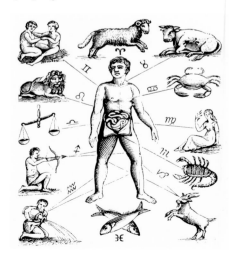

The Zodiac

Aries *Above*

Aries, the ram, is a masculine, cardinal, **fire** sign in the house of **Mars** and represents uncontrolled energy. As the first sign of the zodiac, it is a symbol of the renewal of solar creative power, **spring** and beginnings in general. It is said to transform the primordial waters of Pisces into the thunderbolt of creation. In Greek tradition, Aries (the name is Latin for ram) was the winged ram of the Golden Fleece, which carried Phrixus and Helle from Io; Phrixus sacrificed it to **Zeus**, who placed it in the heavens. People born under this sign (which is ascendant between March 21 and April 20) are courageous, active and amorous but can also display egotistical, destructive and impatient characteristics. The sigil of Aries represents the ram's head and horns but can also signify a human **head** and nose.

Taurus *Above*

The sign of the **bull**, Taurus is a fixed, feminine, **earth** sign ruled by **Venus**. It symbolizes fertility, solidity and stubbornness. The second sign of the zodiac, in ancient Greek tradition Taurus (the Latin word for bull) represented life, as bulls were once sacrificed in fertility rites. Like the bull, Taureans (born between April 21 and

May 21) are patient, strong-willed and tenacious but can have a tendency toward obstinacy, possessiveness and sensuality. The sigil of Taurus can represent either the bull's head and horns or the human throat and larynx; it is, moreover, reminiscent of the full and crescent **moons**—both signifying fertility.

Gemini *Above*

The third sign of the zodiac is Gemini, the sign of the twins (in Latin, *geminus* means twins), representing duality. It is a mutable, male sign of the **air**, in which **Mercury** is ascendant. In Greco-Roman mythology, Kastor and Polydeukes (Castor and Pollux) were the immortal sons of Zeus (Jupiter). When Kastor died, Polydeukes pleaded to die too, and **Zeus** reunited them in heaven. Gemini is regarded as a sign of the intellect, and the positive characteristics which those born under this sign (between May 22 and June 21) can exhibit include communication skills, versatility and compromise. They can also suffer from the traits of contradiction, confusion and immaturity. Gemini's sigil represents two people holding hands, signifying the duality of opposites such as black and white, male and female, life and death, good and evil, negative and positive. But, because the sigil is joined,

it also represents the doubling of power achieved though unity.

Cancer *Below*

Cancer (which is the Latin word for crab) is a feminine, cardinal, watery sign under the influence of the moon. The constellation emulates the crab's sidling gait by moving sideways toward the south. In Greek mythology it was placed in the heavens by the mother-goddess, Hera, as a reward for nipping Herakle's foot. Those born under the fourth sign of the zodiac (between June 22 and July 22) are sensitive, traditional and nurturing, but they may also be over-protective, too emotional and highly opinionated. Cancer's sigil can be interpreted in numerous ways: as the crab's pincers, as its lopsided movement, or as combining the masculine and feminine principles. In ancient belief, Cancer was the "gate of men"—*Janus inferni*—through which the soul enters the body.

Leo *Above*

Leo, named by the Latin word for **lion**, is the fixed, fiery, cardinal, masculine fifth sign of the zodiac, ruled by the **sun**. It was said to have been placed in the heavens by **Zeus** after Herakles strangled the Nemean lion. Leos (born between July 23 and August 23) are regarded as being natural leaders as they are brave, generous, creative, energetic and strongminded; conversely, they can tend toward pride, vanity and autocratic behavior. Because it is dominated by the sun at its most powerful, Leo represents the center of life. Its sigil depicts the link between divinity and humanity, but it can also be seen as a lion's mane or tail or as a corruption of the initial letter of Leo's Greek name (*Leon*), *lambda*, or L.

Virgo *Above*

Virgo is the sign of the virgin (its name is Latin for virgin): it is a mutable, feminine, **earth** symbol and is ruled by **Mercury**. In Greek mythology, Astraea, the goddess of innocence and justice, was transformed into this constellation. It could also represent fertility goddesses such as Demeter, and it was said that deities were born under this sign. It is a sign of discrimination, for the virgin considers no man good enough for her. Because Virgo is governed by Mercury, it can symbolize the hermaphrodite. Traditionally introverted, those born under the sixth sign of the zodiac (between August 24 and September 23) are considered analytical, precise, orderly and moderate but can also be overcritical, pedantic and nervous. Virgo's sigil is variously regarded as symbolizing celestial wings, a woman holding a **wheat** sheaf, female genitalia or the head and body of a **snake**. Further, it could be considered a monogram of the first three letters for the Greek word "virgin"—*Parthenos* (*pi, alpha,* and *rho*—PAR), or the initials MV, signifying the **Virgin Mary** (*Maria Virgo*).

Libra *Right*

Libra represents the balance, or scales, and is a masculine, cardinal, **air** sign in the house of **Venus**. It is the seventh sign of the zodiac and signifies justice and harmony. The scales must be kept perfectly balanced, however, otherwise the good contained in one or the evil of the other will prevail. In Ancient Greece the constellation was considered to be the claws of **Scorpio** or the scales of justice held by Astraea, but the modern sign is drawn from its presence during the **fall** equinox, when night and day last for an equal amount of time. Librans (born between September 24 and October 23) can be gentle, balanced and observant yet self-centered, indecisive and lazy. Libra's sigil represents either two balances or the sun sinking into the horizon; in addition, the lower line can signify worldly existence and the upper, spiritual power.

Scorpio *Below*

The venomous scorpion is the eighth zodiacal sign of Scorpio (named from the Latin word); a fixed, feminine and watery sign ruled by **Mars** and **Pluto**, it can signify death. In Greek mythology the boastful Orion was stung by a scorpion, which **Zeus** then placed among the stars; Scorpio was also occasionally symbolized by an **eagle**, **phoenix** or **serpent**. Those born between October 24 and November 22 are characteristically determined, forceful and self-disciplined, but these positive qualities can be overshadowed by those of envy, cruelty and destructiveness. The sigil of Scorpio is said to symbolize the male genitals or the scorpion's legs and stinging tail.

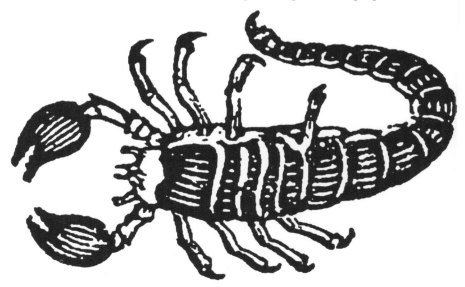

Capricorn *Right*
The tenth zodiacal sign, the **goat** Capricorn, is a cardinal, female, **earth** sign ruled by **Saturn** and represents order and stability. According to the tradition of Ancient Greece, Pan transformed himself into a goat to escape Typhon, thus becoming half goat and half fish, and was then made a constellation by **Zeus**. Its name is a composite of the Latin words for goat (*caper*) and horn (*cornu*). Those born under this sign (between December 22 and January 20) are ambitious, practical, cautious and scholarly, but these qualities can be twisted into those of intransigence, lack of sympathy and selfishness. The sign was once represented by Capricornus, the mythological goat-fish, and the sigil reflects this fabulous creature's dual realm by representing earth and sea. It can also be interpreted as being the horn of a goat and the coiled tail of a **fish**, or the first two letters—*tau* and *rho*—of the Greek word for goat, *tragos*. Capricorn is the "gate of the gods"—*Janua coeli*.

Aquarius *Below*
Aquarius is the eleventh sign of the zodiac and is symbolized by the water-carrier. It is a fixed, masculine, **air** sign, governed by **Saturn** and **Uranus**. The **water** (*aqua* in Latin) being poured signifies the water of knowledge but also creation and destruction—in Sumerian belief, it was decanted onto earth by the

Sagittarius *Above*
Sagittarius is personified in the zodiac by the centaur bearing a **bow and arrow** (its name is the Latin word for mounted archer). It is a masculine, mutable, **fire** sign, dominated by **Jupiter**. The ninth sign represents the perfect man: a combination of animal and spiritual power and divine potential. Chiron, the immortal centaur who was killed by Herakles' poisoned arrow, represents man's animal and spiritual nature, and his bow and arrow stand for power and control (because the arrow is pointed at the perfect angle). In general, Sagittarius is a symbol of higher **wisdom** and philosophical thought. Sagittarians (born between November 23 and December 21) are purposeful, optimistic, adventurous and loyal but can also be fanatical, unrealistic and impatient. The sigil of Sagittarius is an iconic arrow and bowstring, signifying the mundane and temporal basis from which spiritual inspiration may rise.

sky god, An. Aquarians (born between January 21 and February 19) are said to be honest, sociable and liberated, and are imbued with a love of learning; on the other hand, they can be irresponsible and reticent. The two wavy lines of the sigil can symbolize life-giving water, the stirred-up waters of the **unconsciousness**, the flood which heralds the end of a cycle or the **serpents** of wisdom.

Pisces *Below*
A pair of **fish** signify the twelfth zodiacal sign of Pisces (from the Latin), a mutable, female, **water** sign in the houses of **Neptune** and **Jupiter**. The ancient Greeks believed that Aphrodite and Eros transformed themselves into fish to escape Typhon and were then commemorated in this form in the sky. Because they point in opposite directions, the fish represent the past and future and the end of the zodiacal cycle, looking toward the next. Pisceans, whose sign is ascendant between February 20 and March 20, are regarded as intuitive, adaptable and sensitive, yet they can sometimes display insecurity, ambivalence and dreaminess. The sigil of Pisces is a clear representation of the two conjoined fishes. On a more profound level, they are said to symbolize the human and cosmic worlds bridged by the **earth**, human and spiritual nature and involution and evolution.

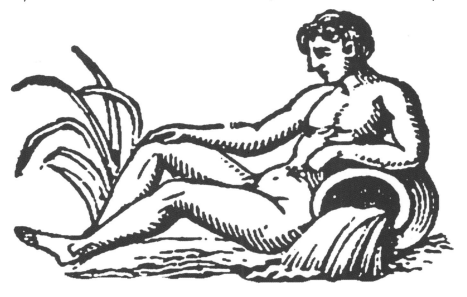

The Chinese Zodiac

Horse *Right*

The horse of the Chinese zodiac (the seventh sign, which corresponds to Libra), personifies grace and ardor. Because horses are intelligent, this sign is one of logic and practicality. The year of the horse signifies adventure and tension.

Tiger *Above*

In Chinese tradition, **Buddha** invited every animal to spend New Year with him; only twelve appeared, however, so he decreed that a year would be named after each of these faithful creatures. Humans born in the year of these chosen animals are regarded as sharing their characteristics. To the Chinese, the tiger is king of the animals, and the third sign of the Chinese zodiac (which equates to **Gemini**) is thus one of courage. Those born under this sign are seen as brave, passionate and audacious; conversely, they are sometimes rebellious, reckless and unpredictable. The year of the tiger is believed to be marked by upheaval, diplomatic incidents and war, but it can be a good year for auspicious change and inventive ideas. The zodiacal tiger is associated with wood, **winter** and the east, as well as with **lightning**.

Dragon *Below*

The dragon is a potent Chinese symbol of luck, and those born in the year of the dragon are considered to be charismatic, generous, strongminded and protective. More negatively, however, they can be selfish, intolerant and demanding. The fifth beast of the Chinese constellations corresponds to **Leo** and is linked with the east, the color blue-green and the rain of **spring**. Although the year of the dragon can bring setbacks, it is a good year for marriage and children, financial matters and ambitious schemes.

Snake *Left*

People born in the year of the snake—the sixth sign of the Chinese zodiac—are believed to be blessed with **wisdom**, which can, however, be transmuted into base cunning. They are considered aggressive, humorous and to possess powers of healing but may be jealous and show signs of duplicity. In Chinese astrology, the snake corresponds to the south, fire and **spring**. It is the equivalent of **Virgo**. The year of the snake is one of contrasting fortunes: thus, while prospects for business negotiations and romance may be favorable, scandals and surprises are also likely.

Monkey *Above*

The monkey is the ninth beast of the constellations that shelter under the twelve celestial branches of the Chinese year tree. Humans associated with this sign are said to be ingenious, curious, diplomatic and well-organized, but these admirable traits can be transformed into laziness, egotism and secrecy. This zodiacal sign (equivalent to **Sagittarius**) is equated with metal and **summer**, and the year of the monkey promises an entertaining period of fantasy and optimism, in which difficult projects may be carried though successfully.

The other signs of the Chinese Zodiac are: Rat, Ox, Rabbit, Goat, Cock, Dog and Pig.

Alchemy

Androgyne *Above*

Mercurius, or **Mercury**, is one of the most important symbols of alchemy. In their search for spiritual enlightenment, alchemists sought to transform elemental matter (*materia prima*) into perfection. Mercury (quicksilver) was crucial as the transforming agent in this process, bringing together opposing forces. The hermaphrodite figure (also known as the Androgyne), shown here standing on the **sun** and the **moon** (the male and female elements), represents the ephemeral.

Fire *Below*

The adherents of this early form of scientific philosophy regarded fire as the central element. It is considered both a unifying and stabilizing force, and most alchemical practices begin and end with fire. It is symbolized by an upward-pointing **triangle**, signifying rising flames, and hence solar power and life. In alchemy fire is contrasted with **water**.

Water *Right*

Emphasizing its opposition to water, the alchemical sign for water is the sign of fire inverted and can signify a cup ready to receive water. It is lunar rather than solar. When the two opposing symbols are interlocked, the union of the contrasting elements of fire and water is attained, creating "fluid fire" or "fiery water." Alchemists considered the elemental pairs of **triangles** as representing the *forma* (essence) and *materia* (substance), and hence the spirit and soul of everything in existence.

Air *Above*

The alchemical sign for air is a **triangle** whose apex points upward, its upper part crossed through by a **horizontal line** (although sometimes the tip is removed). The symbol is reminiscent of that of fire and represents passive heat, from which its association with air is derived. In alchemical thought, air is in constant opposition with **earth**.

Earth *Above*

Demonstrating the connection by opposition of the two elements, the alchemical symbol for earth is that of the air, but inverted. Composed of a **horizontal line** (which can sometimes cut off the apex) placed across the **triangle** signifying water, the earth sign thus represents stagnant **water**, which eventually solidifies into matter.

Mercury, Sulphur and Salt *Below*

The triple-headed **dragon** illustrated here is drawn from a seventeenth-century alchemical treatise. Each of its heads is marked with an alchemical symbol: mercury, representing the ephemeral (*spiritus*); sulphur, symbolizing fiery energy and the soul (*anima*); and salt, which signifies the corporeal (*corpus*). These three alchemical "philosophical" elements were the most important components of the "first material" (*materia prima*), which could potentially be transformed into the philosopher's stone (*lapis philosophorum*)—the stone of **wisdom**. This concept also has macrocosmic significance. Fiery, solar sulphur was believed to be in constant opposition to volatile, lunar mercury, but they could be reconciled by alchemy, and the salt would then act as a preservative. When combined in the body of the dragon, all three elements serve as a reminder that success depends on a harmonious three-fold solution. The dragon is therefore a symbol of the balance that results in the ultimate perfect union (*coniunctio*), for which man and alchemist alike should strive.

Secret Societies

Rose Cross *Below*

Combining the symbols of Christ's resurrection and redemption, the Rose Cross (also known as the Rosicrucian or Rosy Cross) was originally the emblem of the Society of the Rose Cross, a religious sect founded in 1484. From the seventeenth century, however, the emblem was adopted by the secret society of philosophers interested in alchemy and mysticism, who interpreted the Rosy Cross as the blood of Christ spilled on the cross. The symbol can also signify divine light shining down upon an earthly world of suffering and sacrifice, as well as Christ and the **Virgin Mary** and regeneration.

Masonic Compass and Set-square *Above, right*

Freemasonry is a secretive, international, male society believed to originate from the time of the building of Solomon's temple, but which in its modern form dates from the eighteenth century. It combines religious symbolism with that of building, workmanship and light. Its aim is the "world union of light," by means of self-improvement with "stone-masonry work" and the construction of the "temple of humanity." Thus masonic symbols combine religious imagery with the instruments of construction and architecture, such as compasses, trowels, hammers and T- or set-squares. A pair of compasses can be related to the letter

A, itself a symbol of the beginning of all things. Because they are used in geometric calculations and architecture, they also symbolize the act of creation and the spirit. God is likened to the architect and master-builder of the universe. Perfect right angles can only be drawn with a set-square (T-square or mason's square), and so it is a symbol of uprightness, lawfulness and the earth. Both the compass and mason's square are instruments of measurement and thus represent judgment. As well as having resonance in the symbolism of Freemasonry, compasses and the mason's square were the emblems of the Chinese emperor Fu Hsi, a bountiful ruler and inventor. These instruments also represent the liberal art of geometry and the union of sky (the **circle**) and earth (the **square**). The letter G, from which radiates spiritual light, stands for God, geometry and geomancy.

Masonic Hammer *Right*

Like the **compasses**, the hammer can be equated with construction and with the creative act—in a cosmic as well as a mundane sense. Shown here with compasses (symbolizing the spirit) and set-square (signifying rectitude), the powerful

arm wielding the hammer symbolizes the mind's strength directed toward the achievement of reason. The compass angle is likened to levels of spiritual development, and specific angles carry symbolic meanings: 90°, for example, symbolizes spiritual and material harmony. Furthermore, the relation of compasses and set-square to each other is also important: when they are crossed (as here), base matter and higher spirit are combined and balanced; when the compasses are shown over a set-square, mind is dominating matter, and vice versa when the positions are reversed.

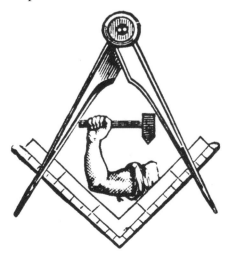

THE MAGICIAN

Tarot

Magician/Juggler *Above*
The Magician (sometimes called the Juggler) is one of the twenty-two major arcana of the Tarot, an esoteric system of

THE HANGED MAN.

divination. Set before him are a cup, **swords**, a pentacle and a **wand**, representing both the four elements of life and the suits of the Tarot. In his hand he brandishes a magic wand, and above his head hovers the sign of infinity. In his positive aspects the Magician symbolizes confidence in life and charm in negotiation; in his negative, the reverse.

Justice *Right*
Like her symbolic counterpart as one of the four cardinal virtues, in Tarot the figure of **Justice** is blindfolded so that her sight will not betray her into prejudgment, and she bears two crossed **swords** of justice (or scales), which signify spiritual enlightenment. Justice is the eighth of the major arcana (although it was once the eleventh until its position was reversed with that of Strength), and is a second-group card. It represents integrity, balance and lack of prejudice; when reversed it symbolizes a false decision, bias and punishment.

Hanged Man *Left*
The Hanged Man is the twelfth card of the major arcana, and its significance is not as sinister as it may initially seem. This Tarot card shows a man hanging by one leg from a crossbeam, whose flowers can equate it with the **Tree of Life**; his other leg is bent at the knee (representing the number **four**—that of completion). His face is surprisingly serene. In some versions coins are depicted falling from his pockets—a symbol of the sacrifice of worldly goods. The Hanged Man belongs to the second group of cards and can be interpreted as denoting spiritual **wisdom**, divination and self-sacrifice in order to attain higher values. Negatively, it represents lack of devotion, selfishness and apathy.

Sun *Right*
Tarot's Sun card almost always bears the positive significance of happiness and success; even when reversed, its portent means only lesser degrees of happiness. The Sun is the nineteenth of the major arcana, a member of the third group and

JUSTICE

is dominated by a figurative solar representation. A child is shown mounted on a **horse**—in many traditions a solar animal—but sometimes twins (or **Gemini**) are depicted, signifying perfect union. Further solar symbols contained in this card are the **sunflowers**.

THE SUN .

Lovers *Below*

The sixth card of Tarot's major arcana, the Lovers, has traditionally been represented in two ways: the first shows a man choosing between two women (one chaste, the other wanton), presided over by an arrow-aiming Cupid. The second portrayal is of a man and woman under the supervision of an androgynous deity and represents the union of masculinity and femininity to create the perfect being. The second concept, depicted here, represents Adam and Eve in the garden of Eden; behind Eve can be seen the serpent lurking in the Tree of Knowledge. The Lovers is one of the first-group cards, representing attraction, a difficult choice (not necessarily in love) and the importance of making the right decision.

Ace of Wands *Above, right*

Tarot's minor arcana are divided into four suits: Cups (Goblets or Coupes), Pentacles (Coins, Deniers, **Circles**, Wheels or Disks), **Swords** (Epées) and Wands (Maces, Batons or Scepters). Each suit is either masculine (Swords and Wands) or feminine (Cups and Pentacles), and represents an element: Cups represent **water**; Swords, **air**; Pentacles, **earth**; and Wands, **fire**. Wands is the first suit. The Ace of Wands card symbolizes fire, and the smoking hand clasping a flowering staff represents strength, creation, birth and fertility.

Divination and Games

Pa Kua *Right*

The Chinese system of pa kua (trigrams) is used for divinatory purposes. It is said that the eight trigrams were revealed to the emperor Fu Hsi (c. 2852 BC) in the patterns of a **tortoise** shell. Yarrow sticks were originally used to represent them. The pa kua are described in *I Ching*, "The Book of Changes," where they appear grouped around the **yin-yang** symbol and represent the ever-changing elements of the **universe** and their interaction. Each trigram consists of a different combination of three lines that denote either the positive and active masculine (yang) or the negative and passive feminine (yin) principles. The lines may be broken in the center (yin), or continuous (yang). Each represents a personal characteristic, a body part, a time, a number, an element, a planet, a color, a direction and an animal. These eight trigrams are multiplied by eight to produce the sixty-four hexagrams (koua) from which interpretations of human situations are made and the future predicted. Arranged in an octagon (whose circumference represents time, and contents space), the trigrams are read anticlockwise and from top to bottom. Trigrams once decorated the clothing of temporal and spiritual leaders and, like the yin-yang sign, they can be used as amulets. The names and significance of the hexagrams pictured here are as follows: *Ki Tsi* (setbacks caused by the ignorance of subordinates); *Ta Kuo* (a dangerous position); *Lu* (travel or homelessness); *Li* (the necessity of behaving correctly); *Hang* (a happy marriage); *Pi* (deceptive appearances); *Kwan* (the need for objectivity); *Yi* (success and travel); *Tsui* (a political encounter); and *Kan* (a military retreat).

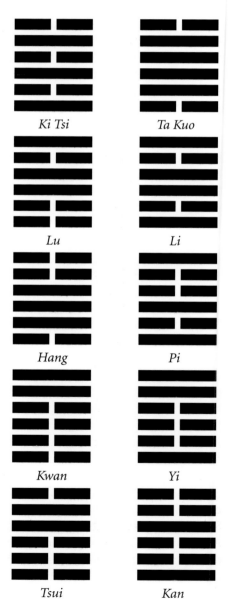

Ki Tsi *Ta Kuo*

Lu *Li*

Hang *Pi*

Kwan *Yi*

Tsui *Kan*

Playing Cards

Playing Cards *Right*
Although their significance is less profound and esoteric than that of **Tarot** cards, playing cards are nevertheless symbolic and are sometimes used in fortune-telling. Each suit of cards has its own significance, as have the thirteen cards contained within the suit. The four suits of playing cards together represent the four elements of the **earth**, winds, **seasons** and cardinal directions. The thirteen cards of each suit represent the thirteen lunar months. Together the cards make up a detailed allegory of the universe. They collectively represent life—with all its joys and woes—and the struggle of opposing forces for victory. The fifty-two playing cards together represent each day of the year. They originated in Central Asia, then spread to India and to fourteenth-century Europe. Playing cards in general are an attribute of vice personified, and symbolize a wasted life (as they do in representations of the deadly sin of sloth).

Hearts *Above*
With its fellow red suit of Diamonds, Hearts symbolize the warm seasons of **spring** and **summer** and contain the powers of light. Hearts are a sign of the center both of life and the world. Linked with Tarot's **Cups**, Hearts represent knowledge, watery creation, love, fertility and the chalice. The King of Hearts symbolizes water and Neptune; the queen, love and goddesses of love such as Venus; while the knave represents the god of war, Mars. In fortune-telling, Hearts signify joy.

signify **fire**, energy and will, as well as wealth, work and luck. The King of Clubs is likened to **Zeus**, the queen to Hera and the knave to Apollo. In divination, any card in the suit of Clubs generally represents happiness.

Diamonds *Below*
Along with Hearts, the suit of Diamonds symbolizes the seasons of warmth and light. The Diamond represents feminine power, in contrast to the Club. As with the other suits, each card has its own meaning, and the court cards are particularly significant: the ace represents the single entity, the king the spirit and father, the queen the soul and mother, the jack the ego and the joker the ethereal. These interpretations are carried further with each suit: the King of Diamonds is the king of **fire**; the queen represents the fuel which feeds fire; and the knave is a warrior. Diamonds can be associated with the Tarot Pentacles suit signifying earthly matter, money, courage and energy. In fortune-telling they foretell spitefulness and annoyance.

Spades *Above*
Along with the black suit of Clubs, Spades—whose symbol signifies a leaf, or the cosmic tree, and thus life—represent the cold seasons of fall and winter as well as the power of darkness. Spades can be compared with the **Swords** (of which they are additionally an iconic representation) of Tarot, and can variously symbolize intellect, action, **air**, destiny and (particularly in association with the Ace) death. The King of Spades is equated with **Saturn**, the queen with war and Pallas Athena and the knave with **Mercury**. In divination, as well as representing death, clubs can bring unhappiness, illness and financial ruin.

Clubs *Above*
Clubs (or trefoils) are black and, along with Spades, represent **fall**, **winter**, night and darkness; they are a symbol of the male principle, in opposition to Diamonds. Like the Wands of Tarot, Clubs

Chess

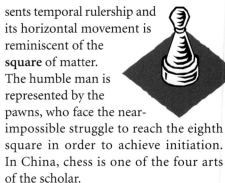

With its checkered board and black-and-white (or sometimes red-and-white) opposing armies, the game of chess symbolizes a clear-cut battle for domination between opposing forces such as good and evil, death and life, light and dark, heaven and earth. As playing requires intelligence and foresight, chess can also signify cosmic reason. Because the moves of the specific pieces within the boundaries of certain squares are exclusive to them, the game can, moreover, represent the dynamism of time and space. Chess carries differing symbolism in various cultures: the Western game is based on the hierarchy of the medieval royal court, for example, while in India the pieces represent the caste system. To the Chinese, the king is at the center of his world—here, too, the game is one of government and of the bitter struggle to impose order (involving sacrifices on both sides), played out on the battlefield of a chessboard. The round board of India symbolizes the round of existence within which man moves of his own free will—to disaster or victory—as he does on the conventional square board. In general terms, the king of either color represents the **sun**, the **heart** and ultimate rulership, while the queen (or vizier) is the **moon** and the spirit, with freedom of movement. The bishop (or **elephant** in the Spanish and Arabic game) signifies spiritual

rulership; his diagonal moves symbolize the intellectual path on white squares and the devotional way on black. The knight is an initiate, and his L-shaped movements represent the jump of intuition. The castle (also known as the rook—from the Arabian roc—or chariot in Spain) represents temporal rulership and its horizontal movement is reminiscent of the **square** of matter. The humble man is represented by the pawns, who face the near-impossible struggle to reach the eighth square in order to achieve initiation. In China, chess is one of the four arts of the scholar.

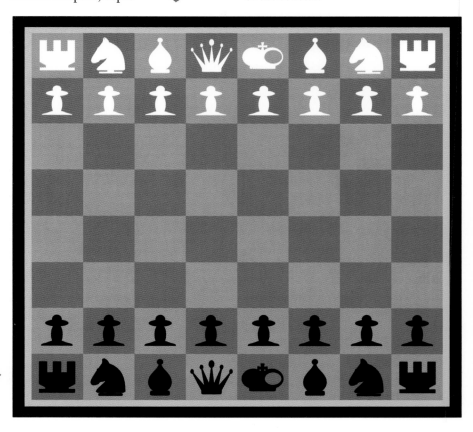

Shapes

Circle *Above*

Although an apparently simple sign, the circle is a universal symbol rich in meaning. The circle, which has neither beginning nor end, represents a never-ending cycle and is thus the primary symbol of eternity (as is the related ouroboros **snake** symbol). It can also signify the cosmos, divinity, unity, perfection and life. In Ancient Egypt, as well as in many other cultures, the circle, which echoes the solar disk in shape, represented the **sun** god and was a sign of the divine presence. Stone circles, such as England's Stonehenge, are believed by some to have been centers of sun worship. In some interpretations, the central point in a circle represents the center of infinity or the cosmic origin (and is also the symbol of the sun and gold). The circle's similarity with the sun also makes it a sign of life. Inherent in its shape is an implication of a dynamic, endlessly turning motion, which equates the circle with time and with the relentless rules of cosmic law. Because it resembles the numeral "0," it is a sign of embryonic potential that has yet to be realized. In many Eastern traditions, including Islam, the circle symbolizes heavenly perfection. In China, the white circle signifies **yang** and represents both masculinity and heavenly energy. As a **magic circle**, the shape has great protective power in occult practices and is also important as a meditational symbol (see, for example, in **mandalas**). In psychological interpretation, the circle represents the ideal self which has achieved the perfect balance.

Spiral *Right*

Like most shapes, the spiral is an ancient symbol redolent with profound symbolic interpretations. Because it resembles the movement of waves and **water** and is an ideogram of **thunder** and lightning, it was once regarded as a sign that emanated life and considered a conduit through which all energy—physical or spiritual—flows. The spiral can be both lunar and solar, for it signifies the phases of the **moon** and the rising, setting and generative power of the **sun**. In Celtic tradition, the spiral was an important symbol of fire, although many other cultures equated it solely with water (perhaps due to the spiral curve of sea shells). As a result of all these associations, the spiral was generally been considered a potent fertility symbol and was often likened to the womb. In common with the circle, the spiral shares the symbolism of continuity and cyclical movement, but it also signifies involution and evolution: while it contains elements of the old order, it branches out into new spheres and thus represents change and development. Its form further equates it with the whirlwind, itself reminiscent of the breath of life, thus identifying it as a dynamic creative force. In addition, in association with the **labyrinth**, its winding shape can represent a mystery which the initiate can only discover by following its sinuous path.

Square *Overleaf*

The square stands in direct contrast to the circle, both in shape and interpretation. While the dynamic circle is considered to represent the celestial and cosmic, the static square signifies matter and earth. Because it is a perfectly balanced shape, however, it is a positive symbol. The square's primary symbolism is that of the earth. With its **four** equal sides, it can also signify stability—the collective balance of the elements, seasons and cardinal directions, otherwise always in opposition, are all associated with the number four. For this reason, the square is perhaps the most important of all Hindu symbols, signifying the anchor that assures the order of the universe— a function it performs in the traditions of many other cultures, too, including

those of China and Christianity. To the ancient Egyptians, the square represented achievement. In the Orient, in contrast to the **yang** circle, the square symbolizes **yin** and femininity. According to Jung, the psychological definition of the square is that of earthly reality and of a personality that has yet to integrate all its facets fully. The square can also signify dependability, honesty and integrity.

Triangle *Right*
Just as the square is inextricably linked with the number four, the triangle's symbolic importance lies in its **three** sides. three is an important cosmic number signifying a multitude of triads, including birth, life and death; heaven, earth and man; body, soul and spirit; father, mother and child. In Ancient Egypt, by combining will, intelligence and capacity to love, it represented man's soul. In Judeo-Christian iconography, the equilateral triangle symbolizes the **Holy Trinity**—the three-in-one. Linked to this concept is the isosceles triangle (the luminous delta) that represents the cosmos, at whose center is the omniscient **eye of God**. Two triangles make up the **Seal of Solomon**, which represents the union of opposites; this is also a central feature of the Buddhist **Sri-Yantra**, a complex meditational symbol. Like the ancient Egyptians, the Mayans built stepped pyramids with temples at the apex. The pyramids represent the cosmic mountain. The triangle is the sign of **fire** (or masculinity) when its apex points upward and, when inverted, it signifies the opposite element

of **water** (and femininity). It can also be seen as an ideogram for aspiration, graphically representing the struggle to climb the sides of the triangle in order to reach its top and thus achieve either one's earthly ambition or a heavenly ascent.

Horizontal Line *Above*
Like its counterpart the vertical line, the horizontal line seems an uncomplicated symbol. Its appearance, however, is deceptive. Its most important significance is as a symbol for the **earth**, the horizon or the base. In contrast to its vertical opposite, the horizontal line represents the temporal world and rational thought, and is a passive and static sign. In China, however, it is a **yang** symbol denoting active, masculine power. The **cross** combines the opposing elements contained in horizontal and vertical lines, uniting them into a harmonious and powerful whole. In mathematics, a short horizontal line between elements indicates deducting the latter from the former— and the line carries several other specialized mathematical meanings. A combination of horizontal lines form the basis of the Chinese I Ching divinatory trigrams and hexagram.

Vertical Line *Right*
The vertical line may seem merely a simple stroke, yet it is full of symbolic meaning—and not just because it is a vital component of many other geometrical signs. It can be likened to the *axis mundi* which links the **earth** to the heavens and, indeed, to any other crucial link between lower and higher orders. It represents the spiritual plane and imaginative fantasy. In its similarity to the letter "I" and numeral "1," it represents the self and also paramount importance, thus also representing authority and absolute power. In logic, the vertical line represents demarcation; in mathematics, division.

Mandalas and Yantras

Mandalas *Right*

The mandala (Sanskrit for "circle") is an important mystical visual metaphor for the **universe** and existence and is used as a meditational aid in Buddhism and Hinduism. The mandala is a geometric cosmogram whose design can vary, but it is generally based on a **circle** (representing the universe), whose center symbolizes perfection or the tantric world axis, Mount Meru. The center can also be represented by Buddha or by a deity in peaceful or wrathful form. The circle may enclose a **square** (representing the **earth**), which sometimes has four entrances to the cardinal points, one in each of its sides. Whichever combination of shapes is used, each symbolizes different aspects of matter and energy. The mandala is believed to concentrate creative energy within its form. Frequently represented in Chinese, Japanese, Tibetan and Hindu art (such as this cloth painting), mandalas are also drawn directly onto walls and were once traced in earth for monastic initiation rites. An early form of mandala was the temple whose architectural layout consists of successive circular and square levels, as seen in the stupas of Borobudur, Indonesia (c. 800 AD). The chakras of kundalini yoga can be represented by a mandala. When used in meditation, the transcendent potential is experienced as a progression from

outer through inner experience to a point of equivalence or unity. Upon ultimate arrival at the center, one may find spiritual fulfillment. Each detail of the mandala is designed to help focus the mind until its true nature is experienced (in Buddhism, as the union of form and emptiness). So sacred is the mandala in the Orient that it is drawn to the accompaniment of specific rituals and can itself be regarded as an object of worship (*puja*). Jung identified the mandala as an **archetypal** symbol of the human quest for perfection—it is now used in psychotherapy as a means of achieving a complete understanding of the self.

Yantras *Left*

The tantric yantras (Sanskrit for "instrument") are variations of mandalas which do not contain lettering or representations of deities. Their geometric symbols mystically represent creation and the interaction of the cosmic and earthly worlds. The most potent yantra is considered to be the Sri-Yantra, which symbolizes the cosmos and consists of a **square** and concentric **circles** which contain **nine** intersecting **triangles**. The shapes signify the respective male and female cosmic aspects of **Shiva** and Shakti. The central point (bindu) represents the absolute.

Greek scripts. Because the scholars who studied it could understand Greek, they were able to decipher the hieroglyphics whose meaning had previously eluded them. The task took over twenty years, however, before Jean-François Champollion finally cracked the code in 1822. The Rosetta Stone can now be viewed in the British Museum in London.

Alphabets

Hieroglyphics *Above and below*
The Egyptian system of writing consisted of three forms: hieroglyphic, hieratic and demotic. Hieroglyphics were by far the most complicated and, because they were considered sacred (as a gift of the god **Thoth**), were mastered only by the priestly caste, for use in religious rituals. As a result of this elitism, when the traditions of Ancient Egypt disappeared, so did the meaning of the hieroglyphics (that is, until the discovery of the **Rosetta Stone**). Over nine hundred hieroglyphics have been identified: most are ideograms and phonograms representing the creatures and plants of the natural world, as well as some man-made objects. Some of these images convey meaning directly, while others (determinatives) have phonetic value. They can be read from right to left, from left to right, or even up and down. The hieroglyphics illustrated here symbolize water, a mouth, twisted flax, a vulture, a snake, a hillside, a flowering reed, a door bolt, a pool and a quail chick.

Rosetta Stone *Below*
An intricately carved basalt slab discovered by Napoleon's army in 1799 in Rosetta, in northern Egypt, the Rosetta Stone provided the key to the decoding of previously enigmatic Egyptian hieroglyphics, a script that became extinct in the fifth century. Inscribed in the reign of Ptolemy V (c. 196 BC), the stone contains parallel columns of text carved in hieroglyphic, Egyptian demotic and

Phoenician Alphabet *Above*
The Phoenician alphabet, the predecessor of Western alphabets such as the Greek and Roman, itself evolved from the very first alphabet, the North Semitic. Unlike modern Western alphabets, however, it was written from right to left and comprised only twenty-two consonant characters. Illustrated here are the characters beth ("B"), mem ("M"), nun ("N") and zayin ("Z"). From the seafaring culture of Lebanon, the Phoenician alphabet was brought to neighboring Greece, where it was modified and added to (with the letters upsilon, phi, chi, psi and omega) to form the Greek alphabet. A good example of Phoenician script can be seen on the Moabite Stone in the Louvre in Paris; dating from the ninth century BC, it tells of the victory of Mesha, the king of Moab, over the Israelites.

αβχδεφγηιφκλμνοπθρστυϖωξψζ

Greek Alphabet *Above*

The Greek letter alpha equates to the "A" of the Roman alphabet, and omega to "Z" (not that omega represents "Z," however: it is the long "O" sound placed at the end of the Greek alphabet to distinguish it from omicron, or the short "O"). Together alpha and omega thus signify the beginning and end of the Greek alphabet. This is their simplistic interpretation, but in Christianity their conjunction is altogether more profound. In the Book of Revelation in the Bible, God states: "I am Alpha and Omega, the beginning and the ending." The two characters were thus established as a symbol of the infinity and totality of God, and, since the early days of Christianity, they have been used as a monogram (sometimes combined with **chi-rho**, cruciform or tau cross) with which to signify both God and Christ. In this context, in Christian art alpha and omega can themselves be symbolized as an **eagle** and **owl**, a bird or **fish** or as day and night. In non-religious translation, the characters can be interpreted in a cosmic sense, denoting the beginning and end of the cycle of time (or of all things in general), which are conjoined to form a continuously rotating **circle** within which everything in the **universe** is contained.

Roman Alphabet *Right and center*

A, B and C are the first three letters of the Roman alphabet and are used together as a convenient contraction with which to symbolize the alphabet as a whole. The expression "ABC" is a childish one, usually used in association with small children when they first learn the sequence of letters in the alphabet.

During times when illiteracy was the norm, people who were unable to spell out their name made their mark on documents such as birth certificates with an X, after which they often then kissed the **cross** as a sign of their sincerity (today

an X is often placed at the end of a letter to represent a kiss). In Christian iconography, X is the first letter (chi) of the Greek name for Christ and is also the saltire cross (*crux decussata*), or cross of St. Andrew, which represents harmony and perfection, as well as being the alternative form of cross upon which the saint chose to be crucified. It also represents the number ten in Roman numeration (which is the perfect number), while in mathematics it denotes multiplication, a Cartesian coordinate and, in algebra, a variable in a function. The letter X can also be an identifying sign which "marks the spot" on maps or postcards. In addition, in contrast to a check (or tick) sign, an X signifies an error, while on road and other signs it warns that something is forbidden or has been canceled. The use of expressions such as "Mr. X" or "Planet X" derives from the letter's significance as an unknown quantity in algebra and in such cases indicates anonymity. For this reason (and also as a continuance of the illiteracy tradition), ballot papers are crossed with an X. A further significance of the letter X is its representation of a

military obstacle or boundary (deriving from its use as such by the Romans).

The character Y is deeply significant, the forked (ypsilon or furka) cross that represents the figure of man. As such, in Pythagorean analogy, while the foot of the Y signifies innocence, the forked arms symbolize the difficult choice which every person must make at some point in their life—whether to follow the good (the right) or evil (the left) path. The Y cross is replicated on clerical vestments and

ABCDEFGHIJKLMNOPQRSTUVWXYZ

objects and, through his highly raised arms, depicts Christ's agony on the cross, as well as the "lifting up of hands" which is a sign of submission before God. Also called the cross of the thieves of Calvary because the thieves who were crucified alongside Christ were said to have been nailed to Y-shaped crosses, the Y cross was used to identify thieves in the Middle Ages. The alchemists used the letter Y as a symbol with which to represent the **Androgyne**. In algebra, *y*, along with *x* and *z*, symbolizes a variable, or unknown, quantity; it is also a Cartesian coordinate denoting values on the vertical axis in graphical representation.

Numbers

According to Pythagoras, who said that "everything is disposed according to numbers," and to Aristotle's statement that they are "the origin and…substance of all things," numbers can be collectively regarded as agents that organize and regulate the universe. Although each number has its own specific significance, in Western cultures the numbers one to ten are regarded as the basis of numerological symbolism, while the Oriental tradition stresses the significance of the first twelve. Numbers can be said to hold the key to the secrets of the universe and to possess magical powers. Although they had great significance before ancient Greek times, systems of esoteric belief (such as **alchemy** and Kabbalism) have placed emphasis on their occult powers since the time of Pythagoras. In general interpretation, even numbers are feminine, negative and passive, while odd numbers are masculine, positive and active. The higher the number, the more complex its significance, because the addition or multiplication of primary numbers incorporates and intensifies their individual meanings. Today numbers are used in onomancy, a system of divination that uses the numerical equivalent of the letters of a person's name to make predictions, and in numerological interpretation.

Zero is the number of potential. It is the point from which all other numbers spring. This significance is underscored by its similarity in shape to the seed, **egg** and womb, each of whose primary importance lies in their fertile possibilities. Because the shape resembles a **circle**, zero symbolizes eternity. However, it can also represent nonexistence and death because of its numerical value.

Just as the first letter of alphabets, such as the Greek alpha, symbolize primal beginnings and creation, so the number one is the numeral of generation. As the point of the mystic center, it is the numeral of creative power or the supreme deity and is thus a symbol of unity, totality and enlightenment. It can also represent the figure of man. In modern terminology the expression "number one" refers to one's own importance as an individual. In Kabbalism, the number one, sephira *Keter* (Crown), represents inspiration.

In its association with the **line**, which has two points, the number two (the binary) represents both balance and the passage of time. The Chinese system of numerology is based on this number, for in Taoist belief the cosmos is made up of two forces—**yin** and **yang**—which, although in opposition to each other, are also complementary. Thus the binary represents the two sexes, although in popular Chinese belief it can also signify an easy life. As in China, in esoteric belief the number two is an ambivalent symbol of duality, embodied in the alchemical **Androgyne** (Hermes or **Mercury**), in the zodiacal sign of **Gemini** and in the two heads of the Roman god **Janus**. Both parts must be perfectly balanced in order to avoid disharmony. However, in Pythagorean belief the binary is the first number of the female principle. As *Hokhmah*, the Kabbalistic sephira, two symbolizes wisdom.

The number three (the ternary) shares the significance of the three-sided **triangle**. It is a self-contained entirety that represents all aspects of creation, therefore constituting a symbol of sacred **trinities** such as those of Christianity and Hinduism. It has cosmic significance as the Taoist triad of man, the earth and the sky and in most cultures also represents the underworld, earth and heavens; birth, life, and death; the past, present and future; or the mind, body and spirit. Three is the basic masculine number but, because it combines and reconciles the numbers one (representing divinity) and two (duality), it can also symbolize the soul. In traditional Chinese belief, the number three (san) is linked with childbirth, and is the numeral associated with endings. To the Kabbalists, the third sephira of the **Tree of Life**, *Binah* (Understanding), signified vitality and intelligence.

The symbolism of the numeral four (the quaternary) is related to the quadrilateral **square**. This numeral is therefore a symbol of order, rationality and symmetry and represents quaternaries such as the cardinal directions, the **seasons**, the elements and the phases of the **moon**. Like the square, the quaternary is a solid, stable number, whose solidity represents both the **earth** and the four-limbed **human body**. As *Hesed* (Mercy) in the Kabbalistic sephiroth, four represents life-giving power.

According to Pythagoras, five is the number of man, who has five fingers, toes and senses, and whose body has four limbs and a head, and can be divided into five equal parts. The ancient Greeks identified five elements that make up man: his body, animal soul, **psyche**, intelligence and divine spirit. The number five is related both to the pentagram and the "golden number" or "divine proportion" that is believed to create architectural harmony. In Kabbalism the sephirotic **Tree of Life** contains five primary numbers, significant because they are divisible only by themselves and the number one, of whose unity they are also a part; *Pechard* (Justice) the fifth sephira, signifies duty and strength. In Hinduism, too, the number five is symbolic, representing the five elements of **fire**, **air**, **earth**, **water** and ether (the quintessence), and it is a symbol of life. Because it combines the numbers two (**yin**) and three (**yang**), in China wu (five) brings good luck. This is reflected in the five felicities: happiness, longevity, joy, wealth and riches.

The number six signifies universal harmony, stability and balance, as reflected in its relationship to the hexagon and Solomon's seal (or the **Star of David**), which combines the union of the triangles of fire and water. Six is regarded as the number of beauty and perfect union in the Kabbalah and is represented by *Tiferet*, the sixth sephira. In China, six signifies longevity and celestial power. In Christian belief, however, six is ambivalent: it is sacred because God created the world in six days, but the Book of Revelation identifies it as the number of evil, and says that the beast of the apocalypse bears the number 666. In modern symbolism, throwing a six in a game of **dice** represents **victory**.

7 Because the number seven (the septenary) combines the ternary and quaternary—heaven or divinity and earth or mankind—it unifies the macrocosm and microcosm and signifies cosmic order. In the Bible, the septenary represents entirety, and governs time and space. The seven "planets" (the **Sun, Moon, Venus, Mercury, Mars, Jupiter** and **Saturn**) were once believed to represent the powers of divinity and nature, to govern the seven days of the week and to symbolize the seven heavens through which the soul had to pass before attaining eternal life. Seven is particularly important in Judaism: the **menorah** has seven branches, the new year begins in the seventh month, and the year of the Sabbath occurs every seventh year. It is ambivalent in Christian tradition, since it is the collective number of both the cardinal sins and virtues and also signifies vengeance. There are seven emblems of **Buddha** in Buddhist belief. In Ancient Egypt, the septenary was a symbol of eternal life; there were seven gods of light and seven of darkness. Moslems believe that there are seven heavens (as do Jews and Buddhists) and hells, seven earths, seven **gates** to paradise and seven prophets, while the Islamic pilgrim must walk round the Ka'aba at Mecca seven times. The septenary is the number of hierarchies, for there are seven colors of the **rainbow** and seven musical notes. In China, qi (seven) is the symbol of woman. To the Kabbalists, the seventh sephira, *Nezah* (Firmness) represents victory.

8 In common with the number four, and because it combines the terrestrial **square** and eternal **circle**, the numeral eight (the octonary) is believed to be an agent of universal order. This is illustrated in the eight-spoked **wheel** of the Buddhist **Dharma Chakra**, the eight petals of the **lotus**, the eight symbols of good augury and the eight paths of Taoism. It is the number of greatness in Japan. The octonary is also important in Hinduism, some of whose gods, including Vishnu, are often represented with eight arms. Indian **mandalas** that are based on multiples of the number eight represent the reflection of the celestial world on earth. In the Kabbalistic sephiroth, *Hod* (Splendor) also represents the cosmic law. The octonary is associated with rebirth because it is the sum of the numbers one (representing divinity), three (signifying the soul) and four (symbolizing the body). Christian baptismal fonts are therefore usually octagonal in shape. Eight is also the number of the initiate who has passed through the seven stages of trial, or the seven heavens, to reach the eighth plane of perfection. In Chinese belief, eight is the number of prosperity.

9 As a triplication of the ternary triad, the number nine represents the powerful triplication of the three worlds and of the body, intellect and soul. It therefore symbolizes eternity, completion and incorruptibility. Its association with the **circle, triangle** and **square** further underlines its synthesizing powers. In Christianity, this numeral represents harmony and divine perfection and is the number sacred to the **Virgin Mary**. In Hebrew belief, nine was the number of truth, while *Yesod* (Victory)—the ninth sephira of the Kabbalistic sephiroth—signifies potential. Jiu (nine) is the number of eternity in Chinese tradition and is a celestial number whose importance outshines all others. Indian **mandalas** based on multiplications of nine symbolize the **universe**.

10 By combining the numbers one and zero—respectively representing divinity and potential—the number ten (the decad) signifies spiritual achievement and a return to unity. In decimal systems, ten symbolizes a new starting point. Because it contains all its preceding numbers, it is additionally a cosmic numeral. In many cultures, including the Oriental, the decad is the number of perfection, and the Pythagorean tetrakis, which combined the numbers one, two, three and four, was regarded as a number of mysterious divine power. The sephirotic **Tree of Life** of the Kabbalah was made up of ten sephira, collectively representing unity, within which *Malkhut* (Kingdom)—the tenth sephira—itself symbolized thought and action.

13 In the Western world, thirteen represents death and is traditionally the unluckiest of numbers—it even arouses panic in triskaidekaphobics (the Greek word for the fear of this number). The conventional explanation for this reputation derives from Christianity: thirteen people (Christ and his twelve disciples) were present at the Last Supper. In France, the number thirteen is known as *le point de Judas*, referring not only to Judas's betrayal of Christ, but also to the fact that he was the first to leave the table and the first to die. In Norse mythology, a banquet was held for twelve gods in Valhalla; when the uninvited Loki (the trouble-making god) appeared, the "good" deity, Baldur, died. The letter "m," the thirteenth letter of the Hebrew alphabet, was believed to bring misfortune as it sandwiched "e" in the Hebrew word for death, *mem*. Today, house numbers or storeys of buildings are frequently euphemized as 12½ or 12A, while Friday the thirteenth is considered especially ominous. Yet thirteen is considered sacred in some Native American cultures, while in Ancient Greece it represented **Zeus**, the thirteenth and most powerful god. The Aztec calendar was divided into thirteen-day periods.

Nature Symbols

Of all symbolic sources, none has provided greater inspiration than the natural world. Its universal constituents, such as the Sun, Moon, stars and planets, flora and fauna and, indeed, the human body, are common to all cultures and to all people.

Since the dawn of humanity, we have gazed up at the sky and pondered the significance of the sun and moon; we have looked around us at the multitude of plant, animal and bird species and wondered about them; and we have regarded each other and considered the purpose of our existence. In trying to find answers to these profound questions, the components of the natural world have been attributed a rich and varied symbolic function that operates at a far deeper level than pure superstition. Indeed, in ascribing significance to the members and phenomena of the natural world, humankind was expressing its belief that each had a part to play in the cosmic drama and that their individual symbolism collectively mirrored and constituted the universal whole.

Predominant in the interpretation of natural symbolism are the concepts of positive masculinity, the sky and light—as epitomized by the sun—in opposition to negative femininity, the earth and darkness—symbolized by the moon. Fauna, in particular, can be categorized as symbolizing either solar or chthonic power, and the eagle and lion are regarded as primary exponents of goodness and solar might, while the slithering snake signifies the powers of darkness and evil. The color of fur or feathers similarly defines a creature's symbolism: a black raven or crow, for instance, is a sinister portent, while a white lamb represents innocence.

Trees have a cosmic significance. Because they are rooted in the ground but rise up toward the sky, they symbolize the *axis mundi* that connects the earth and the heavens. As verdant fruit-bearing vegetation, they can also be collectively identified as the Tree of Life or the Tree of Knowledge. Fruit, flowers and plants are themselves generally regarded as symbols of natural abundance and also of life itself. Like the symbols of animals, birds, marine creatures and insects, however, each tree species has an additional and unique significance that has evolved over centuries of mythological, religious and superstitious belief.

Just as all terrestrial life has been attributed symbolic meaning, so have the celestial planets, which are believed to govern both the constellations and earthly creatures: each has its own sign, role and sphere of influence. The inevitable changing of the seasons—which symbolize primarily the eternal cycle of life, death and rebirth—and the unpredictability and mystery of other natural phenomena have inspired strong emotions of fear and awe. Thunder and lightning, for example, were long considered symbolic manifestations of the wrath of the gods; a rainbow still signifies reconciliation and hope; while clouds and mist represent obscurity.

As will be seen in the following pages, the natural world provides a rich palette for the painting of vivid and universal symbolic images such as these.

Opposite: According to the superstitions of ancient and medieval seafarers, monstrous creatures, intent on destroying ships and consuming their crews, lurked in the deeps. The giant octopus pictured here has malevolently entwined its tentacles round the ship in order to drag it down to its doom on the seabed. It is a terrifying representative of chthonic and underwater might waging a constant, evil battle against both man and the benevolent celestial powers. The octopus's association with hell is further underlined by its practice of squirting black ink.

The Cosmos

The Universe Beyond *Above*
Astronomy and astrology fascinate humans trying to make sense of their position in a microcosm of the great universal macrocosm. When set against the vastness of space—our own galaxy of the Sun, stars, Moon and planets and the infinity beyond—man's significance seems little. From prehistoric times, people have attempted to figure out their place in the scheme of things and their significance in relation to both the **Earth** and space. The cosmic tree, rooted in the earth and rising to the sky, was believed by most cultures to unite Earth and heaven and to symbolize the *axis mundi*. Several philosophies note a parallel in the concept of universal man and according to the Christian theologian Origen: "You are another world in miniature…in you are the sun, the moon and also the stars."

 Sun *Right*
The sun is one of the most important symbols and has res-

onance in all world cultures. As the primary source of light and warmth, the crucial force for creation and maintenance of life, its cosmic, generative role was recognized by the earliest civilizations. Its active energy was regarded as being male and spiritual and, because it is the most powerful and brightest star, it was believed to be the eye of the all-seeing sun god, the universal father; thus it was the "eye" of the Greco-Roman god **Zeus** (Jupiter), the Egyptian god **Horus**, the Hindu Varuna, the Norse god Odin (or Wotan) and the Islamic Allah. Heroic and passionate, male solar divinities were worshipped by the Persians (Mithras), ancient Egyptians (Ra, Horus and Osiris), the Greeks (Helios/

Apollo) and the Romans (Sol). The Incas believed that the Sun was a divine ancestor, and the pharoah of Egypt and the emperor of Japan were also said to be descended from the sun. Although usually male, some traditions, including African, Native American, Maori, Oceanic, Japanese and Germanic, regard the Sun as a female deity. Because it rises in the East and sets in the West, it is a symbol of both resurrection and death. In some traditions, its passage across the sky during the day is likened to a chariot of the gods. The Sun is associated with intelligence and enlightenment: to the Hindus, the Sun is equated with Brahma and Indra and represents man's spiritual self. In alchemy, the Sun corresponds to the intellect and to gold, but, in a belief shared by some Native American cultures, there is also a black sun (*sol niger*), which symbolizes both death and *prima materia*. The rising Sun is a symbol of hope and new beginnings, while a rayed Sun signifies illumination from the center. It is a popular symbol on national flags, appearing on those of Japan, Taiwan, the Philippines and Uruguay. It is also much used in heraldic art:

the depiction shown here is the "sun in splendor" and was the badge of Edward IV of England. The sun's astronomical symbol is believed to be derived from Egyptian **hieroglyphics**, although it was prevalent in a number of ancient cultures. In astrology, the sign can be interpreted as meaning the spiritual consciousness and creative energy of the individual. It is also associated with gold in **alchemy**, annual plants in botany and Sunday.

Moon *Below*
In most cultures, the Moon was regarded as the regulator of natural cycles and time, the passive, feminine counterpart of the Sun. Thus it became a symbol of the lunar consorts of male solar deities. Moon mother-goddesses such as Astarte in Phoenicia, Isis in Ancient Egypt, the Greco-Roman goddesses Hecate and Artemis (**Diana**)—also known as Phoebe, Cynthia, Selene and Luna—and even Christianity's **Virgin Mary**, all have the crescent moon as their attribute. Its appearance at night make it a symbol of the dark and mysterious, and it is widely believed to have power over

humanity's fate. Because of its relationship with natural cycles—especially the tides and menstruation—it signifies **water** and female fertility. It also represents the **unconscious**. Due to its phases of waxing, waning, disappearing for three days and then becoming "new," the Moon is a symbol of the cycle of life, death and rebirth. The round, full moon signifies completeness and unity, the half moon death, the waning moon demonic powers and the crescent and waxing moons resurrection from death, creation and fertility. Generally feminine, in some

African, Native American, Oceanic, Maori and Japanese tribes, however, the Moon is a masculine symbol. Many cultures believe that there is variously a man, a frog, a toad or a hare in the moon. In **alchemy** the Moon—*luna*—is linked with silver and purified emotions. The crescent Moon is the most important symbol of Islam, representing sovereignty and divinity. The Moon is symbolized in astronomy by the new crescent moon—a symbol found in the **hieroglyphic** script of Egypt, as well as in other ancient traditions. Signifying the receptiveness of humanity in astrology, the Moon's astronomical sign was also equated with Monday and alchemical silver.

Star *Below*
In general terms, stars signify divine presence, but of less powerful deities than those of the "king" and "queen" of heaven, the Sun and the Moon. Female deities such as the Babylonian goddess Ishtar (whose emblem was an eight-pointed star), the Phoenician Astarte, the Egyptian **Isis** or Christianity's **Virgin Mary** (*Stella Maris*) are often represented with a crown of stars as queens of heaven. Because they light up the dark night sky, stars—"eyes of the night"—signify spiritual enlightenment and wisdom, as well as human aspiration. Some cultures, moreover, believe that stars are the souls of the dead. Fiery and unpredictable, comets have been regarded as portents of doom and disruption and as a signal of the anger of the sun god. Stars of various forms appear on the national flags of a quarter of the nations of the world.

Planetary Symbols

Mercury *Above*
In Greco-Roman mythology, Mercury (Hermes) was the winged messenger of the gods who carried the **caduceus** staff. Mercury's astrological symbol is therefore a graphic representation of the caduceus. To alchemists, the sign was that of the **Androgyne** and represented the element of mercury (or quicksilver), and today it signifies biological hermaphrodites. In astrology, it is the sign of the intellect.

Venus *Above*
The planet Venus—the Morning Star—is named after the Roman goddess of love and beauty, and the astronomical symbol is believed to represent her necklace or mirror. The horizontal cross bar was added in the sixteenth century. To alchemists, this sign symbolized copper, while in astrological interpretation, it is a sign of the benefactor. The Venus sign also represents Friday and in biology it indicates **femininity**.

Earth *Above*
Earth can be represented by two symbols: either a **cross** enclosed by a circle or a **circle** surmounted by a cross. The circle enclosing the cross is believed to be an ancient **sun** or **wheel** cross and represents Earth and the points of the compass. The cross surmounting the circle signifies the orb of a ruler. Both signs came into use in the sixteenth century and signify the globe of Earth dominated by Christianity. This symbol can additionally represent churches on maps.

Mars *Above*
The red planet was named by the Romans after their god of war, and the astronomical symbol of Mars portrays his **shield** and **spear**. The symbol represents Tuesday. It was adopted by alchemists to represent iron, and in astrology, it represents the aggressive ego. It is also the biological sign of **masculinity**.

Jupiter *Above*
Jupiter is the largest planet and so was named after the supreme Roman god,

Jupiter (**Zeus** in Ancient Greece). The astronomical symbol is composed of the letter Z (the initial Greek letter—zeta—of Zeus) with a cross bar. In astrology it can represent the soul supported by matter (the cross). The symbol signifies tin in alchemy, perennial flora in biology and Thursday.

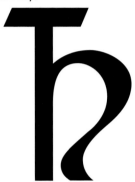

Saturn *Above*
The Romans equated Saturn with the Greek god, Cronos. Because Saturn orbits the Sun every twenty-nine years, a human might see it only two or three times. Thus it came to represent death, and Saturn's astronomical symbol consists of Cronos's **sickle** (or scythe). To astrologists, the sign symbolizes the soul's domination by matter and therefore sorrow. This sign signifies lead in alchemy, treelike plants in biological representation and Saturday.

Uranus *Above*
Uranus was only discovered in 1781 by an Englishman, Sir William Herschel, who named it after the Greek god of heaven. The planet was originally represented by the symbol shown here (which could also represent morning), but, because it was considered too similar to that of **Mars**, it has been replaced in gen-

eral usage by a sign which is a graphic shorthand for "Herschel's planet" in tribute to its discoverer: a planetary orb bisecting the initial letter, H.

Neptune *Above*
Despite its Roman name, Neptune was unknown until 1846, when it was discovered by the German astronomers Johann Galle and Heinrich d'Arrest. Neptune was originally symbolized by the initials L and V (after Urbain Le Verrier, who had calculated the planet's position, but had been beaten to its discovery). It is now represented by **Neptune's trident**. In astrology, it is the sign of both the escapist and the idealist.

Pluto *Below*
The planet Pluto was named after the Greek god of the underworld, who was also known as Hades. Its symbol has the dual significance of representing the first two letters of the planet's name and the initials of the American astronomer, Percival Lowell, who first predicted its existence in 1905—twenty-five years before its discovery in 1930. To astrologists, the symbol represents the subconscious, death and rebirth.

Weather

Rain *Above*

Rain is a universal symbol of the life-giving bounty of the gods and of fertility (the rain drops of the sky god were believed to fertilize the earth). Rain thus represents life but also purification, both because it falls from heaven and because it shares the cleansing properties of **water**. In a related concept, a deluge can be interpreted as the sky god's wrathful determination to purify a corrupt world. The expression "raining cats and dogs" derives from the medieval belief that these creatures were the **familiars** of **witches** and possessed the power to make rain. Witches were said to assume their forms when they rode on storms. In Norse tradition, cats were unusually sensitive to changes in the weather and were even said to influence it, while dogs were the messengers of the storm god Odin, heralding wind; therefore, while cats symbolize a downpour, dogs represent the accompanying wind.

Clouds *Above, center*

The symbolism of clouds is of nebulousness, mystery, obscured truth and hidden secrets—the expression "living under a cloud" indicates a personal disgrace. Because clouds can bring **rain**, they can also symbolize nature's bounty and human fertility. The gods of many religions, including those of China and Japan, were believed to live in clouds because clouds obscure the sky and appear to have substance. The gods would sometimes emerge from their clouds to reveal themselves to humans. The Judeo-Christian scriptures say that God occasionally conceals himself from man's view in the clouds, and in Christian iconogra-

phy, God is sometimes represented by a hand emerging from a cloud. It was said that Christ ascended to heaven in a cloud (in later artistic representations this was transmuted into a **mandorla**) and will one day be carried down to earth on one. In Islam, clouds are regarded as a symbol of the sacred mystery of Allah. In China, however, they are equated with the transformation that humans must undergo in order to obtain spiritual enlightenment. The Chinese word for cloud is a homonym for "fortune," and so clouds are regarded as symbols of **good luck**. Also, because they produce rain yet appear solid, they are **yin** and **yang** and a sign of harmony. The ancient Greeks believed that clouds, which resemble the woolen fleeces of **sheep**, were the flock of Apollo, while in Norse mythology, the Valkyries rode on them.

Rainbow *Below*

The elusive, ethereal and transient rainbow, with its beautiful spectrum of colors, is a symbol of the **bridge** or union between heaven and earth. In Norse mythology, for example, it was known as *bifröst* ("the trembling way") and linked Asgard, the abode of the gods, with Midgard (earth). In Ancient Greece, it was an attribute of Iris, the messenger of the gods, as well as of **Zeus** (Jupiter) and Hera (Juno), rulers of the sky. In Judeo-Christian tradition, God placed the rainbow in the sky after the Flood as a sign of deliverance and of God's covenant with humanity. In medieval times, it thus also became an emblem of the **Virgin Mary**, signifying reconciliation. Christ is often depicted enthroned on a rainbow at the Last Judgment, so demonstrating both his heavenly power and his mercy. When portrayed in three colors, the rainbow signifies the **Trinity**. In the Christian context, the rainbow is therefore primarily a symbol of hope, yet in earlier cultures (such as the Babylonian, where it was the emblem of the malicious goddess, Tiran-na, and also in early Hebrew tradition, as recounted in the Jewish Apocrypha),

the rainbow was a symbol of divine wrath. In China, the rainbow signifies the sky **dragon** uniting heaven and earth and also represents the perfect union of **yin** and **yang** (so symbolizing marriage). It can additionally foretell disharmony. In an African tradition echoing that of the Chinese, the rainbow is the sky **serpent** that transmits heavenly energy to earth. Indra's bow is a rainbow in Indian Vedic belief, so the rainbow is a manifestation of the god's divine power. On a spiritual level, both Buddhists and Hindus believe that the rainbow represents transcendence to the highest state of enlightenment before the attainment of nirvana. In Celtic mythology, a crock of gold at the foot of the rainbow awaits a lucky finder: translated into modern terminology, the rainbow can therefore represent an impossible dream.

Lightning/Thunder *Above*
The sizzling flashes of electricity that rend the sky during thunderstorms were understandably regarded with terror and awe by early civilizations, in which lightning and its accompanying rolls of thunder were universally considered as manifestations of the wrath of the gods. Originally an instrument of divine punishment in the ancient religions of the Middle East, in the Greco-Roman pantheon, **Zeus** (Jupiter) wielded the thunderbolt, while in Norse mythology, **Thor** (or Donar) was the god of thunder and lightning whose rolling chariot (pulled by **goats**) caused the noise of thunder and whose hammer, Mjöllnir, produced lightning. In China, the lightning goddess Tien Mu highlighted transgressors with lightning in order to identify them to the god

of thunder, Lei Kung. The Vedic Indra brought rain with his vajra thunderbolt (a sign of truth), as did the storm god, Rudra. As the Buddhist dorje, or vajra, the thunderbolt assumes great importance as a symbol of enlightenment and knowledge and is carried by buddhas and the bodhisattva Vajrapani. The dorje, or diamond mace—a decorated staff with a globe at either end signifying the union of heaven and earth—is used in sacred rituals and represents the male principle and divine truth; with a bell it signals an enlightened mind. Thus, as well as signifying punishment, lightning can also represent creative activity, revelation and spiritual enlightenment. In shamanism, in which lightning is considered a **bridge** between the lower and higher worlds, being struck by lightning denotes initiation, while being killed by lightning guarantees instant transcendence to heaven. In Native American belief, the universal deity, the **Thunderbird**, brings both lightning (by flashing its eyes) and thunder (by beating its wings). **Rain**-bringing lightning is a fertility symbol in Eastern tradition and is portrayed in the shape of a phallus. Lightning can be symbolized by means of an **arrow**, a **trident**, an ax, a hammer, a zigzag or the Chinese *ju-i* and Japanese *nyoi*. The phenomenon of thunder is explained in various ways by different cultures: in Ancient Greece, it was believed to be the bellowing of a **bull**; in

Roman times, it was the voice of **Jupiter**; in China, it is the laughter of heaven and the sound of fire; in Buddhism, it is the sound of the law; while in Germanic tradition, it was caused by rowdy gods rolling barrels across the sky in sport.

Mist/Fog *Below*
The shrouding of the landscape in mist or fog obscures previously familiar landmarks, rendering them hazy and mysterious and filling the viewer with uncertainty. Fog was once believed to be the primeval, chaotic matter from which evolved the "mist of fire" that eventually formed and ordered the universe. In most cultures, fog is a symbol of the indeterminate and of an agent that confuses and hides the truth from the observer. Furthermore, in some religions (including the Judeo-Christian), it is believed that fog is a sign that otherworldly forces are at work; with its dispersal will come a revelation of great magnitude. Because it is a transient phenomenon, it can be regarded as symbolizing a transition from one state to another—this significance is particularly true in association with the initiation rites of some cultures and religions, in which it is believed that the initiate has to pass through darkness and mist before attaining the true and clear light of spiritual illumination. Mist can also signify evolution, for it is formed from the elements of **air** and **water**.

Seasons

Spring

The four seasons can be likened to any cycle of four components, including life, the phases of the **Moon** and the positions of the **Sun**. Spring is a time when living things revive: plants send out new shoots, birds lay eggs, animals emerge from hibernation and man's thoughts turn to love. Spring is therefore a symbol of the renewal of life and of hope for the future. Christians associate it with the resurrection of Christ. In the Middle Ages, man was believed to be governed by four "humors"—bodily fluids whose balance determined character; these were equated to the seasons. Spring was the sanguine humor (denoting blood), which granted an energetic and cheerful disposition. The element of **air** can also be equated with spring, for this season implies freedom and possibilities. In Western tradition, spring is symbolized by a lamb or by the color green. For the Chinese, the color of spring is also green: its symbols are the peony and the cherry, peach and almond blossoms, as well as the green **dragon** that guards the East. The people of eastern Mediterranean countries, too, regard the almond blossom as a sign of spring, for it flowers early; in Western Europe, daffodils and crocuses share this symbolism. In relation to man's life-cycle, spring is likened to infancy.

Summer

Summer is the season in which the wonders of the natural cycle are at their peak: the **sun** shines warmly, flowers are in full bloom, crops are ripening and there is a sense of happiness and well-being. Like the other seasons, summer can be compared to a specific element—in this case, **water**, which creates and sustains life. Various symbols have been used to denote summer: in Greco-Roman tradition, it was Dice (or Demeter/Ceres, who was depicted as crowned with ears of **corn** and carrying a sheaf and **sickle**); in medieval Europe, the solar **dragon** or **lion** and the color yellow were emblems of this season. According to Chinese tradition, the flower of summer is the **lotus**, and the scarlet **phoenix** that guards the South also represents this season. Summer is regarded as being the developmental period of man's life-cycle of approaching one's prime.

Fall/Autumn

Fall is perhaps the most ambiguous of the four seasons: there are reminders of the warmth of the past summer, but its colder days also deliver sharp glimpses of the coming of winter. It is associated with the third age of man's life-cycle, in which it represents maturity. In Greco-Roman imagery, fall was personified by a Hora (or by Dionysus/Bacchus), who is laden with bunches of **grapes** and a cornucopia. In Western cultures, this season is represented by a **hare**. In China, fall is symbolized by the white **tiger** or the **unicorn**-like ky-lin that protects the West, by the color white, the **chrysanthemum** and convolvulus flowers, as well as by the red maple tree. In association with the four elements, fall can be likened to **fire**, as fire consumes the past in preparation for a rebirth.

Winter

Winter comes at the end of the cycle of seasons and is a time of coldness, hibernation and death. It is likened to the fourth and final phase of man's life and symbolizes hopelessness, decrepitude, old age and the inevitability of death. In Greco-Roman art, winter was represented by the bare-headed Irene standing beside a leafless tree, by Boreas (god of the north wind), or Hephaistos (Vulcan). In Western tradition, this season was once symbolized by the cold-blooded **salamander**, but could also be represented by a cloaked old man with frosted hair, as well as by a deer or a wild duck. To the Chinese, the plum, bamboo and pine trees are emblems of winter, as is the guardian of the North, the "dark warrior" **snake** that is coiled around a **tortoise**. Winter can be equated with the element of earth, because in death all living things return to earth (which also stores the seeds of new life).

Biological Symbols

Masculinity and Femininity *Above*
In biology, masculinity is denoted by the astronomical symbol of **Mars** (above, left), the aggressive male counterpart of the female symbol of **Venus** (above, right). These signs have been used to represent masculinity and femininity since the eighteenth century, when the Swedish biologist Carl Linnaeus first adopted them for this purpose.

Hermaphroditism *Above*
Hermaphrodite creatures, such as worms, can be symbolized by two signs. The first (above, left) is also the astronomical sign of the planet **Mercury**, because the Greco-Roman god (Mercury/Hermes) was regarded as being both male and female. The second sign (above, right) is an amalgamation of the signs of masculinity and femininity. Hermaphrodites possess both male and female reproductive organs and, in alchemy, mercury was believed to be the perfect union of opposites including the male and female principles.

Recycling *Above, center right*
This graphic symbol, which consists of three arrows forming a perpetual circle, is the modern symbol for material that

can be recycled for future use. In our environmentally conscious age, we consider it important to be able to reuse materials such as paper and aluminum in order not to deplete the world's natural resources more than is absolutely necessary. This symbol is seen on everyday articles such as plastic and paper packaging and bags.

Ecological Symbol *Below*
Today, a **circle** bisected by a horizontal line is best known as the ideographic symbol for ecology, but this is a much-used sign with multiple meanings. It represents the letter *theta* in the **Greek alphabet** and is one of the alchemical symbols for **salt**. In more recent times, it has been used as the basis of traffic signs that indicate stopping or ending and by adherents of Scientology to signify the individual human spirit. The sign appears in at least ten different symbolic systems of natural science (including that of animal classifications, in which it represents the **egg**). This symbol generally signifies absoluteness, which is perhaps one of the reasons behind its choice as the symbol for ecology; in this case, however, it is differentiated from similar signs by a slight narrowing of the center of the horizontal line.

The Human Body

Eyebrow *Above*
Eyebrows are expressive features and can indicate a range of emotions. Eyebrows are especially symbolic in China, where Chinese Lohans (those who had attained enlightenment) had eyebrows that grow to the ground. The movement of their eyebrows was one of the few ways in which strictly chaperoned Chinese women could express themselves freely; stylized eyebrows (often in the form depicted here) therefore came to symbolize love. In popular Western tradition a man whose eyebrows meet above the nose should not be trusted.

Human Body *Opposite*
The human body was regarded by many ancient traditions as representing the cosmos and life in general and was believed to contain the various stages of creation within it. The gods of most cutures are frequently portrayed in human form, and the figure of "universal man" was thought to reflect the components of the universe: the **head** corresponds to the heavens, breath to the **air**, the abdomen to the sea and the legs to the earth. In China, the human body was regarded as being both **yin** and **yang**, and thus in perfect balance. The human cosmic number is five, for man has five senses, five fingers or toes at the extremities of each limb, and his height and width divide into **five** equal parts; "**cosmic man**" is therefore portrayed in pentagramic form. The human body is both macrocosm and microcosm: while it can represent the universe and all that is in it, each individual has a separate part to play within the great scheme

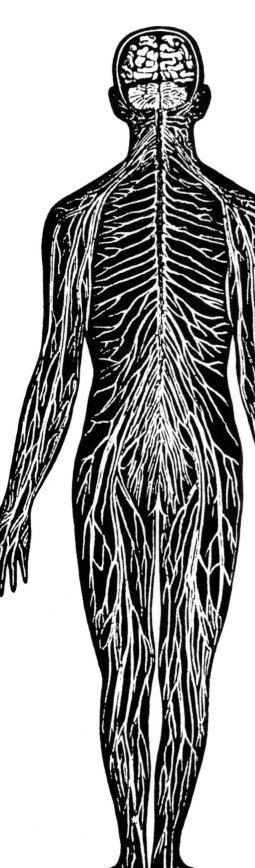

of things. Each part of the body was once believed to fulfill a special purpose beyond its purely biological functions: the heart, for example, was believed to bestow emotions. Following from the belief that man was a cosmic being, it was thought that each sign of the **zodiac** governed a specific part of the body. In medieval analogy, bones (or the body as a whole) were equated with the element of earth, the head (or body heat) with **fire**, the lungs with **air** and blood with **water**. Furthermore, it was believed that man was governed by the four "humors," or bodily fluids, flowing through the body: blood was the basis of the energetic, sanguine humor; gall of the fiery, choleric humor; black gall of the sad, melancholic humor; and phlegm of the calm, phlegmatic humor. Chinese tradition, too, allocated symbolism and influence to each part of the body. In the interpretation of many religions, the human body is regarded as a "temple" of the soul created by their god, whose purpose is to carry out the god's will and to act as a link between the heavenly realm and Earth. Yet although the human body can thus be regarded as a sacred creation, it is simultaneously profane, for man abuses the gift of life and frequently "descends" to the level of the animal world.

Teeth *Right*
Teeth, used for tearing and chewing food, are a clear symbol of animal aggression and strength. Yet as well as representing threat, danger and an intention of at least wounding (and sometimes also devouring), in some situations, bared teeth can also be a signal of defensiveness. In psychoanalytical interpretation, the loss of one's teeth, which leaves one feeling vulnerable and powerless, can thus signify feelings of frustration and helplessness.

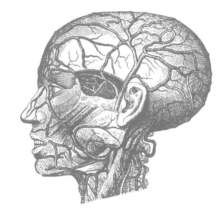

Head *Above*
In the symbolism of most cultures, the head is the most important part of the human body and signifies the life force and the higher self, for it contains the brain—the instrument of reason and of the spiritual and social capacities that distinguish man from beast. Just as important are the head's eyes, nose, ears and mouth, which respectively control the gifts of sight, smell, hearing, taste and speech. Such was the significance of the head as a symbol of life that head-hunting cultures believed the possession of their victim's head would transfer the vitality of the deceased to the victor. It is significant that signs of authority, such as **crowns**, are placed on the head, a practice that reflects the preeminent position accorded to this part of the body. Bowing one's head signifies submission to a higher being, while shaving one's head denotes penitence. Because the head has the power to make the body act either wisely or foolishly, in medieval times, the head was linked with the element of **fire**, for both can be regarded as being both destructive and creative. The head is therefore a symbol of life, the soul, wisdom and rulership.

Wild Animals

Lion *Above*

The magnificent lion is traditionally king of the beasts and is the leading emblem of **royalty**. It is endowed with the various virtues of life, strength, conquest, valor, **wisdom**, pride, authority, courage and protection. Because of its strength, regal bearing, mane and golden fur, the lion is an ancient symbol of the **sun**, and embodies earthly power—making it the enemy of the **eagle**. The lioness, however, represents the **moon**, femininity and fierce motherhood. In Egyptian art, two lions sitting back to back signify the rising and setting sun, the past and future; the pharoah was frequently depicted in the form of a lion. As a fertility symbol, the virile Greco-Roman lion drew the chariots of Cybele and Hera (Juno) and was sacred to Dionysus (Bacchus) and Aphrodite (Venus). Hercules killed the Nemean lion. Other legendary lions include those of Androcles, Daniel and St. Jerome. In Hinduism, the lion is an avatar of Vishnu, the mount of Durga (destroyer of demons), and the attribute of Devi. It is the defender of the law to Buddhists, and **Buddha** sits on the lion throne. In Christian tradition, the lion can personify God. The winged lion is the emblem of St. Mark (and thus also of his city, Venice). However, it can also signify **Satan**. Rastafarians adopted the lion as the symbol of the tribe of Judah. Because the lion was sometimes believed to be born dead and then animated by the breath of its father, it can additionally symbolize resurrection. Moreover, it was once thought never to shut its eyes,

and thus signifies vigilance. Yet because it is a wild and dangerous beast, the lion can be viewed as untamed excess. Many Oriental cultures believe that the lion protects against demons. The lion has many significances in **alchemy**, where the red lion represents sulphur and the green, matter. It is the most popular animal in **heraldic art**, where it signifies power, masculinity and leadership and is the emblem of English sovereigns. The lion is the sun-ruled zodiacal sign of **Leo** and is fiery and masculine.

Tiger *Above*

Unlike other cultures, the Chinese regard the tiger, rather than the **lion**, as king of beasts. It has great symbolic significance in the East, where it is regarded as representing vital animal energy, power, ferocity, royalty and, thus, protection. The tiger protects graves and was a Chinese guardian of hunting—and later of agriculture. The white tiger has **yin** attributes and opposes the dragon, and because it can see in the dark it symbolizes illumination and the new **moon**. Tigers also have **yang** and signify war and valor. They are the emblem of the god of wealth and gamblers because they can also guard money. Five mythic tigers guard against chaos: the red (symbolizing **summer** and **fire**), the black (**winter** and **water**), the blue (spring and vegetation), the white (**fall** and metal) and the supreme yellow tiger (the **sun**, center and the emperor). To Buddhists, a tiger finding a path through the jungle symbolizes spiritual struggle, while in Chinese Buddhism, it is one of three Senseless Creatures, signifying anger. The tiger is the

third sign of the **Chinese zodiac** and symbolizes courage, enthusiasm and generosity but also rebellion, recklessness and unpredictability. It was believed to live for a thousand years in Japan, where it signifies war. For the Hindu, the lion represents loss of control. **Shiva** and Durga ride tigers when destroying demons, so it is also an emblem of royalty and warrior castes.

Bear *Below*

The bear's primary symbolism is that of bravery and strength, and it is therefore a popular heraldic symbol in Europe. The bear is the emblem of Russia and the Swiss city of Berne. Siberian cultures consider the bear an instructor of shamans and also a mythological ancestor (a belief shared by the Arcadians). Among some Native American and northern Asian tribes, a bear cult is practised to pacify the souls of hunted bears. Because it hibernates, the bear can signify resurrection. It is also linked with the **moon** and was sacred to the Greek lunar goddess Artemis (**Diana**), whose acolytes were called bears. The Celtic lunar goddess Berne was represented by a bear, as was **Thor** in Norse legend, where, in addition, the male and female bears Atli and Atla signified masculinity and femininity. The nymph Callisto and her son were transformed by Hera (Juno) into the bear constellations Ursa Major and Minor. In Christian tradition, the bear is a negative creature signifying bad temper, evil, cruelty, crudeness, **greed** and even **Satan**. However, because it was believed that the bear was born formless and was licked into shape by its mother, the bear can

symbolize both the conversion of the pagan and the virgin birth. Bear fat was once believed to have mystical powers of healing. In psychoanalysis, the bear represents the dangers of **the unconscious.** The grizzly bear on the state seal of California signifies determination.

Jaguar *Above*

The jaguar's symbolism is greatest among the native tribes of Central America, whose traditions derive from the ancient Aztec and Mayan cultures. In Mayan belief, the jaguar was considered the master of animals, a creature of the underworld that knows the mysteries of the earth and guides the souls of the dead. Its reflecting eyes were believed to be a passage to the underworld and would reveal the future to those who gazed into them. The Aztec Earth goddess was depicted in pregnancy with the claws of a jaguar, and it was believed that jaguars guarded the four pathways of the world. To the Toltecs, while the eagle symbolized the sun, the jaguar represented the **moon** (as well as **thunder** and **rain**), and the coming of twilight was depicted as a jaguar devouring the sun. Indeed, the jaguar, whose spotted pelt resembles the starry sky, became associated with the Aztec warrior god of night, Tezcatlipoca, who assumed this form after falling to Earth. In today's Central American shamanistic cultures, the jaguar (which is said to have given man **fire** and hunting), is regarded as the premier guide of the **shaman**, who can also assume its form. In western Europe, the jaguar is more prosaically known for its adoption as the emblem of the Jaguar car manufacturer, in tribute to this great cat's speed, grace and strength.

Elephant *Below*

Indigenous to Africa and Asia, the elephant's symbolic resonance is greatest in these continents and, indeed, it can symbolize both India and Africa. There it represents the various qualities of strength, royalty, dignity, patience, **wisdom**, longevity and happiness and is a symbol of **good luck.** Some cultures believe that the elephant is a cosmic, caryatid animal bearing the world upon its back; this image has been carried over into architectural devices. Because it has often been the preferred mount of royalty, the elephant represents status and power. Through its long lifespan, it symbolizes longevity and memory ("an elephant never forgets"). The white elephant is sacred in Buddhism because **Buddha** assumed this form to enter the womb of

his mother, Maya. The elephant has assumed Buddha's qualities of patience and wisdom and is the Jewel of the Law. The Hindu god **Ganesha** has the head of an elephant, thus signifying his sagacity, and the elephant Airavata is the mount of Indra. In Christian tradition, the elephant personifies the virtues of chastity and **temperance** and is also a symbol of Christ trampling a **serpent** (Satan) underfoot. The term "a white elephant" derives from Thailand and signifies a worthless project. Since 1874, when *Harper's Weekly* published a cartoon of an elephant trampling on inflation and chaos, it has been the symbol of the **U.S. Republican Party.**

Camel *Above*

In most cultures, the camel is a symbol of arrogance, wilfulness, laziness and bad temper, yet, in the countries where it is used as a beast of burden, it is endowed with more positive symbolism. In North Africa, for example, because it stores **water** in its hump and draws on its supply sparingly, it can represent sobriety (and, in Christianity, the virtue of **temperance**). Because it sinks to its knees to be loaded with its burden, Christian tradition approves of it as a creature who kneels before God, signifying both humility and obedience. Moreover, because it was the mount of the **Magi**, it is a symbol of royalty and dignity, as well as of stamina. St. John the Baptist was believed to have worn a camel-hair tunic. The Persian Zend-Avesta speaks of a flying camel (dragon-serpent) as being the serpent in the Garden of Eden. The camel is regarded with favor in Islam, for Mohammed fled to safety from Mecca to Koba on the camel Al Kaswa; furthermore, his fabled camel Al Adha was said to have carried him from Jerusalem to Mecca in four strides. In Ancient Rome, the camel symbolized Arabia.

Monkey/Ape *Above*

As man's closest animal relative and in tribute to its intelligence, the monkey of whatever breed has been accorded both respect and distrust. It has ambivalent symbolism of intelligence, sociability, mimicry and cunning, as well as baseness and the vices of **greed** and lust. In Oriental cultures, the chattering monkey symbolizes distraction but, when tamed, intelligence and loyalty. The Three Wise Monkeys which see, hear and speak no evil represent discipline of the mind. **Buddha** was incarnated as a monkey, but it is also one of the three Senseless Creatures, signifying greed. In China, the monkey signifies health, success and protection (but also mischief, ugliness and conceit). The monkey is the ninth sign of the **Chinese zodiac**, representing fantasy and a **trickster** figure embodying base human nature. In Hinduism, where monkeys are sacred and benevolent creatures, the monkey god Hanuman, aide of Rama, represents bravery, speed, cunning and power and can transform fire into spiritual energy. Christian belief saw the monkey as symbolic of the sins of lust, malice, greed, drunkenness, laziness and vanity. In Christian iconography, **Satan** was sometimes portrayed as an ape: a chained monkey depicted victory over Satan and one with an **apple** in its mouth, the Fall.

Stag *Above*

The stag, or hart, is the universally positive symbol of life, **wisdom**, and virility. Because of its branched antlers, it was equated by many cultures with the **Tree of Life**. By renewing its antlers annually, it is synonymous with regeneration; furthermore, through their shape and height, the antlers can also be identified with the **sun**'s rays. In Celtic belief, the stag led souls through the darkness and was the emblem of warriors and hunter gods. In Scandinavia, the four stags of the Yggdrasil represented the four winds.

Its vigorous rutting habits led it to be regarded as the epitome of virility by the Chinese, as well as of happiness. The stag was sacred to Artemis (**Diana**), goddess of hunting in Greco-Roman mythology, and symbolized life. In Christian tradition, it symbolizes purity, solitude and, as the enemy of the **serpent** (**Satan**), Christ. Shamans often dress as stags, hoping to assume the animal's wisdom. In Buddhism, too, the golden stag represents knowledge.

Wolf *Below*

A creature of complex symbolism, the wolf can represent evil, cruelty, ferocity, avarice and the deadly sins of gluttony and covetousness but also maternal love and valor—the latter attributes being derived from the she-wolf that suckled Romulus and Remus, the founders of Rome. The wolf is now an emblem of that city and was once a sign of the tribe of Benjamin. Its nocturnal vision earned it the symbolism of light, and it was an attribute of both Apollo and Ares (Mars), god of war. As a **lunar** creature, it was also identified with the under-

world in Ancient Greece and Rome. In China, a sacred wolf guards the heavenly palace, while to Mongolians it is the ancestor of Genghis Khan. In Hinduism, however, it is the mount of terrible deities and a sign of night. According to Nordic tradition, a cosmic wolf, Fenris, is imprisoned in the bowels of the earth and, at the end of the world, he will escape and devour the sun—the Celts also believed that a wolf devoured the sun each night. The wolf can signify victory when ridden by Odin (and also the Valkyries), although Odin's lupine companions Sköll and Hati signify repulsion and hatred. Native Americans, however, regard the wolf as a friendly spiritual guide. As a predatory creature, Christians came to believe that the wolf devours lost "sheep" (souls), although it is an emblem of Francis of Assisi, who tamed the wolf Gubbio. In medieval times, the wolf was regarded as a creature of **Satan** ridden by **witches**. The popular tradition of the **werewolf** (man by day, rampaging wolf at night) signifies the violence that underlies the superficial calm of civilization.

Coyote *Above*

The cunning coyote is mistrusted, yet also respected, by the Native American cultures of its habitat. This North American prairie wolf is regarded by some tribes as the epitome of evil and, as a lunar creature, it is seen as the bringer of floods, the harsh **winter** months and **death**. Less negatively, however, west of the Rocky Mountains the coyote is considered the chief of animals and is attributed the ambivalent role of antihero and **trickster**—a master of mischief-making but occasionally a friend to humans and the creator of the world order. In the Aztec tradition of Central America, the creator god, Quetzalcoatl, can be represented by twin coyotes during his victory over Mictlantecuhtli, ruler of the underworld.

Fox *Above*

In Western tradition, the fox is a symbol of base cunning, hypocrisy, and trickery, but in some Native American cultures its slyness is transmuted into **wisdom**, and in the East it represents longevity and transformation. In Japan it was considered to be a **rain** spirit and the messenger of Inari, the rice god; it symbolizes longevity but can work for good or evil. A black fox signifies good luck, a white fox disaster and three foxes absolute calamity. The Chinese regard the fox with

suspicion, believing that it can assume human form (usually that of a beautiful girl), as well as those of other creatures; the spirits of the dead can be foxes. The Greco-Roman fox was a stealer of **grapes** and was thus associated with Dionysus (Bacchus), protector of the vine; in the Christian analogy this habit was associated with heresy. It additionally represents the sins of deceit, injustice, greed and lust; because it can feign death to trap its prey, it is also associated with **Satan**. As well as being a creature of great sagacity, some Native American cultures believe that the fox embodies lasciviousness; here it is the ultimate **trickster**, as it is in the Caribbean character Br'er Fox.

Rabbit *Above, right*

Because they are nocturnal, rabbits and hares symbolize the **moon** and hence death and rebirth. Hares and rabbits share most other symbolic interpretations. They are creatures which burrow in earth, are prolific breeders and therefore represent fertility and good fortune. Sacred to Hermes (**Mercury**) as a fleet-footed messenger, the hare was also dedicated to the love deities Aphrodite (Venus) and Eros (Cupid) in Ancient Greece and Rome. In Norse tradition, the hare was the emblem of Freyja and Holda, the moon goddess. The hare-headed Saxon goddess of spring, Eostre (Oestra), is the origin of the Easter Bunny and Easter Egg symbolism of life renewal. In Judaism and Christianity, however, this fecund quality brought about an association with uncleanliness and lasciviousness. In Christianity, the rabbit's swiftness also led it to symbolize both the passing of life and diligent service. Some Native American cultures consider the Great Hare a demiurge (as did the Egyptians); however, as in West Africa and the Caribbean, it can also represent the positive qualities of the **trickster**. The rabbit was an emblem of the Chinese emperor and signified longevity through its connection to the moon. The white hare, as the guardian of animals, signifies divinity and the red and black, good fortune and prosperity. The rabbit is the

Chinese zodiac sign for the feminine and virtuous. To Buddhists, the hare symbolizes self-sacrifice, because a hare offered itself as food for Buddha and in gratitude he placed it in the moon. Their shy habits have led rabbits to epitomize timidity and sometimes cowardice. Through their procreative powers, both rabbits and hares were regarded as magical in the Middle Ages: carrying a foot (the part which came into contact with the life-giving earth) was believed to protect against evil and bring good luck, although the hare could also be a **witch**'s **familiar**. In Western tradition, the March hare symbolizes madness.

Mouse *Above*

An apparently harmless symbol of timidity and humility, the mouse can also signify hypocrisy (in Judaism) and destruction (in Christianity). In ancient times, the shrew was regarded as sacred in Egypt, while in Rome the white mouse was a sign of good luck and an attribute both of Jupiter (**Zeus**) and of Apollo. Because it is a rodent, for Christians it can embody destructive power (it is sometimes depicted gnawing the **Tree of Life**), and thus **Satan**. "Plagues" of mice were regarded as a punishment from God. In the folk tales of the Western European world, mice were regarded as the personification of **witches** or the souls of the dead, although white mice could embody the souls of unborn children.

Bat *Above*

In an enduring traditional belief, the nocturnal bat is an agent of the powers of darkness, death and chaos. The combination of its mouselike body and black, webbed wings has incurred popular suspicion, as has its habit of roosting upside down. It swoops unpredictably so, to Buddhists and the Japanese, it embodies a restless mind as well as ignorance. Yet in some African cultures, because it has nocturnal vision, it can represent both intelligence and dead souls. In medieval Europe, bats were considered **witches' familiars**; **Satan** was portrayed with bat wings, and bats were believed to play an **incubus** role, also sucking the blood of children, like a **vampire**. As a night creature in lonely places, the bat can symbolize melancholy, concealed envy and hypocrisy (because of its hybrid form). In China, conversely, the bat represents a happy, long life and is a good-luck symbol because the words for "bat" and "luck" are homophones (*fu*). In Egypt, too, bat heads were once protective amulets. Because it inhabits caves (believed to be passages to the afterlife), the bat symbolizes immortality and rebirth in some Native American cultures.

Rat *Above, center*

Rats have traditionally been regarded with mistrust as opportunist creatures scavenging off people's misfortunes, deserting sinking ships and accompanying death and decay. In addition, as rodents, they are often regarded as agents of destruction. Yet in Japan, a white rat is the messenger of the gods of happiness and wealth, and in Hinduism a rat is the mount of the elephant-headed god Ganesha, representing endeavor and prudence. In China, the rat is the first creature of the calendar and signifies charm and prosperity, although it is also associated with miserliness and regarded as a carrier of the plague (a view shared in Ancient Egypt and western Europe). Its tendency to flee doomed places has caused it to be considered an animal of augury and **wisdom**: in Rome a white rat was believed to foretell **good luck**. In Christian allegory, the rat is a chthonic creature equated with **Satan**, **witches** and other sinister powers of darkness but is also the emblem of St. Fina, who lived in a rat-infested attic. During the Renaissance, day and night were often depicted as two rats—one black, the other white—representing the inexorable passing of time. In recent years, the agile jerboa (desert rat) was adopted by British soldiers as their emblem during the North Africa campaign of World War II; the mascot was revived in 1991 by their successors in the Gulf War.

Squirrel *Above, right*

In modern symbolism, through its habit of energetically seeking and then storing away supplies of food for consumption during the barren winter months, the squirrel signifies a hoarder. This somewhat mundane interpretation is transcended in Norse mythology, however, by the mischievous red squirrel living in the boughs of the cosmic tree, Yggdrasil, from which it incited conflict between the solar eagle and chthonic serpent. This squirrel was sacred to **Thor**, the god of **fire** and **thunder**, while another, the "Ratatosk," was believed to bring snow and **rain**. In Ireland, the squirrel was the emblem of the Celtic goddess, Mebd. Until the introduction of the gray squirrel in recent times, the indigenous red squirrel proliferated in Europe and its color caused it

to become a symbol of **fire**. In Christian belief, this association, along with its unerring agility, led to its unfortunate equation with Satan, while its hoarding of food caused it to symbolize greed. In Japan, as in South America (where it was once sacrificed to the Mayan gods), the squirrel signifies fertility.

Hedgehog *Below*

Because the hedgehog rolls itself up into a tight, prickly ball when threatened, it is a clear symbol of self-protection. In ancient cultures, however, on account of its rounded shape and defensive exterior, the hedgehog was regarded as an emblem of great mother goddesses such as the Babylonian Ishtar. In other traditions, its sharp spines sometimes identified it as a solar symbol and in Renaissance allegory it also came to be associated with the sense of touch. In Christian interpretation, the greedy and short-tempered robber hedgehog is associated with the sins of avarice, gluttony and wrath and is likened to **Satan**, who steals the souls of men. On the other hand, as a predator of grubs and worms, it was once regarded as an enemy of evil chthonic forces. Like many animals, it is believed to be able to predict the weather and is particularly sensitive to wind changes. According to some popular western superstitions, **witches** can assume the form of a hedgehog in order to milk **cows** dry. In the East, however, the hedgehog signifies wealth.

Domesticated Animals

Bull/Ox *Above*

The bull, or steer, retains its age-old significance as a symbol of masculinity and virility. Its symbolism can, however, be ambiguous: its vitality and male fertility associate it with the **sun** and resurrection, but because it has crescent-shaped horns it can also represent lunar deities and death. The Apis bull was worshipped in Ancient Egypt as a symbol of creation and was often depicted carrying the sun disk of **Ra** between its horns. Conversely, it was also sacred to **Osiris** and symbolized death. In Mithraic and Roman times, the bull was sacrificed annually, for its blood was believed to fertilize the earth. It was sacred to **Zeus**, because in Greek mythology the god assumed the form of a white bull to seduce Europa; their son Minos (keeper of the **Minotaur**) became king of Crete. The bull was also dedicated to Dionysus (Bacchus), Aphrodite (Venus) and Poseidon (Neptune). In some traditions, because of its thunderous roar, the bull was the animal of thunder gods such as the Norse deity, **Thor**. To the Hindus, Agni is the mighty bull, and it is the breath of Aditi; Nandin is the mount of **Shiva**, and both Indra and Rudra can take this form. The Jews call Yahweh the bull of Israel. In Western tradition the bull's strength is tainted with the characteristics of brutality, cruelty and lust. It is a popular heraldic symbol (the emblem of Richard III of England), denoting courage and ferocity. The zodiacal symbol **Taurus** is the celestial sign of the bull. The ox, which shares the symbolic characteristics of strength with the bull, is imbued with less ambiguous symbolism: it represents agriculture, patience, chastity and (along with its yoke) self-sacrifice. To Christians, it can therefore signify Christ, and the winged ox is the emblem of St. Luke. The ox, like the waterbuffalo, has special resonance in Taoism (where it is tamed and ridden by Lao Tzu) and Buddhism (where it is a symbol of Yama) as a symbol of the ego. It is the second sign of the **Chinese zodiac**, and signifies balance and endurance.

Cow *Below*

As the provider of milk, the cow is a universal symbol of motherhood, fertility, nourishment and abundance. Furthermore, because its curved horns are reminiscent of the crescent **moon**, it is a celestial symbol of all mother goddesses, as well as being a chthonic representative of Mother Earth. In Ancient Egypt the cow was sacred to Isis and Hathor, mothers of the gods, as well as to Nut, the "Celestial Cow," whose legs are the four quarters of the earth. In Norse mythology, the primordial cow—the Nourisher—licked the ice to produce the first man. It is a sacred animal to Hindus and may not be killed; variously known as the "melodious cow" and "cow of abundance," its milk is believed to form the Milky Way and, in association with the heavenly bull, it represents female cosmic power. Nandini is the wish-fulfilling cow, and the earth mother Aditi can assume its form; the legs of the sacred cow signify the four castes.

Pig/Boar *Above*

The intelligent pig, or swine, has long been burdened with the negative symbolism of uncleanliness, ignorance and **greed**. In the world of antiquity, however, the sow was a fertility symbol and thus sacred to **Isis** in Egypt and the goddess of agriculture, Ceres (Demeter), in Ancient Greece and Rome, because it roots up earth. Native American cultures identify the pig as a bringer of rain, which fertilizes the land. In the Celtic world, the pig was linked with both the sow goddess Keridwin, "the Old White One," and Phaea, the lunar fertility goddess; it also fed the gods. To Hindus, the sow represents the female aspect of Vishnu, Vajravarahi. The black pig, in contrast, is a sinister creature and was sacred to Set in Egypt; in Buddhism it stands at the center of the Round of Existence, representing ignorance—one of the three illusions that prevent man from attaining Nirvana. Because they consider it an unclean creature, Jews and Moslems are forbidden to eat pork. Christians regard it as a low, coarse animal, symbolic of the sins of the flesh, especially gluttony; it can also be **Satan**, because five marks on the animal's forelegs were believed to be the mark of the Devil. The pig (or boar) is the twelfth sign of the **Chinese zodiac**, representing honesty. Related to the pig is the wild boar, which embodied the positive qualities of strength and pugnacity to the Greeks, Celts and Japanese. The Hindu gods Rudra and Vishnu (who was incarnated as a boar) are celestial boars. In Western tradition, however, the boar can additionally signify brutality and lust, a deadly sin. In this context, it is sometimes depicted being trampled by the personification of Chasity.

Horse *Above*

Considered a noble animal, the horse represents courage, grace and speed, as well as virility in Western tradition, and is solar in the East, signifying both **fire** and the heavens. It was once considered a chthonic creature and can therefore also be associated with **water** and the **moon**, symbolizing **death**; it is also known as a guide to the underworld. In many ancient cultures, the horse was considered an intelligent animal, combining strength and reason with the powers of divination and magic, making it the most significant animal to sacrifice. Its color is an important factor in interpreting its symbolism: the white horse is solar but can also signify the sea and moon; the black horse, however, is a sign of death and destruction. The Greco-Roman horse was an omen of war dedicated to Ares (Mars), Hades (Pluto) and Poseidon (Neptune), who was said to have created the first horse. Moreover, because **Pegasus** was a winged horse, it can additionally represent a messenger of the gods. In Norse belief, the horse was sacred to Odin, whose eight-legged mare was Sleipnir. It was an important creature to the Celts as the steed of the sun god and was also associated with deities such as the fertility goddess Epona. A white horse was a Saxon emblem and later also the device of the house of Hanover. To the Hindus, the horse can be equated with Varuna and thus the cosmos; Vishnu's last avatar will be as the white horse, Kalki. In Chinese Buddhism, the winged horse carries the Book of Law. To the Japanese, Bato Kwannon, goddess of mercy, can take an equine form. In Islam, Mohammed was carried to heaven by the steed Borak, and thus the horse signifies happiness. Christians regard the horse as a symbol of courage, generosity and the swiftness of life. The four horses of the Apocalypse are white (signifying pestilence), red (war), black (famine) and pale (death). The seventh sign of the **Chinese zodiac** is a horse, where it is equated with Gemini and signifies practicality and love.

Donkey *Below*

The donkey, ass or jackass, is a creature of contrasting symbolism, including danger, poverty, obstinacy, stupidity, foolishness and laziness but also virility, patience, courage, meekness and gentleness. In Egypt, the red jackass signified danger in the underworld and was the emblem of Set. Although the Greco-Roman donkey was regarded as the epitome of stupidity, sloth and stubbornness, it also signified brute virility and was thus sacred to Dionysus (Bacchus) and the fertility god Priapus, as well as Saturn (Cronos). Christians sometimes portrayed the ass as a heathen symbol, but because **Mary** rode a donkey to Bethlehem, and Christ into Jerusalem (from which it is said to derive the dark cross on its back), the animal signifies gentleness and humility. The talking ass of Balaam further denotes communication with God. Because it was a sacrificial animal, the donkey can signify **death**; as it carries heavy burdens, it can additionally represent the poor. In China, it is an unambiguous symbol of stupidity; in Judaism, obstinacy. Since its use in 1828 by President Andrew Jackson as a

humorous allusion to his pejorative nickname "jackass," the donkey has been adopted as the emblem of the **U.S. Democratic Party**.

Goat *Above*

Goats have a complex symbolism, both positive and negative. Still used in many societies as a sacrificial animal, the goat can represent vitality and sacrifice. In Ancient Greece it was sacred to **Zeus**, Pan and Artemis; in Hinduism it represented the higher self; while in paganism **Thor's** chariot was drawn by goats (or **rams**). In the Bible, however, unbelievers are termed "goats," and the sins of the world were laid on a goat's head (hence the "scapegoat"). As well as denoting lechery ("goatish") and lust, the goat has a strong connection with **Satan**, who is often depicted in this form.

Ram *Above*

The brave, fierce, energetic ram embodies these aggressive qualities, as well as being a symbol of male strength and virility. Its unmistakeable masculinity and erect horns (reminiscent of both **sun** rays and **thunderbolts**) combine to make it a symbol of sun gods in many cultures. Thus the Egyptian creation gods, Amon-Ra and Khnemu-Ra, were depicted with ram's heads, and the Phoenician god Baal had ram's horns. The Greco-Roman ram was sacred to **Zeus** (Jupiter), Hermes

(Mercury), Dionysus (Bacchus) and Pan. The Hindu god Agni rides a ram as a symbol of the sacred **fire**. In Celtic mythology, where the ram-headed serpent was an attribute of Cernunnos, the ram was associated with war and fertility. The Gaulish deity Benin was depicted as a ram, and rams (or **goats**) pulled the chariot of the Norse thunder god, **Thor**. The ram was a common sacrificial creature in antiquity, when some cultures believed that its blood transferred its attributes. In the Bible, the ram caught by its horns in a thorn bush was sacrificed by Abraham in place of his son, **Isaac**; in Judaism the blowing of the **shofar** horn commemorates this event. In Christianity, the crucified Christ with the **crown of thorns** can be equated with this creature. The celestial sign of the ram is the zodiacal **Aries**, a sign of spring and regeneration.

Sheep *Above*
Because it is a docile and trusting creature, the sheep symbolizes blindness and stupidity; in a religious context, however, similar qualities are not negative as they can denote unquestioning faith. In its juvenile form, the lamb (an ancient sacrificial animal) signifies purity, innocence, meekness and martyrdom. In Christianity, it is thus the **Lamb of God** (*Agnus Dei*)—Christ—who carries the sins of the world. The lamb can be portrayed as both suffering and triumphant or as heralding the Apocalypse. In a reversal of this role, however, Christ can also be portrayed as the Good Shepherd who tends to his flock (apostles and believers). Satan is powerless against the unblemished lamb, which is in addition an emblem of St. John the Baptist. In Judaic tradition, the sprinkling of lamb's

blood at Passover recalls the deliverance of the Jews and signifies obedience to God and the future messiah. The sheep (or goat) is the eighth sign of the **Chinese zodiac** and is a symbol of the artistic temperament and harmony.

Dog *Below*
The symbolism of the dog is truly that of man's best friend, for dogs signify loyalty, vigilance, and courage. The Celts believed that dogs had powers of healing, as did the Greeks, who linked them with Aesculapius. Faithfulness is probably the dog's prime virtue, and ancient Egyptians and Greeks believed that it followed its master to the afterlife. The dog (Sirius) was sacred to the messenger god, Hermes (Mercury) and Artemis (**Diana**), goddess of the hunt, and was also a companion of Hecate (signifying war) and Orion. In many cultures, it was believed that dogs were mediators with the realm of the dead. Thus the Egyptian god Anubis is jackal-headed—**Cerberus** too is depicted as a three-headed dog; the dogs of Hades represent darkness and danger, while in Norse belief the dog Garmr guards the underworld. Some African cultures regard the wise dog as the ancestral father of civilization and bringer of **fire**. In Hinduism, it is associated with Yama and Indra. In a reversal of its usually positive symbolism, Jews and Moslems consider the dog an

unclean beast, a black dog signifying the Devil. Canis Major is the dog star, and the dog is the eleventh sign of the **Chinese zodiac**, representing idealism. In Chinese tradition, the dog can be both **yin**, symbolizing catastrophe, meteors and eclipses, and **yang**, signifying protection.

Cat *Above*
Once sacred to Bast in ancient Egypt, since the Middle Ages (when it became known as a **familiar** of **witches**) the cat has attracted mainly negative symbolism—although in some countries a black cat can be a bringer of **good luck**. Because of its perceived Satanic associations within Western tradition, the cat was regarded a cruel, deceitful, malevolent creature. Female cats were considered promiscuous and epitomized lustful women; their "nine lives" were regarded as suspiciously supernatural. The Celts once sacrificed cats, and Buddhists consider the cat cursed because it did not weep for the death of Buddha. However, other cultures have regarded the cat more charitably: because of its independent nature, in Ancient Rome the cat was an attribute of the goddess of liberty, was sacred to the lunar goddess **Diana** (Artemis) and was also the guardian of homes, and thus a symbol of domesticity. The cat drew the chariot of the Norse fertility goddess Freyja. A cat is revered by Moslems for saving Mohammed from the serpent, and the "M" marking on many cats' foreheads is believed to be the mark of the prophet's fingers. Westerners sometimes equate the cat with the fourth sign of the **Chinese zodiac**, the hare.

Reptiles and Marine Creatures

Snake *Above*

The snake or serpent is a universal symbol, one with the most complex and converse connotations. Ancient cultures believed that because the snake shed its skin, it symbolized immortality, and so it became associated with Aesculapius, the Roman god of healing and also with many Hindu gods. Furthermore, in Indian culture, the Kundalini snake is believed to exist at the bottom of the human spine, symbolizing cosmic energy and life. The ancient Egyptians, Romans and Greeks regarded it as a protective spirit. Largely through its role in tempting Eve, thus bringing about the Fall of Man, the snake came to be seen as crafty and malevolent—the personification of **Satan** and sin. Its slithering movements, scaly skin and venomous forked tongue inspired fear, while its lidless eyes denoted watchfulness and wisdom. Because it is born from an egg, the snake is sometimes regarded as androgynous, and because it often lives underground, it has been supposed to be chthonic, sharing the **dragon**'s symbolism. Its shape makes it a powerful phallic fertility symbol, and the snake has great significance as such in dreams. When shown coiled, it signifies dynamic potential.

Crocodile/Alligator *Right*

Crocodiles and alligators share the same mixed symbolism of death and destruction, as well as life and renewal. Because the crocodile is a creature of both water and land, its significance is complicated beyond that of being a devouring animal. Some Native American cultures regard it as a demiurge, or a cosmic creature that carries the world on its back. In Ancient Egypt, the crocodile had particularly complex symbolism and was so culturally important that it could represent the country itself. It was believed to have been born from the water and therefore represented the vicious chthonic and solar deity Sebek (Sobek), but it could also be the form of the earth god, Geb, as the life force. Alternatively, the ferocious crocodile embodied fury and disorder and was the typhonic attribute of the evil deity Set. The hybrid crocodile Ammit (sometimes equated with Serapis) ate the hearts of the sinful after judgment by **Osiris**, and the dead themselves were sometimes depicted as crocodiles of knowledge. Because it was believed to be tongueless, the classical world regarded the crocodile as symbolic of silence. The biblical **Leviathan** was linked with the crocodile, and in Christianity it shares the symbolism of the **dragon** as the guardian of knowledge, but, also typifies deceit, because it sheds "crocodile tears" to encourage its softhearted victim to approach it.

Lizard *Above, right*

The cold-blooded lizard warms itself in the **sun**; it is thus associated with both the sun and light and, in some religions, represents the seeker of spiritual enlightenment. In Ancient Greece, it was believed to offer itself to Apollo, the sun god, in order to achieve eternal light; this symbolism is shared in Christianity. Furthermore, in ancient times it was believed to renew its sight by looking into the sun, so signifying a renewal of faith. Because it sheds its skin, the lizard is a clear symbol of rebirth. Like the crocodile, the world of antiquity believed it to be tongueless, signifying silence; in Ancient Egypt and Greece it also symbolized **wisdom** and good fortune and was sacred to Serapis and Hermes (Mercury) respectively. Conversely, in non-European countries it is associated with natural disaster such as drought. It is regarded as being the master of evil transformation in some African cultures. In Christianity, it shares the Satanic associations of the **serpent**. The lizard is important in Polynesia, where it is regarded as a god; in Maori tradition it is a demiurge; while in some Australian Aboriginal tribes the lizard Tarrotarro is a culture hero, creator of the sexes. The mythical **salamander** was usually depicted in lizard form.

Turtle *Above*

The turtle (or tortoise) has profound symbolism in Native American cultures and in Southern Asia, where it was believed to carry the world, or to represent the cosmos—its upper shell being the heavens, its body the earth and its undershell the water, or underworld. In Hindu myth, for example, the turtle Chukwa carries the world-supporting **elephant** on its back. For this reason, turtles have frequently been represented in architecture as the caryatid of the universe. The turtle was an avatar of Vishnu and was also Kasyapa, the North Star. More generally (and particularly in China and Japan), it is a symbol of longevity, indestructibility and immortality. It is a spiritually endowed creature in China, where it can be **yin** and symbolic of **water** or **yang**, as the Black Warrior. The marks on the turtle's shell have been considered both a map of the constellations and sacred writing: hence it was also a symbol of **wisdom** and, through its habit of withdrawing into its shell, of spiritual

meditation. In Native American, West African and Caribbean cultures, its sagacity is that of the **trickster**. A creature of both water and land, the turtle generally represents water and femininity, and the Greco-Roman turtle was a fertility symbol, sacred to Aphrodite (**Venus**). Alternatively, in Christianity the turtle is sometimes considered a demonic creature representative of darkness, as well as a symbol of domesticity.

Frog *Above*

In most traditions, the frog is regarded as the antithesis of the malignant **toad**; however, it is still imbued with the conflicting symbolism of **good luck**, fertility and resurrection but also evil, heresy and sin. Because it lays quantities of **eggs**, it is a fertility symbol and was sacred to the frog-headed Heket, Egyptian goddess of birth (and also the Greco-Roman Aphrodite/**Venus**). The green frog symbolized the flooding of the Nile. To the Celts, the frog was the lord of the earth and represented the curative power of **water**. Its three stages of development and amphibious habits make it a symbol of resurrection. In China the frog is a **yin** creature thought to bring **rain**, as is believed in some Native American cultures. Hindus believed that a great frog supported the world and that frogs signify darkness. Early Christians regarded the frog ambivalently: either as a symbol of resurrection or as the embodiment of evil and heresy and of the sins of envy and **greed**.

Seahorse *Below*

In the Mediterranean cultures of Ancient Greece and Rome, seahorses were believed to pull the chariots of sea gods and, as an attribute of the sea god, **Neptune** (Poseidon), they therefore symbolized the power of the **water**. Compounding this positive significance, they were believed to carry the dead safely to the underworld. The seahorse illustrated here with a naiad is from Greek legend. Seahorses remain symbols of **good luck** for fishermen and in popular superstition they have the added benefit of protecting against fever. Their unique form understandably caused the Chinese to regard seahorses as the lesser sons of **dragons**.

Whale *Below, left*

The huge whale was a symbol of power and the regenerative energy of the cosmic waters until it came to be regarded as the devourer of the biblical Jonah, when it symbolized death, the grave and the jaws and belly of hell. In this context, however, it can also signify resurrection, because, once Jonah had renewed his faith after three days, the whale released him. The story can be compared with Christ's death, burial and resurrection. In Inuit (Eskimo) tradition, the whale is a **trickster**. Because of their massive size, early sailors mistakenly tried to land on whales, and so they represented the devil's lure and cunning. Furthermore, the whale can be a cosmic symbol, either as a caryatid of the universe (in Arab and Slav countries and Russia), or as the embodiment of the world or of the **body** and grave.

Dolphin *Above*

A universally popular symbol, the dolphin signifies salvation, speed, **love** and diligence. It is so friendly to man that it was once believed to have been human. In Ancient Greece and Rome, it was regarded it as the king of sea creatures, and so it signified maritime power and pulled the chariot of Poseidon (Neptune). It was also the "woman of the sea," sacred to Aphrodite (Venus), as well as the Babylonian Ishtar and Egyptian Isis. At Delphi, it was dedicated to Apollo, god of the sun, but, in association with Delphi, the dolphin (*delphis*) can signify the womb (*delphys*). It is frequently depicted entwined with an anchor "making haste slowly," representing prudence. It is a symbol of Christ on the **cross** when portrayed on an anchor or pierced with a **trident**; with a ship it represents the church being guided by Christ. Because it was reputed to rescue drowning sailors and, in many traditions, to guide the dead through the waters of death, it also symbolized Christ the Savior. Along with the whale, the dolphin was once equated with the beast that swallowed and then released Jonah and so symbolizes rebirth. In Native American cultures, it can be both a divine messenger and a form of the Great Spirit.

Fish *Below*

As well as being a potent symbol of Christianity, these aquatic creatures of elongated shape represent male fertility (a good haul representing abundance) and also lunar deities. Because the depths themselves represent the **unconscious** mind, the fish can signify creativity and inspiration. Fish can also symbolize female fertility. They were sacred to the Babylonian god of the deep, Ea-Oannes, but also to Ishtar. In Ancient Egypt, the fish was believed to be the phallus of **Osiris** and was additionally sacred to **Isis** and Hathor. Fish, in Greco-Roman belief, were attributes of the goddess of love, Aphrodite (Venus) and the god of the deep, Poseidon (Neptune). Celtic tradition equated the salmon and trout in particular with sacred wells and divine knowledge. To Buddhists the fish represents freedom of mind and faith, for, like **Christ, Buddha** was the fisher of men. The fish is heavenly food to the Jews and can furthermore represent the faithful swimming in the waters of the Torah. Both the Hindu gods Varuna and Vishnu can assume its shape—it was Vishnu's first incarnation as the savior of mankind from the flood, and Varuna is the golden fish water deity—so it is a propitious symbol of wealth, fertility and love to the Hindus. In China the fish foretells abundance (the words are homophones in Mandarin) and is an emblem of both the goddess of mercy, Kwan-yin, and of the T'ang dynasty. **Pisces** is the zodiacal sign of twin fishes, representing human conflict, water and otherworldliness.

Carp *Above*

The carp has little significance in Western cultures, but in the East it is a positive symbol of **love**, courage, dignity and good fortune. In Japan, the carp is a sign of the gracious acceptance of fate and, because it lives a long life, it represents luck. The Japanese word for "carp" is a homophone of "**love**," so it also assumes this symbolism. Moreover, because it overcomes all obstacles when swimming upstream to reach its spawning grounds, it signifies endurance and was an emblem of courage for the Samurai. The Chinese carp shares many of these associations but is also representative of perseverance and literary success because it can leap the Dragon-gate rapids to transform itself into the knowledgeable **dragon**.

Starfish *Above*

The starfish, or sea star, shares much of the symbolism of the **star** because of its shape. In Christian iconography, however, it represents the **Virgin Mary** (*Stella Maris*, meaning "the Star of the Sea"), who assures safe passage over the tempestuous sea and is thus a shining beacon of salvation in the dangerous waters of the world. This significance is further extended to the Holy Spirit, charity and the Christian faith. Because it is a celestial symbol thriving rather than drowning in the sea, the starfish also represents pure and inextinguishable **love**.

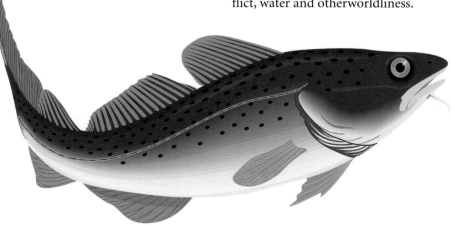

Molluscs

Shell *Above*

The shell is a universally positive feminine symbol of birth, life, resurrection, **love** and **good luck**. Because of its hard casing that protects life (and contains pearls), the bivalved mollusc symbolizes the womb and fertility, and as an aquatic being, it is also feminine, lunar and associated with virginity. In Greco-Roman mythology, Aphrodite (**Venus**), goddess of love, was said to be created from foam and carried ashore on a scallop shell, as was the Hindu goddess, Lakshmi. In Christianity (and in other religions), the shell signifies resurrection and also baptism, because shells were often sprinkled over baptismal water. In medieval times, a scallop shell symbolized a pilgrimage, especially to St. James's shrine in Santiago de Compostela in Spain: St. James was patron of pilgrims and his attribute was a scallop shell. The guardian angel

Raphael also was depicted with a scallop shell. Because it was believed to be fertilized by dew, the shell could signify the **Virgin Mary**, mother of the "sacred pearl"—Jesus. In both Buddhism and Hinduism, the **conch shell** is particularly symbolic because its call awakens the faithful. The shell is one of the Eight Symbols of Good Augury in China and signifies a prosperous journey.

Snail *Right*

Sharing the significance of the **shell**, the snail is a symbol of birth and renewal but also of slowness. Its withdrawal into, and emergence from, its shell (equated with a cave) has rebirth symbolism and can additionally signify the waxing and waning of the **moon**. Through its **spiral**-like shell, it represents the dynamic and cosmic attributes of this shape, along with those of the labyrinth. Some Native American wind gods take its form because, like the gastropod, wind can reach into its habitat. In the ancient

Mayan and Aztec cultures, the snail was associated with deities such as the Mexican moon god, Tecciztecatl. The snail is a symbol of laziness in Christianity and of sinful behavior because it can feed on slimy matter.

Octopus *Below, left*

The octopus (or cuttlefish) symbol is most prevalent in Mediterranean countries, where it was a widely used decorative motif in Minoan and Mycenean art. Its eight spiral-like tentacles associate it with the unfolding of creation from the cosmic center, a dynamic concept shared by the **spiral** shape, the **dragon** and the **spider**. However, this positive association was sometimes contrasted with the belief that, because it squirts black ink, it represented the spirit of the devil and hell. As an aquatic creature, it assumes the symbolism of the **water** and **moon** and can also signify **thunder** and **rain**. It can be equated with the zodiacal sign of **Cancer** and the summer solstice.

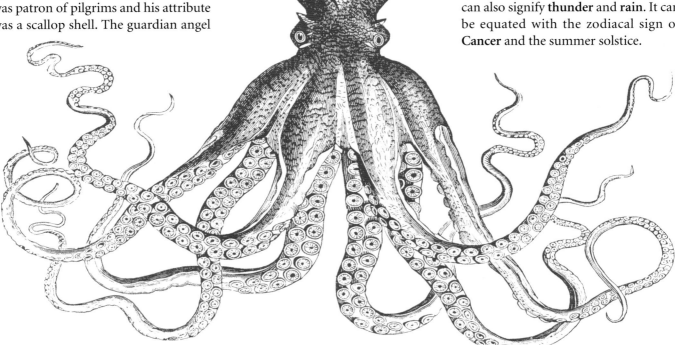

Birds

Eagle *Right*

With its majestic appearance, soaring flight and acute vision, the eagle is a universal symbol and represents the all-seeing sky god. It also represents courage, victory and power, height, **thunder** and storms. To the ancient Greeks and Romans, it was the lightning-bearer for **Zeus** (Jupiter) and represented the victorious Roman Empire on the banners of the Roman legion. In Christianity, the eagle symbolizes the omnipotence of God, faith, Christ's ascension and St. John. The eagle shares the symbolism of the **phoenix** because, in Christian legend, it renewed itself every ten years by flying into the **sun** and then into the sea three times. It thus became a symbol of rebirth and baptism. A **serpent** in an eagle's beak signifies Christ's victory over **Satan**. The eagle-shaped lectern holding the Bible represents the inspiration of the Gospels and power. The eagle is frequently depicted as a solar emblem battling with serpents (chthonic powers) or in victorious conflict with a bull or lion, demonstrating the triumph of spiritual over earthly power. In Native American cultures, the eagle's feathers symbolize the sun's rays; worn as a headdress they represent the Thunderbird and Great Spirit; the eagle can also signify the day and is a messenger between the gods and man. As king of the birds, the eagle is an emblem of royalty, an association developed by its status as the most popular heraldic symbol; it also signifies empires such as the Holy Roman and that of Napoleon. The double-headed eagle of the Byzantine and prerevolutionary Russian empires was derived from the Hittite symbolism of twin gods of power and omniscience. Many states have adopted the eagle as a symbol of nationhood and sovereignty, including the United States, where the bald eagle is the national symbol. It has ambivalent significance when associated with the seven deadly sins and the four cardinal virtues, symbolizing pride and justice respectively.

Owl *Below*

Although sacred to **Athena**, the Greek goddess of learning, and a symbol of **wisdom**, the owl suffers negative associations in most traditions. In many cultures—including those of Ancient Egypt and Christianity—this night bird denoted death, misfortune and spiritual darkness. Although the Celts regarded it as sacred, it was linked with the underworld as a "night hag" and "corpse bird." In Hinduism, it was the messenger of the Vedic god of the dead, Yama. West African and Australian Aboriginal cultures regard the owl as a messenger of sorcerers, and in medieval Western Europe, it was believed that **witches** could transform themselves into owls. For Native Americans; it shares this significance but can also symbolize wisdom. In China and Japan, it was believed to abduct children and therefore signified both crime and ungrateful offspring. The owl symbolizes blindness and is considered an unclean bird in Hebrew lore. Generally, the barn owl and horned owl (shown here) are especially demonic. The screech owl, however, can sometimes play a benevolent role in warning the hunter of danger.

Hawk *Below*

The hawk, falcon and similar birds of prey have the conflicting symbolism of evil and **death**, plus solar light, sharing this significance with the **eagle**. As the king of fowl in Ancient Egypt, the falcon was a sacred royal bird because it was believed to personify the all-seeing **Horus**, the sky god (or the sun god, **Ra**). He and other Egyptian gods are frequently depicted with the head of a fal-

con. Early Christians, however, believed that the hawk signified evil, while a tamed hawk represented the converted pagan, and a hooded hawk symbolized hope for illumination. In Greco-Roman legend, the hawk was the messenger of Apollo and was sacred to Circe, the Greek sorceress. To the Celts, the falcon was the symbol of victory (usually over the hare, which epitomized lust). It was a form that the Norse god Odin assumed and was an attribute of Freyja. In Hinduism, the hawk Gayatri was the vehicle of Indra and carried soma from heaven. It symbolizes the **sun** in China, where it also denotes war. Polynesians believe that the hawk is a prophetic bird with magical powers of healing. The bird illustrated here is a Cooper's Hawk.

Raven *Below*

The raven (along with the crow) is a bird of ambivalent symbolism: although it shares the solar associations of most birds, its black feathers can cause it to be regarded as the epitome of evil. Because it is intelligent and can speak, it was sometimes accorded the attributes of prophecy (usually of ill omen) and wisdom. Some Native American cultures consider it variously as the demiurge, the sly **trickster** or a messenger of the Great Spirit. Ancient Egyptians regarded it as a destructive bird, as did the Jews, believing that it plucked out the eyes of the dead. As the Blessed Raven goddess in Celtic myth, it was a symbol of war, fertility and prophecy; yet as the Raven of Battle and the goddess Badb, it also brought misfortune. Norse cultures, however, believed that two ravens sat on

the shoulders of Odin (Wotan): Hugin ("thought") and Munin ("memory") acted as the deity's eyes. The raven is the emblem of the Vikings and Danes. In Greco-Roman mythology, the raven had positive associations of longevity, fertility, hope and the **sun** but also signified death. It was a messenger of Apollo and was once white, until he blackened it in anger. In China, a three-legged raven lives in the sun, denoting its three phases—dawn, midday and dusk. To the Japanese, it is a divine messenger. In Christian tradition, the raven is equated with **Satan** and sin, although it can be accorded the less malevolent attribute of solitude (from its preference for living away from the flock). Having fed Elijah, it is also a reminder of God's providence and of hope. Noah sent a white raven from the ark and when it failed, it turned black. Alchemists considered it the nigredo, or

dying of the world. It also represents the deadly sin of gluttony. Traditionally, if the raven deserted its nest, disaster was foretold—hence the popular myth that if the ravens ever leave the Tower of London, the English nation will fall.

Crow *Above*

Much of the symbolism of the crow is intertwined with that of the raven and many cultures do not make a distinction between the two. Thus it is a dual symbol of **death** and misfortune, yet it can also have solar attributes. The Egyptians believed that a pair of crows symbolized monogamy. According to the ancient Greeks, Apollo assumed the form of a crow when fleeing Typhon and therefore it was sacred to him and to Athena. The Celtic heroine Branwen, sister of Bran (whose attribute was a raven), was depicted as a white crow. In popular belief, fairies can transform themselves into crows to create mischief. To the Native Americans, the crow is a totem bird that keeps the sacred law and can signify change; like the raven, it can be a **trickster** and messenger of the spirit world.

Vulture *Above, right*

In modern times, the vulture has received bad press due to its scavenging habits and unkempt appearance. However to the ancient Egyptians, it was "Pharoah's hen" and symbolized exemplary motherhood: vultures were believed to be exclusively female and were said to feed their young on their own blood (a myth later applied to the **pelican**). As such, it was sacred to Mut, goddess of maternity, and to **Isis**, who once took the form of a vulture. Hathor was occasionally portrayed with a vulture's head, as was Nekhebet. The vulture exemplified the female principle

and the **scarab** the male (in other cultures the scarab was replaced by a hawk). In Greece and Rome, the vulture was sacred to Ares (Mars), Apollo and Hercules (who killed the vulture who repeatedly tore out Prometheus's liver). It was also the mount of Cronos (Saturn). Like the horn of the **unicorn**, in the Middle Ages, the vulture's claw was believed to detect poison. For obvious reasons, the vulture is closely associated with **death**. Because it picks corpses clean, Native American cultures associate it with purifying **fire** and the **sun**, while in some African traditions, it is considered to know the secret of transformation through its ability to turn dead into living flesh. For Christians, the vulture can signify **Mary**'s virginity, a notion arising from the erroneous belief that the bird's eggs are fertilized by the east wind.

Dove *Below*

The dove symbolizes peace in Christianity and other cultures, but it has many other associations as well. According to Slavic tradition, the soul transforms into a dove on death and in many religions, including Hinduism, the dove is representative of the spirit. Christianity's Holy Ghost is sometimes portrayed as a dove, as are the apostles. In Greco-Roman mythology, the dove was sacred to **Athena** (Minerva), signifying the renewal of life, to **Zeus** (Jupiter)—who was fed by doves—and to Aphrodite (**Venus**), as a symbol of love. The ancient Egyptians considered it representative of

innocence and believed that it sat on the **Tree of Life.** The dove is revered in Islam as the protector of Mohammed. While the dove signifies longevity and orderliness in China, in Japan, it is linked with the war god Hachiman. In the past, the dove was the only bird that Jews permitted to be sacrificed for the mother's purification after childbirth. It can also symbolize Israel. Attributes of ancient fertility goddesses such as Ishtar and Astarte, today doves (and particularly a pair of turtledoves) embody **love.** When associated with the cardinal virtues, the dove signifies temperance. *See also* **Dove and Olive Branch** *in Sacred Symbols.*

Peacock *Above*

The beauty and grandeur of the magnificently plumed peacock have given it a variety of associations. Its stateliness has often led it to be associated with royalty, and some cultures, such as the ancient Babylonians and Persians (who thought that two peacocks guarded the **Tree of Life,** signifying man's duality), seated their royalty on peacock thrones. Roman empresses and princesses had a peacock emblem. Further symbolism of the peacock derives directly from Greco-Roman mythology. The bird-god, Phaon (also known as "the Shiverer"), was identified with a peacock. Hera (Juno)—to whom the bird is sacred—created the peacock from the corpse of the giant, Argus, setting his one hundred eyes in the tail (the tail representing the vault of heaven and the "eyes" the stars). The peacock's distinctive tail markings have been identified with eyes ever since, and in Christianity can represent the "all-seeing" church. As it sheds and renews its feathers, it can signify resurrection, and because it was believed that it could not decay, it symbolizes immortality. In the Hindu pantheon, the peacock is the mount of Lakshmi, Brahma and Kama and is sacred to Sarasvati. Islam describes the peacock's "eye" as the "Eye of the Heart" and associates it with the **sun, moon** and **universe.** Buddhists regard it as symbolic of the Wheel of Life and the sun. It was an emblem of the Buddhist Avalokitesvara and the Amitabha Buddha, also becoming linked with the Chinese and Japanese goddesses of mercy, Kwan-yin and Kwannon. Representing compassionate watchfulness (it was also believed to die of grief if its mate died), the peacock was once sacred in China, where its feather was both an emblem of the Ming dynasty and a symbol of high rank. Because it becomes restless before storms, it is widely associated with rain. The peacock can also be accorded negative symbolism: its ostentation signifies the deadly sin of pride (*Superbia*), and vanity. In Hinduism, it is said that the peacock has the feathers of an angel, the voice of the devil and the walk of a thief, and that it screams upon glimpsing its ugly feet.

Dodo *Above*

The now-extinct dodo was a flightless bird indigenous to Mauritius. It is, therefore, a tragic symbol of the result of the irrevocable extermination of other species by humans and a reminder of our duty to respect the natural world. The expression "as dead as a dodo" can today mean an ultraconservative person or something outdated or defunct.

Ostrich/Emu *Above*

The idiosyncratic habit of burying its head in the sand causes the ostrich to symbolize primarily stupidity and the futile avoidance of unpleasant truth. Historically, it has far more profound and positive significance. Its feathers were important symbols of **justice** and truth in Ancient Egypt, helping to weigh the hearts of the dead in the underworld, as well as signifying the goddess Ma'at, governess of the laws of existence. In antique and medieval belief, many unusual practices were erroneously attributed to the ostrich: it was believed to hatch its eggs by staring at them, thus causing them to become a symbol of meditation. Another theory held that the sun's heat caused the ostrich egg to hatch, and so it became a symbol of creation and life in many cultures, including Christianity, in which it signified the demonic Tiamat (sometimes also portrayed as a dragon) in opposition to Marduk. To some African tribes, the ostrich is a cult bird signifying light, **water** and magical power. The emblem of the Prince of Wales is composed of three ostrich feathers. The emu and ostrich share their symbolism, and this picture is of an Australian emu.

Swan *Above*

The graceful swan has a variety of positive associations, including light, life, grace, purity, **love**, solitude, poetry, music and sincerity. By contrast, it signifies deceit in some cultures since its white plumage covers black flesh. Because it has a rounded body and long neck, swans can represent both masculinity and femininity, as well as **water** and **fire** and, by uniting these qualities, symbolize perfection. In Norse cultures, however, the swan is regarded as the epitome of feminine beauty (the Valkyries sometimes assumed this form). According to an ancient tradition, the swan was believed only to sing when about to die, and the song therefore foretells death (the last work of a poet or composer is known as the swan-song). In Greco-Roman mythology, the swan was sacred to Apollo, god of music, and as a symbol of male virility and the sun, it also drew his chariot. **Zeus** (Jupiter) assumed the form of a swan to seduce Leda and thus it became associated with love. It was also an attribute of Aphrodite (**Venus**), goddess of love, and symbolized chastity. This significance is shared in Christianity, where a swan can symbolize the **Virgin Mary**. The Celts believed that swans were benevolent solar deities, identified by gold or silver chains around their necks. To Native Americans, the swan carries out the will of the Great Spirit and can call up the four winds. It signifies the sun, grace, nobility and courage in Oriental cultures. To Hindus, the swan was the Hamsa bird (combining Ham and Sa in the divine mind) and signified both perfect union and the breath of the spirit. It was also the mount of Brahma and laid the Cosmic Egg. The goose shares many of the symbolic associations of the swan.

Stork *Below*

Today the stork is best known as the mythical bringer of babies to new parents, but it is also a more general good-luck symbol. The stork is a migratory bird—the emblem of the traveler—and, through its habit of leaving for warmer climes in winter and returning in spring, it represents spring, resurrection and new life (in the lands to which it migrates it was often said to take on human form). This probably explains the origin of the stork's symbolism as the deliverer of children, although in northern Europe it was believed that the souls of unborn children inhabited the stork's natural habitat of marshes and ponds. In China, the stork signifies longevity (it was itself believed to live a long life) and the recluse. Its habit of standing immobile on one leg led to its association with meditation. In Ancient Egypt and Rome, it symbolized a child's gratitude because it was said to feed its parents when they could no longer sustain themselves. In Greco-Roman mythology, it also represented woman as nourisher and was sacred to Hera (Juno). Because it kills **serpents**, it is regarded in Christian tradition as an enemy of **Satan** and can epitomize Christ as well as the virtues of chastity, purity, vigilance and prudence. A Swedish legend says that a stork appeared at the Crucifixion, exhorting Christ to be strong by crying *Stryka! Stryka!* (strength).

Pelican *Above, right*

The pelican was once believed to feed its chicks with its own blood by pecking open its breast—thus trading its life for that of its young—so its primary significance is of self-sacrifice and parental love. In medieval tradition, it was said that the female bird smothered her young with love but that the male revived them

with his blood. Alternatively, the male killed them in anger and the loving mother revived them with blood from her breast—both myths, and other variants, signify resurrection. Since the time of Dante, the pelican has been identified with Christ and signifies piety and the **Eucharist** to Christians. Jews, however, regard it as bringing misfortune and desolation. In alchemy it represents resurrection, the antithesis of the raven.

Magpie *Below*

The black-and-white magpie has traditionally been distrusted in the West as a result of its perceived role in foretelling bad luck and death, although the origins of these associations are unknown. Medieval Christians believed that the magpie signified evil, persecution or premature death. It is depicted in scenes of the **Nativity** and can personify **Satan** and symbolize vanity and dissipated behavior. There is an old English rhyme attributing prophetic powers to magpies, which interprets the significance of seeing magpies as

follows: one represents sorrow; two, joy; three, a wedding; four, a birth; five, a christening; six, a death; seven, heaven; eight, hell; and nine, the Devil. In the East, the negative symbolism of the magpie is reversed, and in China it is regarded as the Bird of Joy. The prophetic association is, however, shared in the East, where it is the bringer of good fortune, and its chattering heralds good news and guests. The magpie was an emblem of the Manchu dynasty.

Swallow *Above*
A migratory bird, the swallow's return in **spring** signifies hope, fertility and the renewal of life. Because it was once believed to hibernate (variously in mud, caves or water), it can symbolize resurrection. In common with most birds, it also represents light. In many ancient cultures, including the Egyptian (where it was sacred to **Isis**), it epitomized motherhood. Egyptians also regarded swallows as northern stars swooping above the **Tree of Life**. A potent symbol in both Ancient Greece and Rome, it was unlucky to kill a swallow, as it embodied the spirits of dead children; it was also an attribute of Aphrodite (**Venus**). Along with a **stork**, Swedish legend tells that a swallow was present at Christ's **Crucifixion**, where it called for consolation (*Svala! Svala!*). In Chinese tradition, it is a symbol of daring, danger, fidelity and a positive change in fortune, but in Japan, it can signify unfaithfulness as well as maternal care. The swallow is revered in Islam, as it is thought to make an annual pilgrimage to Mecca. In heraldry, the swallow is portrayed as the footless martlet, because in the Middle Ages it was believed never to touch the ground (a

belief echoed in African cultures, where it represents purity). It also represented younger sons. Furthermore, swallows were said to feed their offspring on the sap of the celandine, which gave them the power of sight, so they became symbolic of God's illumination. In popular tradition, a swallow's nest in the eaves of a house brings **good luck**.

Cock *Right*
The cock, cockerel or rooster generally signifies courage and vigilance but also arrogance and conceit. In Ancient Greece, it was believed to salute the **sun** by crowing at dawn and was sacred to Apollo and many other gods. In most cultures, this practice also caused it to represent both the victory of light over darkness (and hence good over evil) and guardianship. Furthermore, it was regarded as a symbol of **fire** by virtue of its fiery red comb. Conversely, however, Celtic and Norse cultures believed that it was a bird of the underworld. It is a universal fertility symbol and in many cultures was a sacrificial bird, especially at harvest time. In Buddhism, the red cock symbolizes lust in the Round of Existence, while in Shinto Buddhism, it stands on the drum summoning the faithful to prayer. An aggressive creature, the cock epitomizes battle and courage in the Far East. Because of its habit of strutting, it is also regarded as a symbol of conceit—particularly in men. In Christianity, because the cock crowed three times after Peter denied Christ, it became a symbol of Christ's passion, but it later came to signify a saint's repentance and papal vigilance, as well as being a resurrection symbol. In association with alertness against evil, it is a popular motif on weathervanes (weathercocks)—particularly on church steeples. The cock, or rooster, is one of the twelve signs of the **Chinese zodiac**, where it represents a myriad of qualities, including honesty, moral and physical courage, but also arrogance and bossiness. It is an important bird to the Chinese, signifying **yang** and a number of other attributes, such

as war, fortune, fidelity, the sunset, protection and literary skills. According to popular Western belief, the black cock is an agent of **Satan**. The cock is the national emblem of France.

Turkey *Below*
An indigenous American bird, the turkey is an important fertility symbol for many Amerindian cultures, signifying both female fertility and male virility. It was accordingly sacrificed during fertility rites. The Creek tribe traditionally holds a Turkey Dance during its **fire** festival. In addition, the bird has also represented self-sacrifice and altruism to many Native Americans, who termed it the "give-away." It was known as the "Great Xolotl" and the "Jeweled Fowl" and was regarded as sacred by the Mayans, Toltecs and Aztecs. Since the seventeenth century, the turkey has formed the main part of the American Thanksgiving dinner, which commemorates the Pilgrim Fathers' first harvest meal of four wild turkeys in 1621. The turkey was subsequently exported from America to England, where it has become the centerpiece of the traditional Christmas Day lunch. Like the **peacock**, the turkey is associated with inclement weather, because it becomes agitated before storms.

Insects

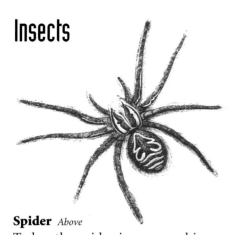

Spider *Above*

Today, the spider is an unambiguous **phobic** symbol yet, through the spinning of its web, it symbolizes life and fate. Because its web radiates from the center and is generated from the spider's body, in some cultures, the web is a symbol of the sun and life-creation. Its intricate and labyrinthine web led the Celts to associate it with the web of life which man must negotiate. To the ancient Egyptians (where the spider was sacred to Neith) and Greeks, where it was a symbol of the *Moirai* (the Fates), **Athena** (Minerva) and Arachne, the web symbolized fate. In Hinduism, as in other traditions, the web signifies the cosmic order with the spider as the center or *maya*—the weaver of illusion. In Oceania and some Native American tribes, the spider created the universe, and in Australian Aboriginal cultures, the Great Spider is a solar hero; while in some parts of Africa, as in North America, the spider is a **trickster**. In Christianity, the cobweb is symbolic of human frailty and futility, with the sticky web a devilish trap for the unwary leading to the spider's identification with **Satan** and evil. Because it immobilizes and then pounces on its helpless prey, the spider represents the terrible Great Mother who creates but also destroys. To Christians, it represents the miser who sucks its prey dry. The Japanese believe that spider women entrap travelers, while the goblin spider is a dangerous shapeshifter. Despite all this, in popular tradition, it is unlucky to kill a spider, which can signify money or good luck (as it did to Romans).

Scorpion *Right*

The scorpion, with its hidden, venomous sting, is an unmistakable symbol of danger and fear, but can also signify protection against enemies. It was traditionally believed that the scorpion could produce an oil to counteract its sting, so creating both toxin and antidote. Thus, in many cultures, including those of Ancient Egypt and Tibet, scorpion amulets were worn to ward off harm. A further ambiguity lies in the scorpion's association with mother goddesses such as the Babylonian Ishtar, and the Egyptian **Isis**. In Sumerian belief, this arachnid had solar associations and scorpion men guarded sacred gateways. To the ancient Egyptians, the scorpion was evil and an animal form of Set, yet the protective goddess of the dead, Selket, was depicted with a scorpion's head. In Greco-Roman mythology, Artemis (**Diana**) was angered by Orion and exhorted the scorpion to sting Orion in the foot. After Orion died, **Zeus** (Jupiter) set the creature in the sky and it became the zodiacal sign of **Scorpio**. The scorpion is a symbol of treachery (personified in Judas) in Christianity, embodying the evil of **Satan** and the sins of heresy, hatred and envy. It was also once an emblem of Africa as well as of the earth.

Butterfly *Below*

Because it evolves from egg to caterpillar to chrysalis and then emerges in its full glory from an inert cocoon, the primary symbolism of the butterfly is that of the soul, transformation and rebirth—the creation of life from apparent death. To the Chinese, the butterfly is an emblem of immortality. Conversely, because of its flighty behavior, the Japanese regard it as a symbol of fickleness and compare it with vain women; a pair of butterflies, however, signifies marital happiness, and a white butterfly represents the spirit of the dead. Christian tradition accepts the butterfly as an emblem of resurrection (the caterpillar signifying life and the cocoon death), but has additionally considered it a symbol of vanity and transience because it lives for such a short time. In Ancient Greece, **Psyche** was represented as a butterfly because both shared the same name. In dream analysis, the butterfly denotes new beginnings.

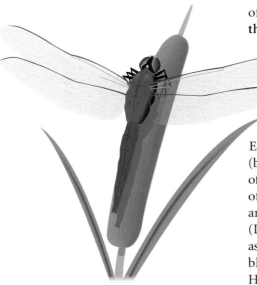

Dragonfly *Above*

To the Chinese, the dragonfly represents **summer** but also instability (because of its unpredictable flight) and weakness. It is a national emblem of Japan (sometimes known as the "Dragonfly Island") because the insect and country share a similar shape. Additionally, it is considered to signify unreliability. Some Native American cultures regard it as symbolizing swift activity and whirlwinds.

Bee *Above*

Like the **ant**, the bee is a communal insect and symbolizes cooperative industry and diligence. Bees can therefore signify vigilance (they were thought never to sleep) and purity because they feed off blossoms and were believed to be parthenogenic. For this reason, the bee is associated with Christianity's **Virgin Mary** and in ancient Greece with virgin priestesses, or *Melissae,* who were termed "bees" (the queen bee being the Great Mother). Because it hoards the product

of its industry—honey—it represents **thrift** (and is therefore sometimes the emblem of banks). Bees were regarded in many cultures as messengers to the gods, so it was necessary to inform them of important events. In Ancient Egypt, the bee represented the Lower Egyptian pharoah, the soul and the sun (by virtue of its golden stripes and power of flight). Collectively, bees were the tears of **Ra**. The Greek bee symbolized work and obedience and was sacred to Ceres (Demeter) and Artemis (**Diana**), as well as being the emblem of Ephesus. In India, blue bees rest on the forehead of the Hindu god, Krishna, and Shiva can be represented by a bee and triangle. Bees form the bowstring of the god of love, Kama, signifying sweet pain, and the bee has been equated with the moon. Since it disappears in **winter** but returns in **summer**, the bee can additionally signify resurrection and hope. The bee was associated with Christ because it can sting if threatened but also produces sweet honey. A bee and beehive represent the faithful and the church in Christianity. Honey and milk are foods of the gods, a symbol of the abundance of the Jewish Promised Land and a sign of Christ's compassion. It was once popularly believed to have preservative qualities and to act as an aphrodisiac, thus signifying immortality and fertility. Since the days of Ancient Greece, honey signifies eloquence ("a honeyed tongue"). The bee was the emblem of Napoleon I, although Napoleon III subsequently termed it a symbol of the workers.

Ant *Top, right*

The humble, hard-working ant is a universal symbol of industriousness and organization. The community of ants in their anthill can be considered both a microcosm of man and his world and a lesson in the power of communal cooperation. The ant was sacred to the harvest goddess, Ceres (Demeter) in Ancient Greece and Rome, where it was regarded as a creature of prophecy. To the Chinese,

it symbolizes orderliness, virtue, humility and patriotism. In India, however, its unceasing activity is regarded as a symbol of the futility and transience of worldly actions. Because the ant hoards food, in Judaism and Christianity, it can symbolize frugality, prudence and foresight. Furthermore, in popular Christian tradition, the ant symbolizes the wise man who can distinguish between true and false because the ant was believed to eat **wheat** but not barley. Today multitudes of ants are a common **phobic** symbol.

Grasshopper/Cricket *Above*

The symbolism of the grasshopper and cricket is inevitably intertwined. In Western cultures, the grasshopper represents irresponsibility because it appears to leap about randomly, but, as a creature of **summer**, it can also signify the delights of the warm season. In Ancient Greece, Athenians indicated noble ancestry by wearing a golden grasshopper in their hair. In China, the grasshopper's fertility causes it to denote abundance and many sons, and when depicted with a **chrysanthemum**, it represents high office. In many countries, the cricket in particular is an auspicious symbol of **luck**, courage and summer. Through the fairytale character of Jiminy Cricket, it has also become symbolic of conscience and the inner voice.

Trees

Tree of Knowledge *Right*

In the Bible, the Tree of Knowledge (sometimes depicted as a vine) grows in paradise and bears the enticing—but forbidden—**apples** that the **serpent** tempted Eve to taste, thus precipitating the Fall of Man. A dualistic symbol, it signifies the knowledge of both good and evil, offering an intellectual awakening, albeit with perhaps ambiguous results, and was variously seen as symbolic of free will, sexual experience and self-indulgence. The alchemical Tree of Knowledge, called *arbor philosophica*, denotes creative evolution. In Judaism, it is believed that God will burn the Tree of Knowledge at the coming of the messiah, whereupon its true meaning will finally be revealed.

Tree of Life *Below*

The Tree of Life—the *arbor vitae*—is highly significant in most early cultures, symbolizing life itself, regeneration and immortality. The Tree of Life can also have the dual significance of the cosmic tree—the *imago mundi*—that stands at the center of the world: its straight trunk can be compared with the *axis mundi*, representing the earthly world; its roots anchor it to the earth and grow toward the underworld; while its branches

stretch for the **sun**, representing man's eternal search for spiritual enlightenment. The Tree of Life is thus a cosmic symbol both of man and of the link between paradise, earth and hell. In both Judaism and Christianity, the Tree of Life is believed to be at the center of paradise and represents the perfection of Eden. In common with beliefs of many other traditions, it bears twelve (or ten) fruits (which can also be forms of the sun or signs of the **zodiac**), that represent the rewards of spiritual growth. Both the tree and its fruits confer immortality and transcend evil. In the Taoist and Buddhist paradise, the **peach** is the fruit of immortality, corresponding in Persia to the sap of the haoma tree (or the almond), while in some Eastern traditions, the fruits are replaced by jewels. Furthermore, in many cultures, a sun is situated in the trunk, signifying the source of all life. Mythical creatures were often believed to live in the boughs of the Tree of Life, as were birds (sometimes representing dead or unborn souls). **Palm** and **olive** trees were popular candidates as the Tree of Life in Babylonian, Chaldean and Phoenician tradition, as are the peach, plum and mulberry in China. In Ancient Egypt, the Tree of Life was represented by a sycamore bearing gifts, while the Norse cosmic tree, Yggdrasil, was an ash, and that of **Thor**, an **oak**. In Mithraic tradition, the Tree of

Life was believed to be an **evergreen** pine; in Germanic myth, it is variously the fir, lime or linden of Wotan; and in shamanistic cultures it is the birch. The Christian **cross** can be regarded as a Tree of Life, signifying victory over death. The Jewish Tree of Life grows in the center of Jerusalem, and in Hinduism, it is personified by the earth goddess Aditi; in Japan, it is named as the mythological Sa-ka-ti. The Tree of Life is universally difficult for the mortal to find and is frequently guarded by a pair of monsters or animals. The Babylonian Tree of Life depicted here, upon which the universe revolves, has branches of lapis lazuli. Inverted trees, such as the Kabbalistic Tree of Life, or *sefiroth*, or that mentioned in the Indian Upanishads, grow downward into the earth, because their roots are in the spiritual world: they thus symbolize the distilling of the spirit into bodily form. In many traditions, there are variant trees of life, and dual trees of life and knowledge or of life and death. The counterpart of the Babylonian Tree of Life was a Tree of Truth.

Christmas Tree *Top, center*
The Christmas Tree has become such a universal symbol that it is now erected and decorated by people of all religions. Its origins lie firmly in pagan cultures. In Norse and Scandinavian tradition, evergreen trees were decorated (and Wotan/Odin's fir tree was burned) in honor of the winter solstice (December 25) to celebrate the rebirth of the **sun**, to symbolize the life-force that prevails even in the barren **winter** months and to commemorate the end of the old year and start of the new. During the "raw nights" (December 25-January 6) of pagan times, when evil spirits abounded, evergreen branches decorated with lighted candles were hung

in dwellings for protection. In antiquity, too, the pine tree, dedicated to Attis and Cybele, was often decorated with ornaments. The Christmas Tree only became a Christian symbol in the nineteenth century, symbolizing rebirth and immortality. The fir tree itself signifies Christ as the Tree of Life, while the **candles** represent Christ as the light of the world—and sometimes souls, or the sun, moon and stars of the Cosmic Tree. **Apples** (today replaced by baubles) were sometimes used for decoration, symbolizing the apple of the **Tree of Knowledge** which caused humanity's original sin, which Christ alone has the power to absolve.

Evergreen Trees *Left*
Because they never shed their leaves, evergreen trees, or conifers, are a universal symbol of longevity and spiritual and physical immortality. Trees such as the cypress are often planted in the cemeteries of Europe, India and China, signifying life after death. The yew is also a graveyard tree and a symbol of mourning and grief. **Wreaths** crafted from evergreen foliage can additionally signify undying fame. As well as having significance in Europe, the pine tree is the prime symbol of longevity and of constant friendship in Japan.

Deciduous Trees *Below*
Unlike evergreens, deciduous trees follow the cycle of nature, shedding their foliage in **winter** and renewing it in **spring**. They therefore signify regeneration, rebirth and the irresistible power of life triumphant over death. Most deciduous tree species have specific symbolic meanings.

Olive *Below*
Just as the **olive branch** is a universal sign of peace, so is the tree, but it also symbolizes knowledge, purification, fertility, longevity, abundance and **victory**. Because it produces a rich oil which can be burned in lamps, the olive tree was sacred in Greco-Roman times to **Athena** (Minerva), goddess of learning. The cleansing properties of its oil make the tree a symbol of purification. The olive tree can live for centuries, so it signifies long life. It is a fertility symbol, and the brides of antiquity carried olive garlands. The olive wreath of **Zeus** was the highest prize of the ancient Olympic Games, representing victory. The olive of the Acropolis had power over the life and future of the Greek people. In Jewish belief, the olive tree symbolizes strength and beauty and was the emblem of the tribe of Asher, while in China, it represents quiet persistence and grace and is the tree of **fall**. Christianity's **Virgin Mary** can sometimes be represented with an olive branch of harmony, instead of a lily.

Oak *Above*

King of the forest, the mighty oak tree is more prevalent in the Occident than the Orient, and thus carries more symbolism in Western countries, where it represents strength, masculinity, military glory and immortality. The oak was widely believed to attract **lightning** and was therefore sacred to the **thunder** gods of most Aryan cultures, including the Greco-Roman **Zeus** (Jupiter), the Norse god **Thor**, and the Germanic god Donar; it was also dedicated to Silvanus, the Roman forest god. The oak was especially revered by Druids (in conjunction with the "female" **mistletoe**) and the Germanic, Celtic and Norse civilizations, who worshiped it in sacred oak groves. In all these cultures, it was representative of divinity and masculinity. Despite its masculine association, however, it is sacred in some cultures to goddesses: some Native American tribes regard it as symbolic of Mother Earth, and in antiquity, it was dedicated to Juno (Hera) and Cybele; the dryads were oak nymphs. The hard wood of the oak was once equated with incorruptibility. Combined with its potential to live to a great age, this belief caused it to signify both strength and eternal life. In Christian iconography, the oak symbolizes Christ's unshakeable faith and virtue, and is often believed to be the wood of the **cross**. An oak under the foot of the mis-

sionary saint, Boniface, represents his conversion of the Druids. In Judaism, the oak is the tree of the Covenant and signifies God's presence. The Romans awarded **wreaths** of oak leaves to those who saved lives in battle, a custom echoed in the eighteenth century when the oak became a German symbol of heroism. From the nineteenth century oak leaves were again used in **victory** wreaths and as military badges. In China, as well as signifying male strength, the oak represents weakness, because, unlike the willow or bamboo, it remains rigid in storms, therefore breaking instead of bending under pressure.

Palm *Below*

In modern, nonreligious iconography, the palm tree promises the delights of tropical countries and is a symbol greatly favored by the tourist industry. It has a far more profound symbolism in religious and historical contexts, however. Because of its height and radiating leaves, it was an early fertility and **sun** symbol. Later, it represented fame, **victory**, peace and righteousness. Because of its solar associations, the Babylonians considered it a divine tree, and it was also sacred to Ra in Egypt and to Helios and Apollo in Greece. The palm was a **Tree of Life** in many early Middle Eastern civilizations: the Phoenician god Baal-Tamar was lord of the palm, and it was an emblem of mother-goddesses, including Astarte and Ishtar. In Ancient Rome, victors were presented with palm branches—the origin of its victory symbolism—and, from early Christian times, evergreen palm leaves were used as funerary emblems, signifying both martyrdom and victory over death. When Christ entered Jerusalem, palm branches were strewn in his path, an event

commemorated by Palm Sunday, when **cross**-shaped palm leaves are blessed and preserved until Ash Wednesday to signify Christ's presence. In the Middle Ages, a palm leaf was a badge of pilgrimage to the Holy Land; those who wore it were nicknamed "palmers". (*See also* **Palm Tree** *in Sacred Symbols.*)

Aspen *Above*

The aspen is a member of the poplar family and is remarkable for its "shivering" leaves that quiver in the breeze. Because of this characteristic, it is a symbol of both fear and indecision. The ancient Greeks believed that it grew in the underworld, and thus the aspen came to signify funerals and wakes. In addition, by apparently mimicking the shivering of fever-stricken patients, the aspen was considered to represent fever and was used as a remedy against this form of illness. In Christian tradition, however, the aspen is associated with Christ in two stories: in the first, its leaves began to tremble uncontrollably (and have done so ever since) when it heard that the cross upon which Christ was to be crucified would be made of its wood; in the second, its leaves were cursed to shiver in perpetuity because it did not bow its head during the Crucifixion. In Christian symbolism, the aspen therefore signifies lamentation or shame.

Fruit and Seeds

Fruit *Right*

Collectively, as depicted in this Flemish still life, fruit represents the bounty of nature. The juxtaposition of many different types of fruit is a wishful symbol of prosperity and of abundant fertility, because it signifies both rich, productive soil and clement weather. Ripe fruit symbolizes maturity. Because it contains the seeds of growth, fruit, like the **egg**, indicates potential, immortality and cosmic origins. The cornucopia—a horn overflowing with fruits and flowers—is one of the most resonant symbols of natural abundance.

Apple *Below*

Cézanne's *Still Life* displays a wealth of apples, a fruit rich with associations in many cultures. The apple was an ancient fertility symbol, and its spherical shape caused it to be identified with the **earth**, totality and eternity. Many traditions believed that apples grew on the **Tree of Life**. As the fruit of the Celtic Silver Bough, they signified fertility. In Christianity, the apple is the forbidden fruit with which the **serpent** tempted Eve, leading to the Fall of Man (an ape with an apple in its mouth represents this). It is thus a symbol of earthly desires and temptation—in Greek mythology, Atalanta, too, yielded to the temptation of golden apples of Aphrodite (**Venus**). This negative interpretation is underlined by the derivation of its name from the Latin word *malum*—"evil." As the fruit of the **Tree of Knowledge**, however,

the apple represents divine wisdom and Christ—the "new Adam"—can be represented by an apple, in which context it signifies salvation. The Norse goddess Freyja rejuvenated the gods with apples from her garden, Asgard; the golden apples of Hera (Juno), guarded by Hesperides and the dragon, Ladon, also symbolized immortality (stolen by Hercules, they became his attribute). The golden apple is a symbol of discord, because, in Greek mythology, Etis (god of strife) asked Paris to chose the most beautiful goddess. Paris preferred Aphrodite to Hera and **Athena** (Minerva); his action ultimately led to his death in the

Trojan war, but the apple became sacred to Aphrodite (red apples particularly signifying **love**). In China, the apple represents peace and harmony. It is also a popular symbol of health, for eating one a day is supposed to obviate the need for a doctor. Today, the apple is an emblem of New York City, the "Big Apple."

Pineapple *Left*

A fertility symbol, the prickly pineapple was an emblem of Cybele, the mother-goddess of Phrygia, while a pillar topped by a pineapple represented the Babylonian god of life and heaven, Marduk. As a life-giving symbol, it is often used as a device of architectural embellishment.

Peach *Above*

The peach has great symbolic importance in China and Japan, signifying marriage, longevity and immortality. Because the Chinese character *t'ao* means both "peach" and "marriage," the two concepts have become linked. Sometimes associated with the **Tree of Life**, peach trees blossom early, thus symbolizing fertility. The peach tree in the celestial orchard, the Chinese garden of paradise, bears fruit only once every three thousand years, so is a symbol of long life; Shoulao, the god of longevity, is frequently depicted in association with this rare peach. The peach tree also has special resonance in Taoism, where it is the Tree of Immortality, providing food for the immortals. To Buddhists, the peach is one of the three blessed fruits. In Christian art, a peach with a leaf attached symbolizes the unity of heart and tongue and hence truth and silence. The peach can also take the place of the **apple** in representing the fruit of salvation.

Grapes *Above*

In common with all fruits, grapes are a symbol of life, fertility and abundance, but they also represent **sacrifice** because of the wine they produce—particularly when blood-red. In the Old Testament,

the grapevine was compared with both the people of Israel and the coming messiah; to Jews it signifies peace and plenty. In Christianity, the grapevine represents Christ, its branches his disciples and the grapes the faithful. When portrayed with a sheaf of **corn**, the vine symbolizes the **Eucharist**. Noah planted the first vine and later became drunk, leading to its symbolizing the deadly sin of gluttony. It is a general symbol of the **fall** season. The symbolism of grapes and wine overlap. Because it intoxicates, wine signified ecstatic communication with the gods. In Ancient Greece, Dionysus (Bacchus) was the god of wine (which was believed to be his blood), and wine could therefore signify both death and eternal life. In Christianity, although wine symbolizes Christ's blood and sacrifice, it also represents youth, life and immortality. In Islam, as in many cultures, wine represents divine **love**, **wisdom** and truth (*in vino veritas*).

Pine Cone *Above*

The fruit of the pine tree—an evergreen—signifies immortality. The pine cone was an important fertility symbol in the classical world. The ancient Greeks, along with the Assyrians, regarded it as a symbol of masculinity because of its phallic shape. It formed the apex of the thyrsus staff, which represented both fertility and immortality. Despite its masculine associations, however, it was an emblem of Artemis (**Diana**) symbolizing feminine purity and also of the Roman goddess, **Venus** (Aphrodite). In Christian iconography, it can form the crown of the **Tree of Life**. Because of its swirling form, it is often associated with dynamic generative and cosmic power.

Fig *Above*

The fig is a symbol of fertility and natural bounty. The leaf represents masculinity and the abundant fruit femininity. In Greco-Roman mythology, its phallic representation of male virility linked it with Bacchus (Dionysus), Jupiter (**Zeus**) and Priapus. In Jewish belief, the fig is a sign of peace and prosperity and is a symbol of Israel. The fig tree is revered by Hindus as the provider of shelter during Vishnu's birth. Its greatest significance, however, is in Buddhism, for the fig, an emblem of **Buddha**, was believed to be the sacred Bodhi Tree under which Buddha achieved enlightenment. In Islam, the fig tree, by which Mohammed made a sacred oath, is regarded as the Tree of Heaven.

Acorn *Above*

The acorn, seed of the mighty **oak**, is a symbol of potential. In Norse and Celtic belief, acorns were symbolic of life, fertility and immortality. Druids swallowed acorns, which were believed to have prophetic qualities, and acorns were sacred to **Thor**, whose **Tree of Life** was the oak. Acorns and oak leaves form one of the circular "hex" signs used by the Amish and Mennonite communities of southern Pennsylvania, the various signs believed to bestow favors such as protection or natural abundance.

Flowers

Rose *Above*

The rose is one of the most important floral symbols in the Western world. Protected by thorns, it is a beautiful, fragrant flower, representing beauty, secrecy, **love**, life, blood, **death** and rebirth. In Ancient Greece and Rome, the rose was sacred to Aphrodite (**Venus**), representing beauty and love, and was believed to have sprung from the blood of Adonis. Dionysus (Bacchus) was garlanded with roses, because they were thought to cool the brain during intoxication. Harpocrates was bribed into secrecy with a white rose by Eros (Cupid) and became the god of silence: this significance was carried over into Christianity, and a rose is often carved onto confessionals or plastered onto ceilings of meeting rooms as a warning that discussions are *sub rosa* ("under the rose"—that is, secret). The Romans scattered roses at funerals as a sign of resurrection. In Christian tradition, it was said that the rose of paradise was thornless, and after the Fall, the thorns serve as a reminder of this catastrophe. The white rose is linked with the **Virgin Mary** (who is the Mystical Rose of Heaven, the rose without thorns) and was a medieval symbol of virginity. The red rose was said to have grown from the blood of Christ and is hence a sign of martyrdom, charity and resurrection. In Islam, the rose signifies both male beauty and the blood of Mohammed, as well as his two sons. The Rose of Baghdad represents the law, the path and knowledge, together symbolizing the truth and Allah. A seven-petaled rose was used in alchemy to represent alchemical relationships and **wisdom**. In Freemasonry, three roses represent light, love and life, while the Rose (or Rosy) cross is the emblem of the **Rosicrucian** society. Different types, colors and species of roses have various specific meanings: the eight-petaled rose, for example, symbolizes regeneration; the blue rose, the impossible; the red and white rose, the union of opposites; and the golden rose (also a papal emblem signifying benediction), perfection. Since **Tudor** times, the rose has been a national symbol of Britain, uniting the red rose of Lancaster with the white of York. A popular heraldic charge, the rose is the cadency mark for the seventh son. In recent times, some European socialist parties (including the British Labour Party) have adopted the red rose as their emblem.

Iris *Above*

The iris and **lily** share much of their symbolism (the iris is a rival contender as the flower of the **fleur-de-lys**), both representing light and hope. Because of its pointed leaves, the iris can be called the "sword lily" and is an emblem of the sorrows of the **Virgin Mary**. The flower was named after the Greek goddess of the rainbow, to whom it was dedicated, and can therefore represent the **bridge** between God and man. To the Chinese, the iris signifies affection, grace and solitary beauty.

Lily *Below*

A symbol of purity, perfection, **mercy** and majesty, in most cultures, the lily once signified light and the male principle (due to the phallic shape of its pistil). In Greco-Roman mythology, the flower was sacred to Hera (Juno), for it was believed to have sprung from her milk, and to Artemis (**Diana**) as a sign of her virginity. According to Christian tradition, it grew from Eve's tears of repentance shed as she left the Garden of Eden. In Christian iconography, the lily is most strongly associated with the **Virgin Mary** (and thus also with the Archangel Gabriel, who is portrayed holding a lily during the Annunciation), signifying chastity, but Joseph is also sometimes shown with a staff blossoming with lilies. The lily's stalk signifies Mary's religious mind, the leaves her humility, the white petals her virginity and its scent her divinity. It has become an attribute of all virgin saints. Christ is occasionally depicted as the judge of the world with a lily in his mouth: in this case the flower represents mercy, while a lily and a **sword** symbolize the innocent and guilty. The lily assumed significance as a royal emblem in Byzantium and in early France (the fleur-de-lys is sometimes considered a stylized lily). With its three petals, the lily signifies the **Trinity** and the triple virtues of faith, hope and charity.

Poppy *Below*

The poppy has the dual symbolism of sleep and remembrance; both interpretations, however, can signify death. Because it produces the narcotic opium, in Ancient Greece, it was sacred to both Hypnos and Morpheus, the gods of sleep and dreams. It was also an emblem of lunar mothergoddesses such as Aphrodite (Venus). Signifying both fertility and oblivion, it was an attribute of Demeter (Ceres) and of Persphone, representing the annual death of nature. In Christian iconography, the poppy can represent Christ's passion and death. In Britain, since 1920 the poppy has been a symbol of the remembrance of soldiers who died serving their country: poppies made by veteran soldiers with disabilities are worn each year on November 11, Remembrance Day. Its origin as a symbol of remembrance was inspired by a poem written in 1915 by the Canadian soldier-surgeon John McCrae: *In Flanders fields the poppies blow/Between the crosses, row on row…*

Sunflower *Above*

As its name suggests, the symbolism of the sunflower is connected with the **sun**: its golden color and ray-like petals, as well as its turning toward the sun as it grows, all identify it as a solar flower. In Mithraic culture, it was the attribute of Mithras, the sun god. It has additional significance in Christianity both as a sign of God's love and of a religious soul; in the latter context, it symbolizes prayer and monastic obedience. More negatively, by its sun-seeking movements, it can signify infatuation, unreliability and phony riches. In Greek mythology, it was the emblem of Clytie (who was rejected by Apollo and transformed into a sunflower) and Daphne. It is considered a magical flower in China, where it represents longevity. It is also a widespread symbol of nobility.

Chrysanthemum *Above, right*

With its primary significance in the Orient, the chrysanthemum is a good-luck symbol, signifying happiness, wealth and longevity as well as meditation and the coming of **fall**. Moreover, its multitude of radiating petals identify it as a sun symbol—the **sun** on **Japan's national flag** is styled after a chrysanthemum. The floral sign of the month of September in Japan, in China it represents October and the fall and harvest (the word *chu* is close to the chrysanthemum's Chinese name, and means "**nine**" and "long time"). To the Chinese, it additionally represents an easy retirement, scholarship and amiability. The sixteen-petaled chrysanthemum is the *mon* (badge) of the Japanese emperor (fourteen petals signify his brothers and sons). The chrysanthemum is Japan's national flower.

Plants

Daisy/Marguerite *Below*

The daisy's symbolism is intertwined with that of the marguerite: both are representative of tears and blood. In association with the **Virgin Mary**, the daisy additionally symbolizes **innocence**, salvation and immortality, sometimes also representing the innocence of the Christ child in Christian art. The daisy was sacred to the Norse mother-goddess, Freyja. As the "day's eye," it is a solar symbol. The marguerite, like the daisy, is likened to a pearl, thus representing tears and the spilled blood of Christ and other Christian martyrs.

Tulip *Below*

Parallel with the Western **rose**, the tulip was the symbol of perfect **love** in Ancient Persia. It was the emblem of the Osman dynasty—the rulers of the Ottoman empire—and of their capital city, Constantinople (Istanbul). Tulips were imported from the Ottoman empire to Holland some centuries ago; such was the enthusiasm of the Dutch for this flower that it is now the national emblem of the Netherlands.

Mistletoe *Below*

Mistletoe is a parasitical plant, needing a host tree on which to grow. It was thus revered in pagan times as a symbol of the femininity that seeks out the nourishment and protection of the "masculine" **oak**. Druids believed that mistletoe was created by a **lightning** bolt striking an oak tree, giving it magical properties. As an **evergreen**, in many cultures, it is sacred to **winter** and a symbol of immortality, while its translucent berries make

it a sign of the **moon** and also thus of fertility. Furthermore, because it is not rooted in the ground, it is sometimes seen as a divine plant, but also signals chaos. Mistletoe played a special role in Celtic rituals. After the winter solstice, it was cut with a golden **sickle** (used both because gold is a **sun** symbol and to avoid its contamination with iron) held in the left hand of a white-robed Druid. It was then caught in a white cloth, as it was believed that it should never touch the ground. This act was meant to release the strength of the oak and was followed by a sacrifice of **bulls**. In Norse mythol-

Foxglove/Hollyhock/Mallow *Above*

The leaves of the hollyhock have greater symbolic significance than its flowers, signifying in many cultures (including Christianity) the desire for forgiveness. To the Chinese, the mallow represents peace, tranquility and humility. In Japan, the hollyhock is sacred to the Kamo-Zinsya shrine in Kyoto, and three hollyhock leaves made up the *mon* (a heraldic badge) of the Tokugawa dynasty. In Celtic countries, the foxglove (whose name is a corruption of the word [little] "folk") is believed to be a flower of the **fairies**. Its leaves produce digitalis, a stimulating medicinal drug.

Mushroom / Toadstool *Below*

Because of their phallic shape and speed of regeneration, both mushrooms and toadstools signify fertility. In China, the mushroom symbolizes long life (because it can be dried and stored), happiness and rebirth; fungus (possibly mushrooms) is the food of the Taoist immortals. Moreover, in Chinese belief, the mushroom only grows in peaceful times, and so represents successful government. Some African and Siberian tribes regard mushrooms as symbolic of the human soul, while in Mexico the sacred mushroom signifies knowledge and enlightenment. In popular Western tradition, small supernatural spirits such as elves and pixies live in toadstools.

ogy, the mistletoe is a symbol of peace, welcome and protection against lightning and evil spirits—although Baldur, son of Odin, was slain by a mistletoe branch. The Golden Bough that enabled Aeneas to enter the underworld was a sprig of mistletoe. The **cross** upon which Christ was **crucified** was once thought to have been made of the wood of mistletoe, and the plant is therefore sometimes called *lignum sanctae crucis,* believed to be an effective remedy for many ailments. Today, as a result of its assimilation by the Christian faith, it is a symbol of Christmas. It retains its associations with freedom and fertility, however, as people are encouraged to kiss under a sprig of mistletoe, perhaps in an unconscious reenactment of the Roman festival of Saturnalia. Mistletoe is the state symbol of Oklahoma.

Wheat / Corn / Maize *Above*

Wheat and maize, or corn, have the universal symbolism of agriculture, natural fertility and harvest. Because wheat is sown, grown and then harvested, it can signify the cycle of birth, life and death, as well as rebirth. Wheat signified the Egyptian mother-goddess, the resurrection of **Osiris**, and, in Christianity, Christ. Egyptians and Romans planted wheat on graves to bring life both in this world and the next. In Ancient Greece and Rome, ears of corn were attributes of Demeter (Ceres), Gaia and **Virgo**, and also sym-

bolized the Eleusian mysteries. Southwestern Native Americans regard corn as a sacred symbol of happiness and prosperity, and wheat germ as representative of man and the cosmos. The Mexican Sun Hero is symbolized by a maize plant and hummingbird, while wheat was sacred to the Canaanite corn god, **Dagon**, as well as the Phrygian mother-goddess, Cybele. In Christian tradition, along with the **grape**, wheat (the main ingredient of bread) is associated with the **Eucharist** and can represent the **Virgin Mary** as the mother of Christ. In heraldic art, the wheatsheaf is known as a garb and is sometimes used as the emblem of bakers. In some Western traditions, a corn doll, representing the corn spirit, is hung in farm kitchens at the end of the harvest to promote fruitful future harvests.

Ivy *Below, left*

As an **evergreen**, in many cultures (including Christianity), the ivy represents immortality and, because it clings while climbing, friendship and faithfulness. This characteristic also led to its significance as representing the feminine need for protection, although the shape of its leaves identifies it as a male symbol. In Phrygian times ivy, was sacred to the god Attis, and in Ancient Egypt it was the plant of **Osiris**, signifying immortality. Because it is prolific, ivy symbolizes the generative power of plants, sensuality and revelry. The Greco-Roman god Dionysus (Bacchus) had an "ivy cup" and was crowned with the ivy leaves that also decorated the Thyrsus (the staff carried by Maenads, itself a fertility symbol).

The Symbolism of Fantastic Creatures

Fantastic creatures do not exist—indeed, have never existed—but have been invented by the human imagination in an attempt to explain the inexplicable. They are common to most cultures and generally perform two major functions: first, as a rationalization for otherwise mysterious natural phenomena; and second, as allegorical personifications of the universal struggle for supremacy between good and evil.

The myths of Ancient Greece and Rome in particular, as well as the pantheon of Ancient Egypt and Hinduism, are populated by gods and creatures whose unpredictability and peculiar skills and characteristics are emphasized by their hybrid form. The body of the merman Triton, who controls the waves, for example, combines a human torso with the tail of a fish; the winged horse, Pegasus, symbolizes a striving for higher things; while the Chimera—a lion/goat/serpent hybrid—represents danger on both land and sea.

Broadly speaking, fantastic creatures can be divided into three groups that symbolize the supernatural powers of the air, earth and sea; frequently at war with each other, their eternal conflict signifies the perennial battle of goodness and light against evil and darkness. Thus, in Hindu belief, the fabulous bird Garuda wages war from the air on the serpentlike nagas, whose realm is the watery depths; in Western tradition, the ultimate chthonic power is the dragon (also known as the worm or serpent), which must be subdued by the power of goodness (although the Oriental dragon is solar, and altogether more benevolent). Just as water itself symbolizes primordial chaos, so do the fabulous creatures that live in it: the biblical Leviathan, whose powers are equaled on land by the Behemoth, and by Ziz in the air; or Scylla and Charybdis in Greek mythology.

Other creatures of darkness include Cerberus, the three-headed guardian of the Greek underworld, and the multiheaded Hydra, both of which were overwhelmed by Hercules during the performance of his labors. Many fabulous underworld creatures are said to guard treasure, and the mythological hero must overcome them before attaining his goal. In this respect, they can symbolize the apparently insurmountable obstacles that stand in the individual's path to success.

Some fabulous creatures symbolize a direct threat to humanity: fearful demonic hybrids like the sirens, the bird-women that lured sailors to their deaths with their sweet songs; or the harpies (vulture women) and the fish-like Lamia which also signified death, as did the vengeance-wreaking Furia and the basilisk, with its petrifying stare. Vampires and werewolves, too, prey on human victims and are all the more sinister because they can transform themselves into different shapes.

Other mythological creatures, like the unicorn, symbolize the virtues of purity and goodness, while some are remarkable for their special qualities: the salamander, for example, which lives in fire, or the phoenix, which sacrifices itself in flames and is then reborn from its own ashes.

All the extraordinary members of this fabulous bestiary in some way or other symbolize aspects of the concerns and anxiety of the human condition.

Opposite: One of the challenges set for Bellerophon by Iobates, king of Lycia, was to kill the chimaera. Bellerophon did so by subduing the winged horse, Pegasus, with the help of Athena's golden bridle, and then riding it to victory over the monster (as depicted in this illustration by Walter Crane). Bellerophon later tried to ascend to Olympus on Pegasus, but Zeus prevented him in this venture, sending a gadfly to sting the winged horse, whereupon Bellerophon was thrown from the horse and fell to earth. Other stories say that Zeus hurled a thunderbolt at Bellerophon, thus killing him. Pegasus symbolizes speed, flight and the capacity for attaining higher spirituality, while the chimera is a harbinger of natural disasters.

TERRESTRIAL CREATURES

Dragon *Above and below*

The symbolic meaning of the dragon is sharply divided in Western and Eastern cultures. In the Orient, where it is the fifth sign of the **Chinese zodiac**, the dragon is seen as a positive symbol, with connotations of joy, health and fertility, protecting man from evil spirits. In the Western Christian tradition, however, the dragon shares the negative, satanic symbolism of the **snake**, representing destructive power, the defiler of innocence and guardian of hidden treasure. Sometimes winged, with a scaly body, **lion**'s claws and lungs of **fire**, its hybrid form symbolizes a primal unifying force, which can be used for good or evil. Psychiatrist Carl Jung also associated the dragon with the mother image.

Unicorn *Above*

A horn grows from the forehead of this horselike mythical beast. Usually white, it is said to have the legs of an antelope, the tail of a **lion** and the head and body of a **horse**, although it is sometimes represented in stag form. It can only be captured by a virgin, and as such symbolizes femininity, purity, chastity and the power of goodness. In Christianity, it can represent the **Virgin Mary** and also Christ, its horn symbolizing the one true gospel. In its heraldic portrayal as the antithesis of the sun-symbol lion, it represents the **moon**, because it was sacred to Artemis and **Diana** in Greek and Roman myth. It also exists in China in the form of the Ky-lin, where it represents the union of **yin** and **yang**, and so fertility and longevity. Many myths are associated with the unicorn: it was said, for example, that its horn could detect poison and that it possessed healing powers, leading it to become a symbol of pharmacists.

Wyvern *Below*

In medieval and heraldic art, the wyvern is a winged **dragon** with two **eagle**'s legs and a barbed, serpentine tail, coiled into a knot. In Western tradition, its symbolism is almost exclusively negative, for it represents war and **Satan**, plague and pestilence, envy and viciousness. Like other dragons, it can, however, also signify vigilance. When it is shown without its wings, it becomes the lindworm, which also symbolizes war and disease. In England, the wyvern was the emblem both of the kingdom of Wessex and of King Harold.

Oriental Lion-Dog *Right*

In China, lions protect against demons, and statues in this form are therefore placed outside holy temples and palaces to guard against the forces of evil. Some believe that they come alive at night and prowl the area. A similar practice is followed in Japan, where the images of lion-dogs also perform a protective function. In the Buddhist religion of both countries, these creatures additionally defend the Buddhist Law. Male lion-dogs are sometimes sculpted resting a paw on a globe, which once represented the **sun**, but now signifies the *cintamani*, or the Sacred Jewel of Buddhism. Females are depicted with a lion cub. Both versions represent protective animal power, ferocity, stamina and vitality.

Opinicus *Above*

Although the opinicus (or epimacus) may resemble a monkey, it is, in fact, a form of **griffin**, with the body and legs of a **lion**, the wings and head of an **eagle** and the tail of a **camel**. It shares the symbolism of the griffin, and therefore represents solar power, strength, protection, vengeance and vigilance.

Griffin *Right*

Symbolic of the **sun**, the griffin, or gryphon, has the head, wings and talons of the **eagle** (king of the birds) and the body of the **lion** (king of the beasts). It was sacred to the Greek god Apollo, god of the sun, **Athena**, the goddess of wisdom and Nemesis, the god of vengeance. It represents the lion's strength and the vigilance and watchfulness of the eagle and was reputed to guard treasure (sometimes interpreted as knowledge or the **Tree of Life**). This hybrid creature came to symbolize Christ and the resurrection in the Middle Ages because of its dual nature and its solar associations. Its duality, however, also led it to be associated with the Antichrist. In its heraldic depiction, the male griffin is shown without wings.

Assyrian Sphinx *Right*

Derived from its Egyptian counterpart, the Assyrian sphinx differs from that of the enigmatic female version of Ancient Greece. The sphinx is winged and incorporates elements of the **lion** and **bull** with a human head and sometimes five legs. Like the Egyptian sphinx, its function is to guard palaces and temples. It is also equated with the lamassu—the guardian spirit of Assyria and Babylon. Both sphinx and lamassu are symbolic of rulership, as well as of the four elements unified. (*See also* Sacred Symbols, Egyptian.)

Chimera *Above*

A creature of complicated hybrid form, the Greek chimera (or chimaera), which dates back to the fifth century BC, was said to have a **lion**'s head, a **goat**'s body and the tail of a **dragon** or **snake**, where each part could also have its own head. The offspring of the monsters Typhon and Echidna, Greek mythology tells that the chimera was a savage creature that bellowed **fire** and terrorized Lycia before it was finally killed by Bellerophon astride **Pegasus**. Like many hybrid animals, its symbolism is that of chaotic, dark and uncontrolled forces. It is a symbol of natural disasters (particularly of storms and volcanic eruptions) on land and sea. It also combines the symbolic meanings of the lion, goat and serpent. In Christianity, it represents **Satan**. Today the word "chimera" means a wild and illusory idea.

Salamander *Above*

The salamander, which is sometimes equated with the **lizard**, can be portrayed in a number of ways. It can be a wingless **dragon** or a **dog** or human hybrid, but it is always pictured engulfed by flames. Its primary significance is that of **fire** itself, of which it is both spirit and guardian. In traditional belief, the salamander is a crea-ture that inhabits volcanoes. Its venomous bite is fatal, and it is so cold-blooded that it lives in fire (which it can extinguish with its body). In medieval times, it additionally symbolized the heat of desire and, because it is sexless, chastity. In Christian iconography, the salamander represents faith and righteousness that survives the fire of temptation and evil. In heraldic art, it is a symbol of bravery. It was an important alchemical sign, signifying fire. The salamander has served as the sign of apothecaries (through its alchemical association) and of insurers (against fire). It was also the emblem (shown here) of François I of France, whose motto was *Nutrisco et extinguo* ("I nourish [the good] and extinguish [the bad]").

Werewolf *Below*

In popular European belief, the werewolf is human by day, but at night (particularly when there is a full **moon**), he is transformed into a **wolf** and rips apart all those who cross his path—especially young girls. Lycanthropy (becoming a

werewolf) has several causes, including being possessed by a demon, being infected by another werewolf, or donning a belt of wolf's skin. The werewolf is difficult to kill, but its death can be brought about by a number of arcane methods, such as by using a silver bullet or a weapon blessed in a chapel of St. Hubert. However, earlier lycanthropic figures, such as Lycaon, king of Arcadia, were said to have been destroyed by being permanently transformed into wolves. Belief in werewolves originated in medieval Europe, and **witches**—servants of **Satan**—were believed to be able to transform themselves into wolves. Because wolves were once populous and widely feared, the werewolf is a symbol of terror and evil as well as of the bestial danger contained within apparently ordinary people.

Cerberus *Above*

Cerberus guards the entrance to Hades—the Greek underworld—and is usually portrayed as a **dog** with a **serpent**'s tail and three heads (representing the infernal trinity), although it can have up to fifty. Its fangs drip with poison. Although friendly to deceased entrants, Cerberus allows no dead soul to leave Hades or living person to enter. Some heroes, however, outwitted him: Hercules brought him to earth but then released him; Orpheus lulled the dog to sleep with his lyre; and Sibyl bought Aeneas safe passage by doping it with a drugged cake. Cerberus represents the irrevocability of death and, in psychology, the self-defensive instincts of the **unconscious**.

Minotaur *Above*

The Minotaur—a man with a bull's head—said to be the offspring of a white **bull** and Queen Pasiphäe, was imprisoned by King Minos of Crete in the **labyrinth** below his palace at Crete. It was fed on girls and boys sent in tribute from Athens. Theseus was destined for this fate but was saved by Ariadne, who gave him a ball of string with which to find his way out of the maze once he had despatched the Minotaur. This hybrid creature is the emblem of Crete and represents man's dark, bestial side, which can be defeated by divine guidance.

Satyr *Below*

The satyr and the similar faun were the forest spirits of Ancient Greece. The satyr attended Bacchus, god of wine, in his drunken revels, possessed the legs and hindquarters of a **goat**, budding horns and goat-like ears and symbolized lustful behavior and profanity. By contrast, fauns, which shared the satyr's physical characteristics, were identified with the god Pan, god of the pastures and forests and were benevolent spirits.

Hobgoblin *Above*

Tales of hobgoblins, or goblins, are prevalent in many cultures, particularly among the pagans of northern Europe. It is believed that in the Dark and Middle Ages, "goblins" were descendants of Neolithic tribes, whose shyness, small stature and rare appearances caused them to be considered nonhuman creatures. Typically more mischievous than malevolent, these mythical small and grotesque creatures were generally regarded as being friendly and humorous, yet frequently also troublemakers. Irish leprechauns typify goblin traits, being good-natured, enjoying practical jokes and harmless unless angered. Hobgoblins (illustrated in this Goya painting) symbolize the power of mischief.

AQUEOUS CREATURES

Capricornus *Above*

Capricornus, the sea god and goat-fish, is closely linked to Ea-Oannes, the Babylonian lord of the abyss. Capricornus symbolizes the life-giving power of **water**. This hybrid form is said to have been created when Pan jumped into the Nile to escape Typhon and represents both land and sea. It symbolizes man's dual ability to reach either for the abyss or for the heights and, through its association with the zodiacal symbol **Capricorn**, the **winter** solstice and the ascending power of the **sun**.

Leviathan *Above*

In the Bible, Leviathan is the "crooked **serpent**," a huge and terrible **fish** which represents the primordial chaos of **water**. In addition, it is associated with the monsters of land and air, Behemoth and Ziz. Leviathan was subdued at the time of the Creation, but Job says that magic can revive the sleeping monster; it will be destroyed by Gabriel (or Behemoth)

at the end of the world, however. According to Hebrew tradition, when the messiah comes, Leviathan will provide the food for the banquet of the righteous. It was said that its eyes lit up the dark sea and its foul breath caused the water to boil. This tradition is less clear on whether Leviathan is a **crocodile**, **whale** or sea serpent. In Islam, Leviathan is equated with Nun and in Norse mythology, with Midgardorm. In Christian belief, the **gate** to hell is symbolized by Leviathan's gaping jaws and it can also represent lower life and worldly power. To Kabbalists, Leviathan is Samuel, the prince of evil.

Dagon *Below*

Although an ancient Semitic god of **corn**, the fierce Canaanite **fish**-god, Dagon, is symbolized by his human upper and fish-like lower half. According to the Bible, he was worshipped by the Philistines. It was during Dagon's festival that Samson pulled down their temple. Dagon can thus signify false objects of worship.

Scylla *Below*

In classical mythology, Scylla was once a lovely nymph who was changed by her rival in love, Circe, into a monstrous creature with six long-necked heads, with three rows of **teeth** in each. In some stories, she has twelve feet and a lower body consisting of a multitude of mon-

sters. Scylla inhabited the rock of Scylla, opposite the whirlpool monster Charybdis, and preyed on sailors in the Straits of Messina, stretching her long necks forward to grab victims from passing ships (including six of Odysseus's crew). Both monsters symbolize the dark powers of the **water** and a difficult journey. They have particular potency in conjunction with each other.

Triton *Right*

Triton is the most famous of all mermen, who are half men and half **dolphin**, the lesser-known consorts of **mermaids**. He directs the waters by sounding a horn or **conch shell**, heard by humans as the roaring of the ocean. In Greco-Roman mythology, Triton was the son of the god of the sea, Poseidon, and his wife, Amphitrite and was also the herald of **Neptune**. Unlike many fabled sea creatures, Triton is generally a positive symbol of control and power (although he was on occasions believed to lose control, making the shores dangerous).

Mermaid *Left and below*

A fantastic creature, half woman, half **fish**, the mermaid is a divinity of the sea symbolizing the **unconscious** (especially the feminine) aspect of the male **psyche**. By association with the **sirens**, the mermaid was once regarded as a harbinger of calamity but came to represent elusive feminine beauty as well as the less idealized characteristics of fickleness and vanity (represented below by the mermaid's mirror). Mermaids are often depicted holding a comb—itself a symbol of magical power over nature that is associated with mermaids because the earliest combs were fishbones—with which to control storms at sea. The most famous mermaid in French legend, the flighty Mélusine, left her human husband to return to the sea. The illustration at left shows a man tempted by an ideal vision of beauty—the unreal, unattainable mermaid.

Makara *Below*

The makara is a mythical Hindu beast, generally portrayed as part **fish** and part **crocodile**, sometimes with the head of an elephant. It can also be represented as a shark, a **naga**, a **dolphin** or an antelope/fish. The makara is the vehicle of Varuna, Lord of the Deep. It is associated with life-giving **water** and thus fertility, but, as a hybrid creature, also symbolizes the duality of man. In the Hindu zodiac, it is the sign of **Capricorn**.

Aerial Creatures

Pegasus *Above*

Pegasus was the winged horse upon which Bellerophon rode to defeat the **chimera** in Greek mythology. Created from the blood of the severed head of the **Gorgon** Medusa, Pegasus also created the Hippocrene spring dedicated to the Muses and thus became associated with intellectual and poetic inspiration. Pegasus symbolizes man's capacity for attaining higher spirituality and for transforming evil into good. On a more mundane level, it denotes air transport or speed.

Nagas *Above*

Nagas—a legendary race of **snakes**—are generally represented as serpents in Hindu tradition, although they can also be depicted as human-headed snakes. It was believed that female nagas could marry humans, and some dynasties claim descent from them. Ananta is the thousand-headed king of the nagas and represents infinity. It was thought that nagas reigned in great splendor in the water and below ground, thus symbolizing the underworld. They also waged war on the skies, symbolized by **Garuda**.

The great god Vishnu sleeps upon a coiled naga, and his mount is the cobra (symbolizing wisdom and eternity); the two intertwined nagas sacred to him represent the fertilized water from which the earth goddess rises. As snakes do in many other cultures, nagas can additionally represent the guardians of material and spiritual treasure.

Hydra *Below*

The multi-headed serpent has many associations. In Greek mythology, the hydra, also called the Lernaean Serpent, was a many-headed serpent, whose heads, when severed, grew back twofold; Hercules conquered the hydra by cauterizing the monster's necks with a log of firewood. In Ugaritic myth, it is the seven-headed monster of chaos, Lotan, which was destroyed during the creation of the earth by Baal; it thus also may be the biblical **Leviathan** and represent the seven deadly sins. Its broad symbolism includes the animal life-force, obstacles in the way of success and world power and creativity through its association with the number **seven** (the number of the universe).

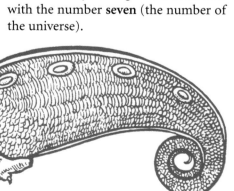

Phoenix *Above*

The phoenix, half **eagle** and half pheasant, is a universal symbol of resurrection and immortality. Its origins are in Ancient Egypt, where it was equated with the **sun** bird, Bennu. The dying phoenix is supposed to build a wooden funeral pyre and set itself alight by the sun's rays, only to rise again from the ashes. Thus it epitomizes recreation from destruction. In Christian tradition, the phoenix denotes Christ's resurrection, while in China, as the **Feng-huang**, it is a sun symbol.

Fairy *Right*

Fairies are small, ethereal and usually winged beings with magical powers. They are traditionally shy of humans, yet can bestow great riches among those that they encounter. The tooth-fairy story is still told to children. Rings of dark green grass are popularly called fairy rings and are believed to have been caused by fairies dancing on the spot. Through their ability to transform, fairies symbolize the latent possibilities contained in the supranormal powers of the human mind.

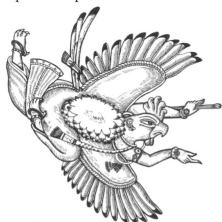

Garuda *Above*

Half man and half **eagle** (and sometimes a wild goose), the "golden sunbird" Garuda is of crucial importance in Hindu and Buddhist mythology as the Bird of Life. Garuda is the king of the birds and is the vehicle of the solar god, Vishnu—the creator and destroyer—and can be equated with the **sun**, the sky and victory. Devotees of Vishnu adopted Garuda as their emblem. According to tradition, Garuda was fully formed when it emerged from the (cosmic) **egg** and lives in the wish-fulfilling **Tree of Life**. As a solar power, Garuda is the bitter enemy of the chthonic naga serpents (particularly Kaliya). For Tibetan Buddhists, Garuda is the mount of **Buddha** and a manifestation of the Botthisattva Vajrapani; therefore, they consider it a fearsome protector against evil. In its association with Vishnu and its battles with the nagas, Garuda symbolizes the sun, immortality and victory in the struggle between life and death and between the forces of good and evil.

Basilisk *Below*

The basilisk—also known as the cockatrice—has the wings, head, triple crest and claws of a bird on the body of a **snake**. Its tail can sometimes terminate in a second head, in which case it is the amphisbaen, which can see both ways. In Western belief, the basilisk was said to have emerged from a yolkless egg laid in dung by a **cock** and hatched by a **toad** or serpent. It had a **crown** on its head and a trifurcated tail. In the East, it was a cock/serpent/toad hybrid. A guardian of treasure, its stare could kill men and death could only be circumvented by forcing it to look at its reflection in a mirror; catching sight of its own image would cause it to die of shock. In Christianity, the basilisk symbolizes the antichrist as one of the four aspects of Satan. It represented sins such as treachery and lust, and disease (particularly syphilis) during the Middle Ages.

Chinese Phoenix *Right*

In China, the phoenix, known as the Fenghuang, is the emperor of birds and one of the four sacred creatures that bring peace and prosperity. It is a composite bird of exquisitely colorful plumage, whose head is the solarlike head of the **cock** and whose swallow's back is reminiscent of the crescent **moon**. Its wings signify the wind; its tails, plant life and its feet, the earth. In addition, each part of its body represents a laudable human quality: its head signifying virtue; its back, correct ritual behavior; its breast, humanity; its stomach, reliability; and its wings, duty. Furthermore, it personifies the unity of **yin** and **yang**. In its feng aspect it is a male, solar symbol representing happiness, while as huang it is female and lunar and symbolizes the Chinese empress. Known as the "scarlet bird" because it guards the southern part of the universe in **summer**, it was believed that its appearance would herald the advent of an auspicious emperor or prophet. It is still a Chinese bridal emblem, signifying unity through marriage. In Japan the Ho-O bird is closely equated with the Chinese phoenix.

DEMONS

Gorgons *Right*

The terrifying Gorgon sisters (Euryale, Stheno, and Medusa—of whom Medusa was chief) had **snakes** instead of hair and were said to be able to turn men into stone just by looking at them. In Greek mythology, Medusa (depicted in this seventeenth-century painting by Caravaggio) was the only mortal of the trio: once a beautiful girl, she angered **Athena** by behaving disrespectfully in her temple and was transformed into a Gorgon who preyed on men. She was finally killed by Perseus, and **Pegasus** is said to have sprung from Medusa's blood. Medusa's severed head became the emblem of Perseus and, when depicted on amulets, it was believed to protect against thunderstorms. A symbol based on the Gorgon's head, the Gorgoneion, was said to have been placed on the protective shield of **Zeus** and Athena (the aegis). Similar images were often placed in Greek temples to ward off evil. The Gorgoneion can represent the terrible Great Mother, fear (particularly of men for women) or the fearful union of opposites, such as beauty and dread.

Harpy *Left*

Originally represented as three beautiful, winged women—Aello (storm), Celeno (blackness) and Ocypete (rapid)—these malevolent spirits of Ancient Greece could summon winds to cause storms on land and whirlpools at sea. In subsequent mythology, the harpies became fierce and filthy hags—half female and half **vulture**—who were sent by the gods to inflict punishment on unworthy men. They symbolized sudden death, as they would snatch or spoil food until their victims (including Phineus, king of Thrace) died. They were also messengers of the underworld, to which they transported the souls of the dead. Harpies are symbolic of death, windstorms and destructive female power. Today the word "harpy" is used to describe a shrewish, cruel or grasping woman.

Siren *Below*

The siren can assume two forms: a bird-woman (as in Greek mythology) or a **fish**-woman, sometimes with two tails. Both forms entice male passers-by to their deaths by singing songs of irresistible sweetness, as told in the story of the Lorelei of the Rhine. They symbolize dangerous worldly temptation along the spiritual path of life.

Lamia *Above*

In Roman and Greek mythology, the lamia was a Libyan queen who was robbed of her children by the jealous Juno (or Hera). Driven insane by this, she vowed vengeance on all children and became a demonic child-devourer. She has the head and breasts of a woman, but the body of a **serpent**. As well as threatening children, she can share the predatory symbolism of the **siren**. She was associated in Hebrew tradition with Lilith, a vampiric night monster.

Pazuzu *Above*

Unlike most evil demons, the Assyrian and Babylonian Pazuzu also has a benevolent aspect, for, by virtue of being the enemy of Lamashtu (the demon killer of babies), he was regarded as a protector of unborn and newborn children. Pregnant women and new mothers would wear amulets portraying this fearsome spirit, who had taloned hands and feet, four wings and a scaled body. However, as the demon of the southwest wind, which was believed to bring disease and death, Pazuzu was also a potent force to be feared.

Tengu *Below*

The tengu of Japanese mythology has the form of a man but possesses the head, claws and wings of a bird. This hateful hybrid creature hatches from an egg, lives in the treetops along mountain ranges and emerges to cause havoc among humans. It appears and disappears suddenly, changing forms and making itself invisible with equal ease. Tengus are malicious: stealing, abducting children, destroying buildings and disrupting religious ceremonies are some of their favored activities. The tengu is therefore symbolic of war, mischief and discord.

Furiae *Below*

The three Roman Furiae were fierce goddesses of vengeance who pursued wrongdoers, murderers and ungrateful children mercilessly in order to vent harsh punishment upon them. The parentage of the terrible Tisiphone ("the avenger of murder"), Alecto ("the implacable one," or "one who does not rest") and Megaera ("the grim," or "jealous one") is disputed, but in some legends they were said to be the daughters of Gaea (goddess of the earth) and **Uranus** (god of the heavens), or of earthly transgressors who had died and entered the underworld. The Furiae

are associated with the Greek Erinyes. They were usually depicted as winged women, whose hair was a writhing nest of vipers and who carried **serpents**, torches or knives. Alternatively, they could be represented as dog or serpent hybrids. They are symbolic of the acknowledgment of a guilty conscience and of the recognition of deserved and inescapable punishment.

Vampire *Below*

Superstitious belief in vampires is centered in Slavonic countries, although other cultures also tell tales of infernal nocturnal creatures who drain the living of their blood. Vampires are believed to be restless, "undead" corpses who receive their sustenance by sucking human blood. Their bite spreads the vampiric infection and they can only be killed by a stake driven through their heart, or, as in Nosferatu's case, by exposure to the sun. Garlic is believed to be effective in warding off vampires, as is a crucifix. The most famous vampire, Dracula, was the creation of Bram Stoker and entered popular culture after his appearance in Stoker's eponymous novel, first published

in 1897; this photograph is from *Scars of Dracula*. Stoker based his infernal character on Vlad V (1456–76) of Wallachia, a fierce warlord who impaled his victims on stakes, but did not, however, exhibit any vampiric tendencies. Vampires symbolize parasites, or bloodsuckers, who draw sustenance from the healthy.

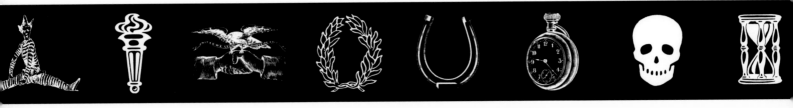

The Symbolism of the Emotions and Inner Mind

It is really only during the last century that the science of semiotics (or semiology)—the study of the role of symbols in informing and influencing the inner mind—has been recognized. Two men in particular, Sigmund Freud and Carl Jung, have shaped our comprehension of the way in which our minds respond to the imagery of symbolism. It was Freud who introduced the concept of dream analysis as a valuable tool in interpreting the messages of the unconscious, while Jung's identification of the archetypal symbols inherent in the collective unconscious represented a major advance in psychological understanding and therapy.

According to Jung, the human psyche has three levels: the ego, or conscious mind; the personal unconscious, which contains our individual dreams, aspirations and memories; and the collective unconscious, which stores our inherited racial memories, often in the form of archetypes. Symbolic archetypes represent shared experiences that are common to us all and include the life-giving, nurturing mother; the powerful, authoritative father; the anima and animus—those parts of our personality that represent, respectively, femininity and irrationality, and masculinity and rationality; and the shadow—our basic, animal nature.

We may seek to hide our true personalities in difficult situations by donning the mask of the persona, thus allowing us to represent ourselves in different ways. This may be a necessary survival ploy, but real peace of mind can only come when we recognize and reconcile all the different and conflicting strands of our psychological makeup. Only then can a healthy balance, or individuation, of the self be achieved. In order for us to do so, it is necessary to heed our intuitive feelings, to attempt to interpret the messages sent to our conscious mind from our unconscious in our dreams and to be aware of our responses to the symbolism that surrounds us, either in our interaction with other people or in our reactions to our environment and personal circumstances.

Our perceptions and responses to symbolism are inevitably intensely personal, and different signs will evoke a variety of responses, depending on the specific experiences, memories and character of the individual. While this chapter cannot pretend to cover the whole range of archetypal and personal symbols that inform and shape the workings of our inner minds and our emotional responses, by exploring the effect of some of the most common symbolic images created and recognized by the unconscious mind, it will give readers a valuable framework within which to broaden their understanding of the evocative language of symbolic images.

Explored in the following pages are archetypal symbols, symbols of identity, direction and transition, as well as those that invoke positive and negative emotions. Together they will lead the reader on a fascinating journey of self-discovery toward, it is hoped, individuation.

Opposite: In the fairy tale Little Red Riding Hood, *a wicked wolf assumes the identity of an innocent child's grandmother in an attempt to lure her into self-sacrifice. The wolf is revealed as an unscrupulous, amoral and crafty male seducer, who tempts, lies and tricks in order to break down the defenses of his unwitting victim. Here, the wolf is an archetypal symbol of unbridled masculine lust—of a sexual predator whose rampaging libido leaves pain and destruction in its avaricious wake.*

Archetypes and the Mind

Persona *Right*

The archetype of the persona is the artificial, idealized face that we present to the world, which does not necessarily reflect our real selves. It is symbolized by the different **masks** we adopt in order to help us lose our personal inhibitions and play a convincing role in a variety of demanding situations—such as at work, at parties or even at home. The persona is a defensive device that ensures our social survival and protects our real selves from potential ridicule or damage. As such, the mask can be a useful aid to coping with a threatening world, but there is a danger that we may begin to identify with it too closely and thus lose our true identity.

Trickster *Below*

The trickster is one of the archetypes (the personification of common and important experiences) identified by Jung and represents the pranks that the unconscious mind can play upon the conscious. The trickster is an antihero—a rebellious, amoral and anarchic figure—who enjoys disrupting, ridiculing and unsettling the psyche. He can be a dangerous figure who can maliciously sabotage our plans, but he can also warn against complacency, vanity and pretension and can force us to challenge previously unquestioned beliefs. The trickster is a universal concept, combining animal and divine qualities. In the stories of many cultures, he appears in the form of a magician or devil. Some gods perform a trickster role, such as the Norse god Loki, the Native American Raven, **Coyote**, Rabbit and Hare, and the Greco-Roman Hermes (**Mercury**). In contemporary culture, the trickster can be identified in the character of Br'er Rabbit and in Batman's Joker. Often represented in dreams by a clown, as a shape-shifter, the trickster is additionally a symbol of mental transformation and heralds an imminent alteration of the status quo.

Psyche *Below, right*

Paul Thumann's painting *Psyche at Nature's Mirror* portrays the beautiful mortal woman of Roman mythology who was loved by Cupid against the wishes of the jealous Venus. Although forbidden to see Cupid's face, curiosity overcame Psyche, and, on lighting a lamp, she recognized the god of love. So shocked was she that her hand trembled, and a drop of oil fell on Cupid, causing him to awaken and then vanish. She embarked on a futile search for her lover, became a slave to Venus and eventually fell into a deathlike coma. Cupid, however, revived her, and the couple were married, Psyche being granted immortality by **Jupiter**. As well as being a symbol of immortal **love**, Psyche (whose name means "the breath of life" or "the soul" in Greek) can represent the journey of the soul through life; like the soul, she is sometimes depicted as a butterfly. She is also the eponymous symbol of the human personality. In the modern psychoanalytical terms of Jung, the human psyche (the whole personality) consists of three levels: the ego (the conscious mind), the personal **unconscious** (containing individual experiences and desires) and the collective unconscious (composed of shared human memories). The psyche has four functions: intuition, sensation, thinking and feeling. The more these are in balance, the more integrated the personality; imbalance can result in introversion or extroversion.

Consciousness *Above*

In dream interpretation, the **sun** is a symbol of the "masculine," conscious mind and is the opposite of the "feminine" **moon** of the unconscious. The movement of the sun therefore represents different levels of consciousness: dawn, for example, symbolizes rebirth, awakening and enlightenment, while the midday sun signifies the highest powers of the intellect. Following this analogy, sunset thus represents the submergence of the conscious into the unconscious, when rational thought gives way to the intuition and emotions of the unconscious mind (represented by the night, the moon and, as also seen in this illustration, **water**). Although sunset can be equated with **death**, it is not a symbol of fear (because the sun will rise again at dawn) but rather one of a calm acceptance of the endless cycle of existence, of an acknowledgment of the necessary interaction of life's components and of consciousness and unconsciousness.

Elemental symbols

Windmill *Below*

Through the movement of the windmill's sails, the symbolism of wind (intangible vitality) combines with that of **air**—(the spirit). Because it functions as a **corn** mill, the windmill can also signify harvest and thus fertility. The wind ultimately produces bread, so the windmill can signify life. In Christian iconography, it is a symbol of **temperance**. Perhaps its most familiar association, however, is with Cervantes's Don Quixote, whose tilting at windmills is regarded as an exercise in futility. The windmill is also a national emblem of Holland.

The Flaming Torch *Right*

Signifying the regenerative power of **fire**, the upright flaming torch symbolizes life. In many cultures, it is frequently used in initiation or fertility rites. In Greek mythology, it was the emblem of Eros and Aphrodite, symbolizing the flame of love; Hercules used it to defeat the Hydra. Conversely, when the torch is depicted held downward, it symbolizes **death**. In Christianity, it came to signify Christ as the Light of the World and was a sign of purification through God's illumination of the spirit. The torch also signifies truth and intelligence and is often used as an emblem of places of learning. When associated with the seven deadly sins, it represents anger.

Compass *Above*

The compass—contained within the **circle** of perfection and quartered by the **four** points of north, south, east and west—is a sign of both life and knowledge; to the inner mind it represents an instrument of direction and identity. In dream symbolism, the compass can orient us safely along the rocky path of life, but if faulty, it signifies a loss of identity and personal direction.

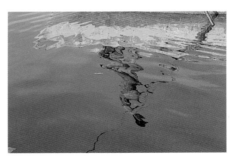

Water *Above*

Along with the **forest** and **maze**, water is a universal symbol of the unconscious mind and can also be linked to the **moon**, femininity and irrationality. Because oceans are boundless and ungovernable, they can be equated with chaos. Unless in an extreme state of turbulence, the unconscious mind is more closely linked to the lake or pond, which appears calm but can hide much activity beneath its surface. In many ancient cultures, it was believed that the Earth was created from primeval waters. Psychologists use this as a metaphor for the birth of ideas in the unconscious mind.

which was believed to be linked to the heart, the circular shape of the engagement and wedding rings symbolizes eternity and completeness. The wedding ring is blessed during the wedding ceremony before being pledged as a binding token of faithfulness and of undying love. Dreaming of a wedding or ring can represent a desire for the reconciliation of the conflicting, yet complementary, parts of one's **psyche** into an integrated whole.

Positive Emotions

Smiley Face *Below*

The origin of the instantly recognizable smiley face is recent, dating from the peace-promoting hippy culture of the 1960s, but it quickly became established as a universal symbol for happiness. The face is yellow, a color usually associated with the **sun** and light, so underlining the sign's simple and positive symbolism.

Thumbs Up *Right*

The "thumbs up" sign is one of an armory of demotic signs available to us through gesticulation. It is a gesture of approval, popularly believed to have originated in the days of Ancient Rome, when the fate of a defeated gladiator was sealed by either an upward- or downward-pointing thumb signal from the emperor (denoting mercy and death respectively). The sign can also signify benevolence and good fortune.

Hearts and Arrow *Above*

Hearts pierced by **arrows** universally symbolize love and union. From ancient times, the heart has signified man's emotional core, while the arrow symbolizes the darts of love fired by the Greek god of love, Eros (the Roman Cupid). The symbol indicates that the hearts of the lovers have been smitten and they are now united. In Christian iconography, a heart pierced by a sword represents the **Virgin Mary**, Christ or saints, but can also signify repentance. The flaming heart signifies illumination and devotion—both secular and religious.

Commitment Ring *Above, right*

The wedding ring symbolizes the uniting of two people in marriage (or a similar commitment). Rings also represent the sacred communion of bishops, cardinals or nuns as the spiritual bridegrooms or brides of the church or Christ. Traditionally worn on the fourth finger of the left hand (or sometimes the right),

Handshake *Below*

The handshake is variously a sign of greeting and farewell, friendship, pardon and entering into a contract. It can represent unity and agreement as well as the doubling of power or potential achieved by partnership. The right hand repre-

sents the life-force, and is the "hand of power," so a pledge is considered stronger when made with this hand. Hands are expressive parts of the body, and a wide variety of hand-gestures can symbolize conscious and subconsious emotions. When two individuals join hands, the physical contact breaches insular reserve and takes the relationship to a more intimate level. Linked hands can therefore symbolize solidarity against hostile forces—as the motto proclaims: "United we stand; divided we fall."

Liberation

Nudity *Right*

To many, Edouard Manet's *Déjeuner sur l'Herbe* depicts a common nightmare scenario: appearing unclothed in public. The belief that nudity is shameful is widespread; in the West, it may predate the Adam and Eve story. While dreams of nakedness can signify feelings of vulnerability, repressed sexuality or the inability to accept one's true self, nudity can also have positive significance. Dreams of appearing naked can signify breaking through inhibitions and embracing honesty and openness, and the desire to display one's true **persona** to the world. In Freud's view, dreaming of self-nudity can be a subconscious expression of the wish to return to the **innocence** and unselfconsciousness of childhood, or a yearning to return to nature. In Manet's scene, the bystanders appear unruffled by the nudity, signifying the liberation of the naked woman whose true self is accepted. Conversely, had they appeared horrified, the scene would symbolize exposure and rejection.

Dance *Below*

The ballerina portrayed in Edgar Degas's *Danseuse sur Scène* appears liberated through dance. Dancing is a form of self-expression, creativity and spontaneity and can symbolize throwing off the shackles of conventional behavior, allowing the individual's true personality to emerge. Both in the physical world and in that of the imagination, dance represents a flight of fantasy—a joyful manifestation of freedom. In dreams, dancing indicates a need to become more extrovert, to partake more fully of life and to unleash repressed creative powers in order to become truly happy. Dancing can signify the rituals of sexual courtship.

Adventure *Right*

Dreaming of sailing on a yacht symbolizes both a desire for adventure and a recognition of the need to embark on a journey of personal development. From the earliest times, ships have been regarded as a symbol of transition and passage—through the sea of life, or from life to death, for example. Furthermore, the ship itself can be a cosmic symbol: while it represents life, the ocean on which it sails represents the **waters** of creation and the ship's mast can be likened to the *axis mundi*. In psychoanalytical analogy, while the ocean represents the **unconscious**, the yacht represents the conscious mind, which has to be steered carefully through the deep waters and their rocky obstacles on the perilous journey of life. Less profoundly, to dream of navigating a yacht can express a yearning for freedom and adventure, for on the unpredictable seas one can explore previously uncharted territory and escape the restrictions of stifling convention.

Curiosity *Below*

The heroine of Lewis Carroll's *Alice's Adventures in Wonderland* and *Through the Looking-Glass* was insatiably curious—a characteristic which led her into many surreal adventures in Carroll's dream world. Curiosity is a healthy quality that encourages the mind to explore new areas and experiences, leading to personal development. Yet curiosity can also be dangerous: it can entice us into perilous situations. Dreams, however, as Alice found in a fictional world packed with psychological symbolism, provide a safe environment in which curiosity can roam unhindered, free of the fear of negative physical consequences. We can thus explore fantasies and desires in an imaginary "trial run," and apply the lessons of our dream experiences to our conscious minds.

Inspiration/Creation

Creative Energy *Above*

This detail from Michaelangelo's *Creation of Adam* depicts dynamic power flowing from God to Adam, thus creating life. At its most basic level, creation is sometimes described as the animation of matter by energy. This applies both to physical objects (the seed that requires solar energy to grow) and to the mind (which requires the mental energy of the unconscious for conscious inspiration). While creation represents the birth of new life, the related concept of creativity is a sign of progress, of a positive breakthrough from mental stagnation, and is extremely important for the maintenance of mental balance, leading to happiness and success.

Embryo *Right, above*

While the **egg**, or seed, is a profound cosmic symbol of potential in many cultures, the embryo takes this significance a step further, for it has been fertilized and is soon to hatch out into a new life. It is thus a symbol of birth, hope and new possibilities. In dream analogy, it represents the rebirth of the self and the opportunity to start afresh. The embryo is therefore a general symbol of creation—both in the literal sense, and in terms of the ideas and solutions latent in the "egg" of the **psyche** that gradually develop in the "embryo" of the unconscious, until they emerge, fully fledged, into the conscious mind.

Lightbulb *Left*

A glowing lightbulb symbolizes a flash of inspiration or the conception of an idea. Just as the power of the unconscious crystallizes into thought in the conscious mind, so electrical energy causes the bulb's illumination. The immediate results of the lightswitch metaphorically underline the spontaneity of the inspiration in the conscious mind. In symbolic terms, this modern invention has clear links with the ancient concept of the transfer of spiritual energy and strength from sources of light (such as the **sun**) to the human intellect.

Success

Laurel Wreath *Right*

Since the Pythian Games in Ancient Greece, the laurel wreath has been an emblem of victory. The **evergreen** laurel was regarded as a purifying plant with powers of immortality. Its significance has survived, while other leaves used for the same purpose do not retain this symbolism: in the Olympic Games wild **olives** were used to crown the victors, while in the Nemean Games it was parsley. First worn by the Romans in triumphal parades after battle, the laurel wreath came to be regarded as both a prize and a sign of divine blessing. Over the centuries, rulers were often portrayed so wreathed, while today those who have achieved excellence in their respective fields can also receive this mark of distinction.

legions passed through garlanded natural arches on their way to give thanks at the temple of **Jupiter**. To them the arch itself symbolized the sky and heavens of which Jupiter was the supreme god. Moreover, it represented a barrier between living survivors and the souls of their dead opponents—a barrier that helped to dispel the victors' feelings of guilt. To the modern mind, the victory arch is an unambiguous expression of successful military might.

Victory Arch *Below*

Since Roman times, military victors have paraded through triumphal arches after battle, and today the Arc de Triomphe in Paris, France (built in tribute to Napoleon I) is perhaps the most famous such monument in the world. Roman

Reaping Rewards *Above*

Jules Breton's *At the End of the Day* depicts a field worker who carries a sheaf of **corn**—a universal and ancient symbol of reward. Good times are commonly represented by a wheatsheaf, connoting nature's bounty, bread (and thus life) and the harvest reaped after arduous labor. Although hardship might be incurred in the quest, perseverance should result in reward—be it in material form, or as the enlightenment of the mind.

V for Victory *Right, above*

The "V for Victory" sign is also known as the peace sign or victory salute and originates from England during World War

II. Initially not a demotic sign, its use was first suggested as a symbol of Nazi resistance in a B.B.C. radio broadcast to occupied Belgium. "V" stood for victory, as well as the French *victoire* and the Flemish *vrijheid*. Shortly afterward, it was transcribed into Morse code for broadcast; coincidentally, this had the same rhythm as the opening bars of Beethoven's Fifth Symphony, with which the sign soon became identified. Winston Churchill famously popularized its demotic use. In some countries, when the sign is reversed it has an insulting significance.

Celebration *Below*

One of the most potent modern symbols of celebration is clinking glasses in a toast. On celebratory occasions, the gathered assembly toast success or good wishes with a glass of champagne or wine—both of which provide a sense of wellbeing and benevolence. Wine played an important part in the ancient rites of Dionysus (Bacchus): it was was regarded as the elixir of eternal life and youth, and its intoxicating effect a means of liberating the soul to achieving a joyful—if fleeting—union with the gods.

Luck/Fate

Chimney Sweep *Right*

In some northern European countries, the chimney sweep is a symbol of good luck. The origin of this symbolism is unknown, but may be a result of his role in the prevention of fire, or of his association with the symbolism of coal in its purification by **fire**.

Four-leafed Clover *Above*

The symbolism of the four-leafed clover as an emblem of good luck stems from the legend that Eve, after her banishment from paradise, took one as a reminder of the garden of Eden. Clovers normally have three leaves, and finding a four-leafed clover is difficult, although not impossible. If the plant has more than four leaves it is thought to bring misfortune.

Money On Trees *Above*

The dreamer who discovers money growing abundantly on trees expresses the sensation of luck in finding an apparently inexhaustible supply of wealth. However, the money tree is obviously an impossible phenomenon and therefore represents unrealistic aspirations.

Horseshoe *Below*

The horseshoe is a symbol of good luck, but only if turned upward, according to some; if its prongs face down the luck runs out. There are many theories regarding the origin of the belief that horseshoes protect against evil spirits and bring good fortune. In Christian tradition, St. Dunstan was asked by the Devil to shoe his single hoof; St. Dunstan did so, but caused Satan such excruciating pain that he promised never to enter where he saw a horseshoe. In popular legend, **witches** rode broomsticks because they feared horses. Another theory was that the horseshoe (being made of iron,

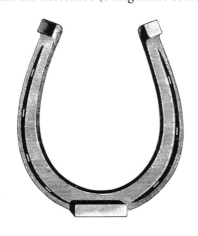

a symbol of **Mars**) counteracted the power of **Saturn** (the god of witches). Because its shape recalls the crescent **moon**, the horseshoe is also a fertility symbol; furthermore, because it resembles horns, it can signify vitality.

Dice *Above*

As well as being gaming devices, dice have symbolic importance as representatives of the fickleness of fate—as attributes of the **Three Graces**, as one of the instruments of the Christ's passion cast beneath the **crucifix** by Roman soldiers and as a symbol of Fortune personified, representing her random gifts. The latter significance has the most relevance today. In both positive and negative senses, dice represent chance.

Direction/Identity

Pointing Finger *Above*

The pointing finger indicates direction, both in the real world and in the more nebulous realm of dreams. A silent indicator of the correct route, by employing this symbol, the unconscious mind can direct its conscious counterpart, helping to resolve conflicts and clarify situations of indecision.

The Unconscious *Below, right*

A densely wooded forest, harboring all manner of wild plants and creatures, is a symbol of the unconscious mind. We do not know—and cannot control—all that our unconscious absorbs. When we dream, snippets of memories long forgotten in our conscious state reappear. Like the unconscious, forests are places of mysterious, uncharted knowledge. They can contain hidden perils, but also buried treasure; we can find in our unconscious minds the key to problems that occupy our waking moments. Dreaming of a forest, however, can also represent a fear of being trapped in the menacing, labyrinthine darkness. Forests thus symbolize danger, as they threaten chaos and disorder. Conversely, if the dreamer does not find it frightening, the forest can represent a place of inner peace and refuge. In addition, the forest is a maternal archetype, symbolizing woman: because of its lush vegetation, it represents the fertile powers of the Great Mother.

Labyrinth/Maze *Below*

The maze, or labyrinth, is an ancient and universal symbol. Its complexity of passages represents confusion and lack of direction. As a metaphor for life, it symbolizes the choices necessary to reach the safety of the center (or of the outside). The terrible power of the maze is symbolized in Greek mythology by the labyrinth in which the **Minotaur** roamed, which was finally overcome by Theseus (who then found his way out using Ariadne's guiding string). In common with the **mandala**, in religious analogy, passage through the maze symbolizes a spiritual journey in the quest for unity with the absolute. In psychological interpretation, however, the maze represents the confusion and contradiction of the unconscious mind. Again, arriving at the center or emerging into the light of day signifies personal individuation and the discovery of self, while wandering blindly in the labyrinth of the psyche signifies a loss of direction.

Innocence *Above*

A young girl dressed in white, such as the figured portrayed in Sir Thomas Lawrence's *Pinkie*, is an archetypal image of innocence and purity—qualities traditionally represented by children (innocence) and the color white (chastity and virginity). Children and adolescents can also symbolize the potential of new beginnings, so in dream symbolism a child dressed in white can either express the desire to return to the unsullied innocence of childhood, or the positive intention to "turn over a new leaf" and make a fresh start.

Protection/Security

Fortress *Below*

As demonstrated by this splendid Babylonian fortress in Iraq, castles and citadels are formidable buildings of defense, whose historical purpose was one of physical refuge from embattlement. Herein lies their complex symbolism, for, as well as symbolizing self-protection and security (if one is on the inside), from the outside, they can represent frustrating obstacles which must be surmounted on the path to progress. In fairy tales, a castle is the stronghold of either good or evil forces, and within it is a prize of incalculable worth (such as a princess, treasure or knowledge).

Depending on the context, the task of the hero is either to attain this treasure by battling with the monstrous guardians of the citadel or, conversely, to protect it from the powers of evil. In dream interpretation, the fortress can represent the secure self, or a self-created prison whose defenses (the unconscious mind) must be broken down before the ideal of self-realization can be won. The fortress can additionally represent positive, spiritual withdrawal from the world, or warn against the dangers of isolation and solitude. When ruined, it signifies feelings of loss and despair.

Walls *Above*

Walls share much of the symbolism of the fortress. On one level, walls indicate personal possession; strangers are discouraged from trespassing. Similarly, walls can signify the protective instinct and the erection of mental barriers. In the positive interpretation, this is a protective measure against potentially harmful influences; on the other hand, wall-building can signify a blinkered view and an out-of-hand rejection of new influences.

Security *Below, center*

In common with most cuddly toys such as teddy bears, the rag doll shown here is a symbol of the security of childhood, when life seemed less threatening, and when we could turn to toys for reassurance and consolation. To a child, the doll or teddy bear not only represents a devoted and unquestioning companion, but also a powerful protector and comforter. Dreaming of a cuddly toy represents a wish to return to a time when we received unconditional love and additionally expresses an urge to escape from the difficult problems of adulthood and revert to the simplicity of childhood. Yet because they are inanimate, nonresponsive objects, soft toys can, more negatively, symbolize a lack of communication. Dolls can also be useful in psychological treatment, for when the personality of the client is projected into them, emotional problems can thus be externalized to facilitate a solution.

Umbrella *Opposite*

The umbrella and the parasol (which provide shelter from the **rain** and rays of the **sun**) are both obvious symbols of protection. In psychological terms, however, this significance is not always positive: it can take the form of extreme introversion, the inability to face the outside world, a reluctance to confront reality and a damaging lack of independence.

Solution

Key *Below*

A symbol of both opening and closing, the key shares the dual symbolism of the Roman god **Janus**, deity of the **doorway**. While the key signifies liberation and the ability to unlock hidden secrets, in its converse aspect, it can also denote incarceration and mystery. In dream symbolism, the key can unlock the unconscious mind and find the solution to a problem. The key figures in many cultures: in Christianity the keys to the **gates** of heaven are held by St. Peter (and are a **papal emblem**); in Greek mythology the key of hell is held by Hecate; in Japan the key signifies happiness; and in Judaism the key of God controls both birth and death.

Illumination *Right*

Like the **rainbow**, light is a symbol of hope and mental "illumination." The anxiety dream (likened to the trauma of birth) of crawling through a pitch-black, constricting and apparently endless tunnel can be terrifying and signifies being forced to travel in a direction over which we have no control. The tunnel is a symbol of the **unconscious** mind, and this dream image sends a message that repressed fears must be confronted and threatening challenges faced in order to banish the feelings of anxiety that can cause severe emotional problems. The relief of glimpsing light at the end of the tunnel is therefore not just a physical deliverance, but also a sense of direction. Light can therefore be regarded as a symbol of the rational and conscious mind with which we can find solutions to the chaos of the unconscious. In the contrast between the darkness of the tunnel and the brightness of the light, a comparison can also be drawn between passing from a state of despair to one of enlightenment and hope for the future.

Jigsaw *Above*

Slotting the final piece of a jigsaw puzzle into place represents an ultimate, triumphant solution. Many mysteries can be likened to a jigsaw puzzle, in which an array of random, seemingly unconnected pieces must be sorted into a precise arrangement before the whole picture can be revealed. The jigsaw is also a metaphor for the unconscious mind presenting "clues" to the conscious mind, where the pieces (archetypal images) are assembled into the whole.

House *Above*

While many cultures have considered the house to be a model of the cosmos, world or **human body**, Jung identified the house as a symbol of the self after a dream that revealed to him the concept of the collective unconscious. Developing this analogy further, the façade is compared to the **persona** and the storeys to different levels of the mind: basement rooms represent the unconscious, the living room is the home of the conscious, the kitchen is a place of transformation and the upper storeys are linked to aspirations and spirituality. Stairs signify a psychic link between these. On a more general level, the house symbolizes the family, protection and stability, a personal refuge from the outside world. Within a house, the persona can be cast off to liberate the true self. This symbolism helps to explain the fact that the house is one of the images most frequently drawn by children.

Transition

Door *Above*

In general terms, the door symbolizes opportunity, or passage from one state or level of consciousness to another. In dream symbolism, when closed, the door represents a hidden mystery or a barrier to which the **key** must be found, while an open door signifies liberation or an invitation to take up a new challenge. Further, a door that opens inward indicates the need for self-exploration; opening outward requires the dreamer to be more accessible to others. Christ's words "I am the door" signify for Christians an entrance to salvation through Christ. **Janus** was the Roman god of the doorway, holding its key and thus the power of transition.

Bridges *Right*

In modern psychoanalytical interpretation, bridges, such as the serene Pont St. Benezet, symbolize the transition from one state of being to another and the opportunity for change. The bridge's near side represents the past, the opposite side a mysterious future, while the waters flowing beneath signify the chaos of the **unconscious** mind. Since antiquity, bridges have also suggested linkage: between the real and heavenly realms, for example; between man and the spirit; or between life and death. When a bridge is difficult to cross, it signifies the difficulties involved in setting aside the past and striving for progress.

Climbing *Below*

In dream cipher, climbing—whether up a ladder, mountain or stairs—is a symbol of the struggle for self-improvement—personally or professionally. Climbing can represent a rite of initiation, personal development and progression though the various stages of consciousness on the route to self-actualization. The achievement is all the greater for the suffering involved in its attainment. Despite the danger, fear and effort involved in scaling the heights, once the summit is finally reached, the climber is rewarded with feelings of exhilaration and achievement. Climbing thus symbolizes transcendence from the lowly aspects of the human condition to higher, more spiritual values. In Freudian thought, climbing can signify a yearning for sexual fulfillment.

Gateway *Above*

Although it shares much symbolism with the **door**, the significance of the gateway, being larger and promising access to greater things, is less specifically personal and represents the entrance to more mystical and profound areas. A gateway can lead to heaven or hell and, on earth, to temporal palaces or spiritual temples. In the Orient, such temples are often protected by fierce guardian creatures; there can also be a series of gateways, representing the various stages of enlightenment. In dream interpretation, however great the barriers to entry, whether an open or closed gateway, the gate (or portal) is a positive invitation to self-exploration and knowledge. The gateway is therefore a symbol of initiation: the initiate must pass through it before transformation to a new, enlightened state of being can be attained.

Death and Mortality

The Reaper *Below*

The Reaper, also known as Death or Father Time, carries a scythe with which to reap those human souls whose time has come. The scythe represents harvest and thus death and rebirth. Through his association with Cronos, the Greek god of agriculture, he often also carries a sickle. Commonly portrayed as a skeletal figure holding an **hourglass**, the Reaper is a *memento mori*—a terrifying symbol of death and a reminder of mortality.

Pocket Watch *Right*

A symbol of the relentless passing of time, the pocket watch or clock is essentially a reminder of the transitory nature of human life. No man is immortal, and as the clock ticks through the seconds, minutes and hours, so it measures life. In dream interpretation, a clock can also symbolize the core of humanity—the emotions of the heart. Usually a symbol of anxiety in dreams, a stopped watch can signify paralysis of the emotions, and a fast watch the feeling of being out of control. However, the symbolism of the clock is not always negative: it can signify new beginnings and the opportunities of the future.

Skull *Above*

The grinning skull, or death's head, is an extensively used *memento mori*, symbolizing man's limited time on earth and inevitable return to dust. In contrast to human impermanence, in many cultures the skull, as the receptacle of the brain, is regarded as the vessel of man's spirit and therefore the fount of life and thought. In **alchemy**, skulls were used in transformation processes.

Hourglass *Right*

The hourglass is primarily a symbol of mortality, a reminder that life is finite. As the sand measuring the passage of time flows from the top to the bottom of the hourglass, so death draws closer with remorseless inevitability. However, because it must be inverted before it can function, the hourglass also symbolizes the life and death cycle, and heaven and earth. In addition, it is a symbol of the Christian personification of **Temperance**.

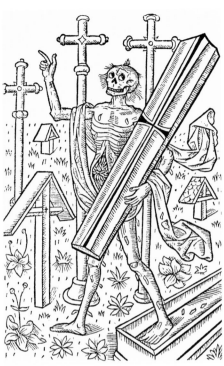

Skeleton and Coffin *Above*

A decaying skeleton emerging from the coffin in which it has been laid to rest is one of the most potent symbols of terror, signifying the undead and negative supernatural power. In dream symbolism, however, the animated corpse does not necessarily symbolize death, but rather the emergence of something buried deep in the unconscious, a trauma previously repressed but which must now be confronted; thus it is the "skeleton in the closet."

Repression/Concealment

Closed Box *Above*
A box which is wrapped up, or otherwise closed, is a symbol of concealment. It invokes intense curiosity as to what may lie inside. As in the cautionary myth of the box that, although taboo, Pandora found too irresistible to ignore, a terrible internal secret (all the evils of the world) may be revealed. In the story, however, the quality of hope remained within the box. Many fairy tales tell of **three** boxes, two of which contain riches and the third devastation. Thus as well as signifying concealment and possibilities for good or evil, a closed box also signifies hopeful emotions regarding the treasure that may lie within. In psychoanalytical interpretation, the box is compared with the destructive (but also positive) potential of the **unconscious** mind, as well as with the protective maternal womb.

Deception *Right*
During the Trojan War, Odysseus ordered the sculptor Epeios to make an enormous wooden **horse** and then pretended to set sail for Greece, leaving the horse outside the besieged city of Troy. The Trojans, believing it to be an offering to the gods, dragged the horse into their city. During the night, the Greek army that had been concealed inside the horse emerged and devastated Troy. In psychoanalytical interpretation, horses represent our natural, primal energies. The Trojan Horse is therefore a symbol of the concealment of the dangerous powers inherent in our **unconscious** which can ambush us even when we feel at our most secure. It is also a warning of potential deception and sabotage (as underlined by the related expression, "Beware of Greeks bearing false gifts") by those who appear innocent and harmless.

Veil *Below*
The veil is primarily a symbol of secrecy and darkness, for the viewer is uncertain of the mysterious countenance concealed beneath. Furthermore, the wearer of the veil does not wish to reveal herself, and so it has protective significance. The veil of mourning represents withdrawal into a solitary world of grief, while the veils worn by Islamic women, brides and nuns symbolize chastity and submission, yet also marriage (in the nuns' case, with

Christ). However, the veil is an ambiguous symbol, for, when it is lifted—as these Spanish women have done—it is a symbol of revelation, truth and knowledge.

Modesty *Above*
In this Italian painting, the **Virgin Mary** at prayer displays the virtues of humility and modesty. Decently dressed and veiled, with downcast eyes, hands clasped in a gesture of supplication, this image of the Virgin represents the ultimate in the acceptance of God's will. Yet while modesty is generally regarded as a quality to strive for, in dream symbolism, it can represent subservience and the sublimation of the real self to an unrealistic, perhaps psychically damaging ideal. Covering oneself with clothing is a dream symbol for inhibitions and the concealment of the **persona**, as well as modesty.

Stress

Suitcase *Right*

Because a piece of luggage, such as a bag or suitcase, is associated with travel, it symbolizes the personal emotional baggage that each of us carries with us through life's journey. Depending on the contents of the suitcase, it can either urge us to discard superfluous anxieties and memories that are hindering our development (if it is crammed with inconsequential items), or (if it has been packed sensibly and sparingly) it can identify the knowledge and experiences that are necessary to our survival. Dreaming of relinquishing or losing luggage can therefore signify a desire to be relieved of burdens—an interpretation which, when taken to its extreme, can ultimately be regarded as indicating a death-wish.

Rollercoaster *Below*

Riding a rollercoaster is a metaphor for the ups and downs of life. As a symbol of the inner mind, it represents ascent and descent into the conscious and unconscious minds. Because we have no control over the speed at which the rollercoaster travels or over the course that it takes, it can represent a loss of direction. The dangerous thrill of the hair-raising journey can be intensely pleasurable, however, and in this context the rollercoaster is linked with the need for excitement and risk-taking.

Juggling *Below*

The juggler is a symbol of balancing life's components in order to prevent the balls (representing elements of either personal life or psyche) from falling and disrupting performance. Most people feel under pressure to reconcile commitments, such as family, work and personal needs, into a harmonious whole; sometimes the pressures are so great that loss of control will result unless the "juggling" skills are highly developed. This analogy applies to the parts of the psyche that are juggled by the conscious mind. A juggler can also be interpreted as a **trickster** figure who, with one (deliberate) slip of the hand, can disrupt harmony.

Burnout *Below*

Mental burnout can be symbolized in a number of ways, including the escape of steam from the ears (indicating a severe build-up), or a **candle** burning at both ends. In this context, steam and **fire** are symbols of destruction, and both warn of the dangers of overextending oneself—either as a result of external pressure or by overriding personal ambition. A nervous breakdown—sometimes called "meltdown" or "burnout"—can cause irreparable damage to the psyche.

Obstacles

Isolation *Above*

An uninhabited island is symbol of isolation, because it is separated by **water** from other land masses and their communities. Although we may exhibit solitary tendencies and enjoy our own company, ultimately, in the words of John Donne, "No man is an island," and we need the company and interaction of others in order to maintain mental equilibrium. To dream of an island may thus indicate the need for the solitude of a peaceful haven (which, in certain measures, is also beneficial), or warn of the dangers that result from becoming cut off from the rest of society or avoiding facing problems. In a further interpretation, the island can be identified as the stability of the conscious mind, and the surrounding sea the unpredictability of the **unconscious**. Because it is difficult to reach, it can also symbolize an unattainable ideal.

Imprisonment *Below*

The bars of this cage symbolize the imprisonment of the parrots. Prisoners are, by definition, held against their will and are prevented from escape and liberation by the bars of their jail. Personal freedom is crucial to the integrity of the mind and physical well-being, and deprivation of liberty leads to a profound mental decline. Dreams of being imprisoned can, on one level, signify feelings of real or imagined guilt for which one expects punishment, or can represent an impending situation that is perceived as a loss of freedom (such as marriage, the birth of a child or starting a new job). On the other hand, captivity can also be symbolic of repression—either of one's aspirations and desires, or of one's bondage to a dominating external force. In dream symbolism, caged animals, such as these parrots, represent our most basic urges and energies, whose release is essential, for continued unconscious repression will result in damage to the conscious mind. The uniform of a convict may serve a practical, identifying purpose but also suppresses feelings of individuality that the prisoner may cling to in an attempt to assert his personal independence.

Manipulation *Above*

Puppets, or marionettes, are inanimate figures whose movements are provoked by threads, wires or sticks controlled by a puppet-master. They can symbolize the loss of free will and inability to act independently—the manipulation of one's mind by another person or exterior force. If the dreamer is acting as the puppet-master, his unconscious is expressing a desire to control others.

Red Tape *Below*

Bureaucratic red tape is among the most frustrating obstacles experienced in everyday life, and this interpretation carries over into the dream world. To be prevented from achieving goals by a smug and immutable official who is backed by the power of unintelligible legal regulations is a clear image of repression. It also indicates a lack of communication between the conscious and unconscious minds. The unconscious is, in effect, sabotaging the creative aspirations of the conscious, and the red tape that symbolizes this repression must be cut or unraveled before frustration erupts, resulting in serious damage. Red tape—a binding object the color of danger—can also be a warning to confront frustrations in order to understand and dissolve them, if possible, or to accept them if a straightforward solution is impossible.

Warning and Temptation

Greed *Right*
The gods granted the legendary King Midas of Phrygia his wish that everything he touched should turn to gold. Unfortunately, his greed was so consuming that although he became rich and fulfilled his wish, he also found consequences he had not foreseen. His food turned to gold and he could not eat, and his touch transformed his daughter into a golden corpse (as illustrated here by Walter Crane). After the distraught Midas had prayed to the gods for release, he was commanded to bathe in the Pactolus River, whereupon the curse was broken and the sands of the shore became golden. Midas is thus a cautionary symbol of the dangers of excessive greed and warns that the destructive potential of wealth outweighs the material benefits it bestows.

Temptation *Above*
This detail from a painting by Hieronymus Bosch graphically illustrates the temptation that we all face at some point, to abandon the path of "goodness" for an ephemeral or destructive reward. Death is represented entering the bedroom of a dying man, around whose bed rages a battle for possession of his soul. An **angel** stands protectively behind the doomed man, urging him to resist the bribes enthusiastically offered by the satanic demons, whose acceptance would result in his eternal damnation. Despite the fact that bags of loot will be of no use to him in the next world, the man's temptation is obvious. In dreams, temptation should not necessarily be viewed in religious terms, but as any attractive option that appeals to our greed and threatens to lure us into behaviour that conflicts with our true selves.

Phobias *Above, right*
While phobias can simply represent a straightforward fear of the phobic object, they can also be regarded as symbolic of something unconsciously feared. Anne Anderson's watercolor illustrates Little Miss Muffet, who, in the nursery rhyme, was frightened from her tuffet by a **spider**, making her perhaps the best-known arachnaphobic. Arachnaphobia is common and is often experienced in nightmares, as well as in actual encounters with spiders. The spider represents fate (because of the thread that it spins, which is likened to the thread of life); creation (on account of the web that it weaves); and malevolent and venomous destruction (because it immobilizes victims in its web and then kills them). In ancient as in modern times, the spider can represent the devouring mother who ensnares her children in her web and destroys them. Arachnaphobia can therefore be variously interpreted as a fear of life and death, of the damaging powers of a dominating mother and, more mundanely, as an extreme dislike of these scuttling, eight-legged arachnids.

Time Bomb *Below*
The time bomb, with its fizzing fuse burning inexorably toward devastation, symbolizes a danger buried deep within the unconscious mind which, unless attended to, will inevitably explode to cause psychological damage. It is therefore a symbol of warning, signaling to the conscious mind a need to address unresolved issues which, if ignored, will blow up—with potentially disastrous consequences to the psyche.

Bibliography

Note: Sources vary—sometimes widely—in the history, roots and meaning of symbols. This is not surprising, as symbols change over time and can have different meanings and associations in different cultures. The author and editors have made every attempt to use authoritative sources and to present a clear and concise description of the symbols included in this book.

Alchemy: The Secret Art, Stanislas Klossowski de Rola, 1973, Thames & Hudson Ltd., London.

American Indian Myths and Legends, eds. Richard Erdoes and Alfonso Ortiz, 1984, Pantheon, New York.

Astrology: The Celestial Mirror, Warren Kenton, 1974, Thames & Hudson Ltd., London.

The Bible and the Saints, G. Duchet Suchaux and M. Pastoureau, 1994, Flammarion, Paris.

Bloomsbury Guide to Human Thought, ed. Kenneth McLeish, 1993, Bloomsbury Publishing Ltd., London.

Brewer's Book of Myth and Legend, ed. J. C. Cooper, 1995, Helicon Publishing Ltd., Oxford.

Dictionary of Jewish Lore and Legend, Alan Unterman, 1991, Thames and Hudson Ltd., London.

Dictionary of Symbols, Tom Chetwynd, 1982, The Aquarian Press, HarperCollins, London.

A Dictionary of Symbols, J. E. Cirlot, 1995, Routledge, London.

Dictionary of Symbols, Carl G. Liungman, 1991, W. W. Norton & Company, Inc., New York and London.

The Element Encyclopedia of Symbols, ed. Udo Becker, 1994, Element Books Ltd., Shaftsbury, Dorset.

The Encyclopedia of Signs and Symbols, John Laing and David Wire, 1993, Studio Editions Ltd., London.

The Guinness Encyclopedia of Signs and Symbols, John Foley, 1993, Guinness Publishing Ltd., Middlesex, England.

Hall's Illustrated Dictionary of Symbols in Eastern and Western Art, James Hall, 1994, John Murray (Publishers) Ltd., London.

Heraldry, Henry Bedingfeld and Peter Gwynn-Jones, 1993, Bison Books Ltd., London.

A History of God, Karen Armstrong, 1993, Ballantine Books, New York.

The Hutchinson Encyclopedia of Living Faiths (4th edition), ed. R. C. Zaehner, 1988, Helicon, Oxford.

An Illustrated Encyclopaedia of Traditional Symbols, J. C. Cooper, 1978, Thames and Hudson Ltd., London.

Illustrated Guide to Dreams, Valerie Francis, 1995, Bison Books Ltd., London.

Indian Art: A Concise History, Roy C. Craven, 1976, Thames and Hudson Ltd., London

Magic: The Western Tradition, Francis King, 1975, Thames & Hudson, Inc., New York.

The Mammoth Dictionary of Symbols: Understanding the Hidden Language of Symbols, Nadia Julien, 1996, Robinson Publishing, London.

Man and His Symbols, Carl G. Jung, 1964, Arkana, Penguin Books, London.

The Mythic Image, Joseph Campbell, 1974, Bollingen Series C, Princeton University Press, Princeton, New Jersey.

Mythology: An Illustrated Encyclopedia, ed. Richard Cavendish, 1987, Macdonald & Co. (Publishers) Ltd., London.

The Native Americans: An Illustrated History, eds. Betty and Ian Ballantine, 1993, Turner Publishing, Inc., Atlanta, Georgia.

The Oxford Companion to the Mind, ed. Richard L. Gregory, 1987, Oxford University Press, Oxford.

The Oxford Guide to Heraldry, Thomas Woodcock and John Martin Robinson, 1988, Oxford University Press, Oxford.

The Penguin Dictionary of Religions, ed. John R. Hinnells, 1984, Penguin Books Ltd., London.

Sacred Symbols: Ancient Egypt, 1995, Thames and Hudson Ltd., London.

Sacred Symbols: The Celts, 1995, Thames and Hudson Ltd., London.

Sacred Symbols: Mandala, 1995, Thames and Hudson Ltd., London.

Sacred Symbols: The Tarot, 1995, Thames and Hudson Ltd., London.

The Secret Language of Dreams, David Fontana, 1994, Pavilion Books, Ltd., London/Duncan Baird Publishers, London.

The Secret Language of Symbols, David Fontana, 1993, Pavilion Books, Ltd., London/Duncan Baird Publishers, London.

The Supernatural, Douglas Hill and Pat Williams, 1989, Bloomsbury Books, London.

Symbols, Signs and Signets, Ernst Lehner, 1950, reprinted 1969, Dover Publications, Inc., New York.

The Tree of Life: Image for the Cosmos, Roger Cook, 1974, Thames and Hudson Ltd., London.

The Truth about Witchcraft Today, Scott Cunningham, 1988, Llewellyn Publications, St. Paul, Minnesota.

Who's Who in Mythology, Alexander S. Murray, 1994, Bracken Books, London.

Witchcraft: The History and Mythology, Richard Marshall, 1995, Saraband Inc., Rowayton, Connecticut.

The Woman's Dictionary of Symbols and Sacred Objects, Barbara G. Walker, 1988, HarperCollins, New York.

The Wordsworth Dictionary of Beliefs and Religions, ed. Rosemary Goring, 1995, Wordsworth Editions Ltd., Hertfordshire, England.

Acknowledgements

The publisher would like to thank Richard Marshall and Lisa Callahan for their valuable editorial comments, and the following individuals and agencies who supplied illustrations:

AKG, London: 6; Aris Multimedia Entertainment, Inc.: 101 (top right), 112 (left); The Bettmann Archive: 11 (bottom), 26 (top), 45 (top), 60 (center), 61 (center), 75 (bottom right), 84 (top & bottom center), 88, 107 (right), 117 (right), 126, 131 (top left & bottom), 133 (bottom left), 135 (top), 138, 140 (bottom right), 144 (bottom right), 152 (top left & bottom), 153 (bottom right), 155 (left, center, above right); BFI Stills, Posters and Designs: 137 (right), 146 (top); Corbis/Bettmann: 11 (top), Corel

Stock Photo Library: 8, 9 (top), 10, 12 (top), 14, 15 (top), 16 (top), 27 (top left), 28 (top right), 30 (top left), 31 (top center & right), 33 (top left), 35 (top), 36 (bottom left), 37 (top left & right), 38 (top left & bottom), 50 (center), 52 (bottom right), 53 (top), 54 (center), 55 (center), 74 (top), 81 (bottom), 98 (top & bottom), 99 (center), 100, (bottom), 101 (below left), 104 (bottom), 105 (left), 110 (bottom), 120 (top & bottom left), 123 (top left), 143 (top & bottom left), 144 (top left), 145 (center & bottom left), 147 (top right), 148 (center left), 149 (top left), 150 (center & bottom), 152 (top right & center); Earthstar Stock, Inc.: 121 (top & bottom left); Giraudon/Art Resource, NY: 64; Mary Evans Picture Library: 68 (bottom); Northwind Picture Archives: 67 (center, hand-colored by Nancy Carter); Planet Art: 36 (bottom right), 41 (top), 43 (top), 47 (top & bottom right), 50 (top right), 54 (center left), 60 (top), 79 (top), 118 (top), 124 (center right), 136 (top); Prints and Photographs Division, Library of Congress: 50 (bottom left), 125 (top);

Reuters/Bettmann: 17, 45 (bottom right); © Michael A. Smith: 15 (bottom), 50 (top left), 83 (top), 93 (bottom), 94 (bottom), 119 (right), 141 (top left), 143 (bottom right); © Michael Tincher: 43 (bottom), 44 (bottom right); UPI/Bettmann: 66 (bottom right); Wyoming State Museum—Division of Cultural Resources: 43 (right); © Charles J. Ziga: 13, 16 (bottom), 17 (top), 20, 22 (center & bottom), 23 (bottom), 24 (top & bottom), 25 (top), 26 (bottom), 28 (bottom left), 35 (bottom), 42 (top & bottom right), 43 (left), 44 (top & bottom left), 46 (all), 48, 54 (bottom), 55 (top & bottom), 59 (bottom right), 80 (top right), 82 (bottom), 85, 93 (center), 103 (bottom), 106 (bottom), 108 (below right), 110 (center), 111 (center left & right), 112 (right), 113 (top left & right), 114 (top right), 115 (bottom), 121 (center), 123 (bottom), 124 (bottom), 125 (center right), 129 (bottom), 140 (top), 141 (bottom right), 147 (bottom), 149 (top & bottom), 149 (bottom right), 150 (top right), 154 (top left/right & bottom left).

Index

*Page numbers in **bold** type refer to illustrations.*